The Guarded Age

For my parents, Anne and Arnold Betz

The Guarded Age
Fortification in the Twenty-First Century

David J. Betz

polity

Copyright © David J. Betz 2024

The right of David J. Betz to be identified as Author of this Work has been asserted in accordance with the UK Copyright, Designs and Patents Act 1988.

First published in 2024 by Polity Press

Polity Press
65 Bridge Street
Cambridge CB2 1UR, UK

Polity Press
111 River Street
Hoboken, NJ 07030, USA

All rights reserved. Except for the quotation of short passages for the purpose of criticism and review, no part of this publication may be reproduced, stored in a retrieval system or transmitted, in any form or by any means, electronic, mechanical, photocopying, recording or otherwise, without the prior permission of the publisher.

ISBN-13: 978-1-5095-4404-2
ISBN-13: 978-1-5095-4405-9 (pb)

A catalogue record for this book is available from the British Library.

Library of Congress Control Number: 2023932510

Typeset in 10.75 on 13pt Adobe Janson
by Cheshire Typesetting Ltd, Cuddington, Cheshire
Printed and bound in Great Britain by TJ Books Ltd, Padstow, Cornwall

The publisher has used its best endeavours to ensure that the URLs for external websites referred to in this book are correct and active at the time of going to press. However, the publisher has no responsibility for the websites and can make no guarantee that a site will remain live or that the content is or will remain appropriate.

Every effort has been made to trace all copyright holders, but if any have been overlooked the publisher will be pleased to include any necessary credits in any subsequent reprint or edition.

For further information on Polity, visit our website:
politybooks.com

Contents

List of Figures	vi
Preface	vii
Introduction	1
1 The Rise of the Walls	13
2 Civilization, War, and Guardedness	31
3 Contemporary Military Fortification	45
4 Storming the City	74
5 Securing the City	101
6 Hiding in Plain Sight	129
7 Luxury Forts to Data Bunkers	164
Conclusion	185
Further Reading	189
Notes	192
Index	224

List of Figures

3.1	Sadr City	52
3.2	The fort at Menaka	54
3.3	Hesco barrier	57
3.4	ANP headquarters	59
3.5	Qalat's tea house	61
3.6	The West Bank 'separation fence'	69
3.7	Saudi Arabia's high-tech fence	70
5.1	The Fortress on the Strand	105
5.2	City of London's 'Ring of Steel'	117
6.1	The American embassy in Beirut	136
6.2	The American embassy in London	137
6.3	The Kabul Airport evacuation	141
6.4	JFK Airport	142
6.5	Armoured security hut, Islamabad Airport	146
7.1	Enclosed neighbourhoods in Johannesburg	169
7.2	Steyn City	173

Preface

In about 1980 an uncle gave me a copy of *Castles: A History and Guide* by R. Allen Brown, a Professor of Mediaeval History at King's College London where, as it happens, I am now Professor of War in the Modern World in the Department of War Studies. Half of the book is a gazetteer of castles throughout Europe and the Middle East. It is sitting on the desk in front of me now and I am proud to say that I have tick marks next to nearly all of them, recording my visits over the years. In other words, the genesis of this book is what I felt was a minor indulgence that has extended into adulthood: I really like castles. In fact, I am into fortifications of all kinds. If there is a trace of a hill fort nearby, let alone a proper fortress, or a derelict bunker, then I am impelled to go look at it. Few things please me more than coming across a machine gun pillbox or a spigot mortar position. No abandoned coastal artillery battery is safe from my interest. I am grateful to my family for forgiving a hundred interrupted road trips and family holidays.

I did not think to apply this interest to my active research until comparatively recently. The fact is that contemporary strategic studies, which is broadly speaking my professional field, is not very interested in fortification. The subject is generally treated as historical in nature and even rather retrograde. Modern warfare is supposed to be about manoeuvring not static positions; and firepower, it has long been supposed, is far too accurate for fixed fortifications to be of much utility. A few years ago, for reasons explained herein, I began to doubt these assumptions. It seemed increasingly obvious that fortification strategies were rather central to the efforts of states to secure themselves as well as to advance their interests externally.

As I investigated these developments with the intent of correcting a misapprehension in the relatively narrow field of strategic studies, or military affairs, I came to see that the pattern of 'hunkering down', of fortifying, was widely manifest throughout society in realms far beyond the strictly military, notably in the rapidly shifting urban landscape.

As a castle-obsessed kid growing up in Canada where fortifications were rare, I developed a mental habit of imagining them. Many an otherwise intolerably boring school day was made agreeable by quietly daydreaming about how, if I was to defend this school (or whatever building I happened to be stuck in) against an attack, I would do it. What walls would have to be reinforced? How to deal with the windows? What sort of gate? How about a moat? What I normally sketched out was some vaguely mediaeval mutation of a twentieth-century building but with a portcullis and machicolation, a battered plinth, and arrow loops and the like.

It was a surprise, then, not entirely pleasant, to learn while researching this book that there is now a large, rapidly growing, and very creative industry employing many thousands of people who are in the business of building a huge variety of fortified architecture. The result does not look mediaeval, nor is there any reason it should. It is not just that the construction materials and techniques available to designers today are very different, it is also that the character of the physical threat against which these fortifications are meant to defend is also very different. Our 'castles' do not look a lot like their distant ancestors but there is no doubt that ours is a highly castellated age. Essentially, the object of this book is to explain how that happened. How has fortification come to be such a big part of what is supposed to be an information age defined by openness and fluidity?

If that intrigues you, then this book is for you. If you are just interested in castles, then this book is also one you will find worthwhile. We are going to talk about some things that you have possibly already observed happening in the world around you; we will learn why they are happening in the way that they are, and make some educated guesses about where things are headed in future. By the end you will not only know your bastions from your barbicans but also, more importantly, how and why that knowledge is important and useful *right now*.

There are many people to whom I am indebted for helping with this project, but particularly my wife, Taisha, and children, Charlie and Lily, for putting up with the protracted distraction and grumpy introversion that comes with researching and writing a book. I am very grateful also to my sister, Catherine Betz, for her massive effort in editing a rather sprawling text into what I hope is now a lean and mean one. All fault of course is my own.

Introduction

The Poo Pond, Kandahar Airfield, Afghanistan, 30 August 2010

Two thousand years from now what will archaeologists make of the wars of the late twentieth and early twenty-first centuries? What will they find perplexing as they attempt to reassemble the history of our time from whatever fragments they find in the dust? I found myself asking these questions one evening in late August 2010, as I was jogging around the NATO base at Kandahar airfield in southern Afghanistan.

At that time the base was about the size of a provincial town with a daytime population of about 25,000 people, falling to just over half of that at night when the locally engaged Afghan workers returned to their homes outside. It was big enough to host a range of amenities, including a notorious boardwalk with fast food restaurants and shops selling cheap carpets, T-shirts, knock-off 'antiquities', and other war-themed souvenirs.[1]

In hindsight, the outside jog was ill-advised, and I should have stuck to the treadmill in the excellent base gym: it was hot and constantly dusty (evening 'cool' is a relative concept in south Asia in summer), in the dim light there was constant risk of being squished by gigantic military vehicles, and my meandering route took me past the notorious Kandahar Poo Pond. If the boardwalk was the 'heart' of the base, as one reporter described it, then the Poo Pond was, well, you can guess. The technical term is 'sewage treatment lagoon'. Anyway, as I circled the open-air pool of human excrement, cordoned off by a rope with signs declaring 'Biohazard: Do not Enter!' (as if that was on my mind), my thoughts were philosophical.

It had been a strange day. Earlier, returning from lunch to our office in a shipping container, my colleagues and I had brought back strawberry milkshakes, one of the several dessert items available in the cafeteria that day. The plan for the afternoon was to have a meeting with a couple of staff officers from the headquarters of Regional Command South (RCS), based at Kandahar, but shortly after the meeting started the alarm siren warning of a Taliban rocket attack blared out. This happened often and fruitlessly enough to be more annoying than frightening as the rockets were badly aimed and usually failed to explode. Nonetheless they could be dangerous if you were unlucky enough to be near where one came down.

We were taught that when the siren went off, we were to immediately seek shelter – if outside, in one of the many small concrete shelters scattered around the base, or if inside then under a desk or table, ideally with one's helmet and flak jacket on. So it was that I, a grown man, found myself hiding beneath a desk with several other grown men sipping milkshakes and chit-chatting while waiting for the loudspeakers to sound out that the attack was over and we might return to normal. That is my war story.

As it happened, one of the things we were discussing that day was a recently published United States Congressional Research Service report entitled 'Warlord, Inc.', which had concluded that a main source of Taliban funding was protection money paid to it by logistics subcontractors to lay off attacks on NATO supply routes.[2]

Guarded Age Warfare

The reason I was there in the first place was that I'd been invited as a civilian academic by the RCS headquarters, then under British command, because my research at the time centred on 'information age' conflict, specifically on the problems of fighting a worldwide 'war of ideas', as the 'Global War on Terror' was then widely conceived. My brief was to help the military get its collective head around how to fight and win such a war. In other words, I was dealing with all manner of intangible aspects of war, the ever-shifting perception of the whys and wherefores of the conflict in the minds of a range of interested onlookers.

Everyone was looking for a 'strategic narrative' of the conflict to unite all the messages to various audiences, from the domestic populations of the intervening countries to the populations of other countries in the region (and the Islamic world more generally), as well as the Afghans themselves. In search of this narrative, I was given access to a range of interlocutors starting with government and military officials in London, then NATO headquarters staff in Kabul, commanders, planners, and information operations specialists at the regional command level, all the way down to a handful of those in direct contact with Afghans in little bases and outposts.

By the time I was circling the Poo Pond on my run I had come firmly to the point of view that said strategic narrative was rather like the mythical El Dorado, the lost city of gold that had once obsessed the conquistadors. It did not exist. I had been studying war and warfare and contemporary strategy for many years and had developed a reputation as a specialist in an aspect of it that many people thought very important. Ultimately, though, I really had no good answer to the question that had been posed to me.

In truth, I had flown halfway around the planet to a country wracked by three decades of war to drink the world's most expensive milkshake. Then I went home, wrote up my notes and published an article as a good academic ought. The gist of that article was that the war had been lost already, which I put down to a failure to communicate a convincing narrative to Afghans as well as to the home populations of the intervening countries. It was an argument that stayed resolutely in the realm of strategic communications.[3]

The fact was, though, that practically every minute I was in Afghanistan was spent inside a highly fortified military installation – a castle in effect, sometimes more of a 'marching camp' – that was almost always (though I did not realize it at the time) built on the ruins of earlier fortresses going back through time: NATO castles jury-rigged around Soviet constructions resting on British Empire foundations built in some places out of stones carved by armies as far back as those of Alexander the Great.

Occasionally we flew by plane or helicopter from base to base, as though we were island hopping in some archipelago. A couple of times we moved a short distance by road but always in an armoured vehicle with plenty of guards. In short, I had not really been in Afghanistan in any meaningful sense; I had been in a series of army-guarded places that could have been in any hot and dusty place. Moreover, what was true of me as a civilian academic was also true of nine tenths of everyone serving there in uniform.

I had an inkling that this was a very important problem for our strategic communications efforts, but beyond the well-worn argument about the credibility-killing, trust-eroding 'say-do' gap I was not able to be more precise.[4] This book is partly an attempt to correct that failing. A very big problem with our communications was the giant gap between what we said in words and what we demonstrated with our actions and, specifically what interests me, with the obvious matter of the kinds of things we *built*.

This book also argues that the issue is much greater than Afghanistan or strategic communications. It is all encompassing – a fact that made writing it hard as there is a lot to work through. The one big message of this book it is that even now in the supposed information age, physical stuff still matters – a lot.

The Language of Architecture

To me, this seems at first glance to be a bit of a paradox – certainly I found it contrary to expectation. After all, the words 'information age' have connotations of intangibility and fluidity that seem incongruous when placed alongside 'fortification', which is practically an epitome of tangibility. If you ask a normal person to 'picture a fortress' they tend to imagine a historical artefact, a ruined castle perhaps, or maybe a fantastical confection like those in a Disney theme park. What they would not imagine is a piece of currently relevant military architecture that is the backdrop to their daily lives.

As for fluidity, when it came to warfare what I expected to see – something agile, something *moving* – turned out to be the complete opposite. Although I was sceptical of the idea, the decades of talk about an information-technology-driven 'revolution in military affairs' (RMA) supposedly enabling relatively small, light, fast-moving armies to fight more decisively and quickly, must have rubbed off on me. The war in Afghanistan had instead an extremely static and highly positional character that both surprised and interested me. I did not expect to come away from the experience with such a strong belief in the critical importance of military engineering *right now*.

This book is not about the Afghanistan war, however. There is a huge literature on the subject, and I have little to add to it that I have not already said elsewhere. It is, rather, a book about the relationship of fortified architecture, global society, and war more generally. It touches upon a very wide range of issues, notably the perception of risk and the danger that our fearful responses to it are causing more harm to society than good. That said, I have one more relevant Afghanistan-specific comment.

When it came down to it, NATO's 'body language' in Afghanistan was very different from the official rhetoric about the war. It is scarcely credible to say to people 'we are here for the long run, everyone who cooperates will be protected in a prosperous new Afghanistan', from the inside of a gigantic but also ramshackle fortress which you rarely leave, and where you have been living in tents beside a lake of sewage for twenty years. The contradiction was supremely obvious to Afghans. What is astonishing is that it was not obvious to NATO.

Ultimately, I think that the world has been propelled by events into a state of profound guardedness, as seen in the proliferation of fortification strategies employed not just by armies but by governments, civil groups, corporations, and individuals. The situation is frequently at odds with liberty. The book attempts to explain how and why it has occurred by letting the structures speak for themselves.

In my opinion, buildings have a kind of 'language', they say interesting and important things about the preoccupations and ideals of their builders. The 'dialect' of the language of buildings that interests me, to continue the metaphor, is that of fortifications. What I am saying is that I have taught myself to speak 'Fortress-ese' and I am going to use that skill to translate what the contemporary built environment says about you and your society, what has happened to it, and where it might be going. It just so happens that Afghanistan is the place where I first realized I needed to learn this language.

It is also a practical place to start the story. Afghanistan has seen a lot of war – not just in recent times, having been at war continuously since the late 1970s. For all recorded history it has betimes found itself the hinge of imperial ambitions of one sort or another, whether Persian, Greek, Mongol, British, Soviet, or American. Since it is also extremely arid and underdeveloped, the layers upon layers of its fortifications – its 'strategic stratigraphy' as I shall discuss further on – are very visible.

The book, however, is not only concerned with military fortification. It is not even primarily concerned with that. Quite soon after I began to study the matter closely, I started to see fortresses everywhere. I developed the opinion that placing contemporary fortification within the strict category 'military' was an act of intellectual compression akin to squeezing a giant into a dwarf's jacket. You may regard the rest of what follows as a defence of that belief. It turned out there is more that is interesting and important about fortification going on outside of the military sphere than within it.

To illustrate, I shall indulge in one more personal 'war story' which helps to explain the form, trajectory, and selection of cases you will encounter in the overall argument of the book.

The Battle of King's College London, 30 June 2015

It was about midday, sunny and hot, when through the open window of my office I heard the gunfire start. First there was a slow and steady 'pop-pop-pop' and then a second or two later came an almost continuous crackling of rapid bursts that carried on and on. I was at first confused at what I was hearing because it was so incongruous. After all, I was sitting in my comfy office in the King's Building of King's College London where the War Studies Department is located. It's not completely unusual to hear vaguely military sounds here in the city. The distinctive double-rotor sound of RAF Chinooks coming out of their base in Odiham, Hampshire, practising urban flying in the helicopter airspace corridor over the Thames, is typical. The sound of close-quarter combat, though, is unexpected. Britain was not at war – not at home at any rate.

It was the screaming and shouting that caused recognition to dawn on me. There was unmistakably a battle going on in my building. Peering out my office window on the seventh floor I saw police snipers working their way across the rooftop of neighbouring Somerset House into positions overlooking the Strand quadrangle. What was going on? Should I run? If so, to where? I had no idea which route out if any led to safety. I could just as easily be walking into danger as away from it. Should I barricade and hunker down in place? Since the front wall of my office is made entirely of thin frosted glass, while the side ones are little more than hollow-core drywall, this did not seem a very healthy idea either. Bullets would tear through that like nothing at all. A grenade in the corridor would have showered the room and me in glass fragments.

There did not appear to be any good options. The 2002 Moscow theatre siege – in which forty or so Chechen terrorists took hostage nearly 900 people, 170 of whom died in the rescue operation – sprang to mind. So, too, did the November 2008 incident in Mumbai in which ten terrorists killed 160 people in a series of coordinated gun and bomb attacks that wracked the city over four days, and the then-recent January 2015 attack by terrorists in Paris in which seventeen people were killed, including eleven employees of the *Charlie Hebdo* satirical magazine. If it had happened in those places, why not in central London – or any place for that matter?

Perhaps I was just unlucky?

As it happened, no; my luck was good. The Battle of King's College London, as I have called it, was in fact just a large and realistic exercise against a very plausible threat. 'Operation Strong Tower', as the exercise was officially called, was designed as a two-day 'noisy and visible' practice for 1,000 armed police, soldiers, SAS, emergency services, and other government personnel practising their ability to respond to an attack like those mentioned above.[5] It had been advertised but I had forgotten about it.

The findings of the exercise were not publicized, but police and city authorities said it was only through such testing and exercising, refining tactics, and learning that they could be confident in their ability to respond to an attack. I was glad to not have been perforated by shrapnel and glass.

The New Normal

I was also not unperturbed, however, for it is a fact that the potentiality at any given time of such scenes recurring on the streets of the world's cities is high, which further piqued my interest. As an independent review into London's counter-terrorism preparedness would conclude, the ever-present prospect of coordinated terror attacks using a variety of means to cause mass casualties was the 'new normal' of urban life.[6]

This concept of the 'new normal' began to preoccupy me seriously. What would it mean if it were true? I had studied war and military strategy for thirty years, nearly always in a context in which my own country's involvement had been in an expeditionary capacity. In other words, I was an expert in wars that occurred somewhere in the distant abroad, not at home. I had just written a book on the effect of 'connectivity' on war which argued that a main consequence was that we could no longer expect that distance and solid frontiers would insulate the 'home front' from 'over there'. Wars that originated any place could be fought, in part, in practically every place – including on our own streets.[7]

From the perspective of 2022, the validity of the assessment of the 'new normal' is hard to gainsay. To continue the list of attacks that I started earlier, in Paris in November 2015 terrorists methodically shot or blew up 130 people, including ninety in the Bataclan nightclub alone. In June 2016 a terrorist shot to death forty-nine people in an Orlando, Florida nightclub. In July the same year, a terrorist in Nice, France drove a heavy truck into a crowd of people celebrating Bastille

Day, killing eighty-nine and wounding another 450. A full and complete list of these sorts of attacks would be gratuitous and superfluous.[8] Everyone knows this danger exists.

A Notion of Death and Destruction

In 1989, on the eve of the end of the Cold War, the annual BBC Reith Lectures were given by the French poet and critic Jacques Darras. Titled 'Beyond the Tunnel of History', the ostensible purpose of the lectures was to reflect on the bicentenary of the French Revolution, but the main focus was on the social meaning of the built environment. The thrust of Darras's argument was that there is always a relationship between the physical features of any city – the morphology of its public squares and parks, its main buildings, and thoroughfares, and so on – and the ambitions and fears of the political culture it embodies. Speaking particularly of the latter, he declared:

> what we can now see as contributing to the strength and resilience of many of our great European cities is that they have had to integrate into themselves the notion of death and destruction which is always potentially lurking there, but at the same time they have triumphed over death and destruction to become the great metropolitan centres that so many of them are today.[9]

The notions of death and destruction that shaped London, for example, in the past are different from those shaping it now; but it is being extensively reshaped, as are all major cities, as we shall see in detail in the following pages.

This book focuses primarily on the reaction to perceived threats, rather than on the threats per se. Broadly speaking, it has two main parts, one focused upon military fortification and another, somewhat larger, focused upon civil fortification. When I first became interested in this subject, I had not thought the latter category of fortification existed, let alone that it was distinctively more important than the former.

What I intend to show is how fortification strategies have resurged. We are seeing a new chapter in the long history of fortification that is massive in scale, design ingenuity, and pervasiveness, though perhaps not obviously to many because so much of it is hidden in plain sight. This is a general and global phenomenon – its effects may be perceived in military operations and in civil (especially urban) life more generally. The guarded character of contemporary life has several important manifestations and causes rooted in global politics, economics, and society that go beyond pure security.

Many people are concerned that the reaction is an *overreaction*, that the measures taken to guard society are more harmful and more costly in many respects, sometimes by far, than the threats being protected against.[10] This is my own opinion, also – for reasons I shall explain below. But whether it is right or wrong, popular delusion or wise policy, there is an observably powerful movement towards guardedness that is especially obvious in our cities. I call it a fortification *zeitgeist*, German for 'spirit of the era', because it seems to possess a certain ineluctability. I do not like what I see but neither can I unsee it.

Plan of the Book

Chapter 1 sets the context for all else discussed in the book. In the main it is a discussion of the disjuncture between the way the future was imagined at the end of the Cold War and the way it has in fact developed. Chapter 2 covers the same period but with a narrower focus upon military theory and practice as well as a discussion of the impact of cultural mood on strategic behaviour. Chapter 3 starts with an articulation of the idea and importance of what I call fortified strategic complexes. It then presents contemporary cases of different types of fortifications for the strategic military purposes of pacification, separation, and consolidation of control of people and territory. That is roughly the first half of the book.

The fortification strategies that typify the guarded age are concentrated more on the civil environment than the military, and particularly on urban areas. This is the focus of the latter half of the book.

Chapter 4 looks in some detail at the history of how the city has been shaped both internally and on its periphery by the long and circuitous interplay of methods and means of attack and defence of urban areas. The main object is to develop the transition from fortification in the military sphere to fortification in the civil environment. Chapter 5 focuses on problems of securing cities from a theoretical perspective to elaborate a conceptual framework for the case studies of contemporary urban fortification, which are presented in Chapter 6, focused on government and public architecture, and Chapter 7, focused on more private and corporate fortification, particularly of critical infrastructure, which is by no means exclusively located in urban environments.

My overall aim is to show you two main things. First, that many everyday elements of our contemporary civilization – *things that you see all the time* – are part of a vast and ingenious fortified strategic complex the object of which is to 'secure' you, whether you want it or not, or recognize it or not. Second, that surprising as that first observation might be, much of the fortification activity occurring so frenetically in recent decades is not new per se; it is a variation of old ideas updated for an age that has its own specific requirements of its fortresses as did previous times. In short, I want to show that fortification is a lively and important part of strategic practice, despite being largely ignored by strategic studies.

I will use examples of past fortification strategies to illuminate present ones, combining theory and practical observation. The premise is that *something* is happening, which I believe is that our age is increasingly fortified and surveilled: guarded, in a word. I intend to bring into full view the details of that development which many people apprehend partially or dimly. Why is it happening in this way? Finally, given an understanding of what and why, where might we be headed?

Methods and Sources

What follows, therefore, is a mixture of military history and strategic theory with social science theory and a lot of direct empirical observation. For the research in these chapters I have attended half a dozen security industry trade shows in the UK and elsewhere, as well as three separate military engineering conferences, spoken with countless managing directors, product specialists and marketers of firms selling fortification devices, consulted with a half dozen architects and designers, questioned dozens of builders, security-product installers, civil and military engineers, real estate developers and entrepreneurs, shopping mall, university, and hotel security managers, police officers and military officers, data centre builders, municipal officials, railway and airport operators, and more.

In trying to understand and explain the increasing guardedness of society I have dipped promiscuously into many disciplines which I will confess are far from my own comfort zone in military strategy. I have relied very heavily in particular on architecture and design, urban studies, and geography, amongst others. I think that my interpretations of and conclusions about some important things differ from the experts in those fields. I can only say in my defence that my dabbling in other disciplines has been respectful. I have borrowed tools from the toolboxes of others and used them as seemed correct to make something of my own that I hope they will find interesting.

One thing which quickly became obvious during this research is that the fortification community of interest is very large and diverse. Most of those involved in it, outside of some of those in military uniform, would not describe themselves as being in the fortress-building industry, which is not surprising as governments (a primary consumer of their products as well as the main regulator) tend to avoid the words 'fortification', 'fortress', or 'fortified enclave' when talking about the domestic scene, for reasons discussed further on. A quick look at the brochures and catalogues of the industry, however, filled as they are with products named 'Bastion', 'Barbican', 'Palisade', 'Citadel', 'Centurion', 'Sentry', and so on, can only lead one to the conclusion that fortification is the correct term, even if it is politically unpalatable.

Over the years in which this subject has interested me I have visited nearly all the places mentioned in the following chapters. The Covid-19 lockdown, however, impeded some of my intended formal field research in places I wanted to revisit with a more explicit aim of data-gathering, or to see for the first time. However, with the help of contacts, many of whom are former students, I managed to conduct extensive 'tours', interviews, and focus groups via Zoom of urban fortifications globally, including favelas in Rio de Janeiro and São Paulo, Brazil; two gated communities in South Africa, two more in China, and another in Papua New Guinea; the fortified middle-class compounds and government districts of Lagos, Nigeria; several fortified residential compounds, offices, and hotels in the Gulf States; the extensive 'Green Zone' surrounding Mogadishu Airport in Somalia; and UN compounds in Timbuktu and Bamako, Mali, amongst others. That this was possible at all is itself exemplary of the paradoxical combination of high 'virtual' connectedness with increasing physical separation that characterizes this guarded age.

I have also visited many of the military fortifications both old and new under discussion here, several in Afghanistan, and many in Europe, from the Kremlin in Moscow, to the walled city of Krakow, to the Iron Age hill forts of Britain. I toured the Jerusalem section of the Israeli security barrier with its main designer, visited the premises of the manufacturer of Hesco Bastion (on which much more to follow) to speak with its designers and engineers, walked two of the more fortified sections of the United States–Mexico border at El Paso in Texas and San Diego, California, and virtually toured three separate fortresses that are part of Morocco's massive Saharan 'Sand Wall'. I corresponded with Gulf-based engineers involved in the construction by Saudi Arabia of linear defences on its border with Yemen, and talked with countless soldiers involved in recent military operations in Iraq and Afghanistan, many of the most interesting of whom were at that time students on the British Army's Urban Warfare Instructors' course taught at the Infantry Battle School in Brecon, Wales.

Many of the examples in the book, however, are drawn from Britain – very often, as above, from the area of central London around where I happen to work: roughly that part of the Strand from Temple Bar to Wellington St, including those buildings enclosed by the Aldwych crescent. Studying contemporary fortifications is a bit like *The Matrix* – after a while you start to notice it everywhere: the armoured glass partitions in the shopping mall food court, the 'impact-rated' planters at the top of the High Street, the hydraulic 'rising road-blocker' at the entrance to the hotel forecourt, the cameras *everywhere*. They all start to stand out and you find yourself compelled to remark on them.

Many of these things are relatively recent additions to the urban landscape, but it is important to note that there is a sometimes surprisingly long history at work, with plenty of relatively old but highly pertinent examples. A personal favourite: the disguised machine-gun ports (now windows) on the front of Leconfield House on Curzon Street in London. These were installed during the Second World War, when the building served as the headquarters of the London military district, as security against possible German parachutists landing in nearby Hyde Park. They were retained after the war when it was taken over as the home of MI5, which stayed there until 1976. Supposedly, they were manned into the 1950s.[11] The fact is that there is a gigantic amount of fortified infrastructure out there, as my children will attest from many happy hours playing the games 'spot the bunker' and 'let's count the cameras' with their dad.

These illustrations, though, however UK- and London-centric, are generalizable of global trends and developments. Readers who are not familiar with Heathrow Airport, for instance, or the financial district of the City of London, may reflect on what is discussed in those parts of the book at whatever major international airport is closest to them or in the central business district of their own city, where, undoubtedly, there will be examples of everything discussed here. In many ways, London, indeed Britain generally, is at the forefront of the fortified state, which is more and more the default condition of contemporary life, but it is not unique nor particularly far ahead.

1

The Rise of the Walls

In 2016, Donald Trump was elected president of the United States to cries of his supporters chanting 'Build that wall! Build that wall!' at rally after rally, up and down the country. His administration pledged to massively scale up and extend the existing fortifications on the border with Mexico, which, while obviously porous to illegal migration, was already quite fortified.[1] People familiar with the geography of the border and the social pressures driving migrants were sceptical. One analyst who had walked and studied practically the entirety of it remarked: 'A wall? A massive concrete fortification? None of this made sense. Walls can be climbed, and fences can be cut, especially when tall, thick reeds make illegal entry that much easier to conceal.'[2] The point is eminently logical. The experience of other places that have tried to stem illegal cross-border movements with much more heavily guarded walls on a *much* smaller frontage suggests that determined migrants are prepared to escalate the levels of force required to get into a place more than border guards are prepared or permitted to escalate their efforts to stop them.

I refer here to the Spanish north African enclaves of Ceuta and Melilla, two autonomous European cities, an incongruous legacy of Spanish colonialism on the coast of Morocco. As early as 1993, the European Union paid an estimated $25 million to build a defensive wall around Ceuta running for eight kilometres, plus two parallel 2.5-metre-high fences with cameras and spotlights every thirty metres, to secure its southern boundary, which in these two spots lies on the continent of Africa.[3] In subsequent years these fortifications have been continuously bolstered.

Nevertheless, results have been poor. From 2016 through to June 2022, there were 145 physical assaults on Europe's southern border defences. In one attack, on 24 June 2022, twenty-three migrants were killed and 140 members of the Moroccan security forces injured.[4] Many thousands of migrants have successfully scaled Europe's ramparts here.[5] The scenes of migrant mobs in the hundreds launching semi-organized escalade assaults on the walls and fences with ladders and ropes, while hurling showers of rocks and bottles at ranks of police wielding batons and riot shields, look like something out of a mediaeval war film.

Ultimately, as we shall see below, even the most dread wall is hardly an obstacle if the people guarding it are absent or unwilling to use potentially very large amounts of force. This has led some to conclude that Trump's promise to build one across nearly 2,000 miles of border was more an act of 'performative statecraft' given that 'the wall' worked better rhetorically, as a political idea, than it did as a real barrier against border crossing.[6] At any rate, the wall was not built.

The point is that it was politically highly popular. People like walls. There is no denying it. The evidence is literally concrete and it's all over the place. We shall discuss this in much more detail further, but for the time being a short exemplary list will be useful. Consider:

i) Since the building of the Israeli 'security barrier' in 2006 – a combination of walls and fences physically separating its claimed territories from those under Palestinian control – dozens of similar walls, many of them much larger, have been completed around the world. Fortification of the boundaries of the European Union has been particularly intense.[7]

ii) Since the 11 September 2001 attacks, every airport in the world big enough to be regulated by the Convention on International Civil Aviation, which means nearly all of them, as well as many private and public buildings ranging from hotels to hospitals and museums to shopping malls, not to mention schools, have been 'target hardened' to a greater or lesser extent – meaning they have been fortified with ballistic- and blast-resistant barriers, surveillance systems, sophisticated access-control systems, and extensive perimeter security measures.

iii) Since the beginning of the Global War on Terror – an old term used to describe a series of ongoing military engagements now more often referred to as the 'Forever War' – armies have adopted a pattern of warfare that is strikingly positional and fortified.

Moreover, it is not only armies that are operating this way but also the representatives of NGOs, international organisations, journalists, and others who are living the 'guarded life', operating out of fortified compounds wherever there is perceived to be risk, which seems to be practically everywhere.[8]

I could go on but, as a rationale for a book based upon the premise that there has been a metaphorical explosion in contemporary fortification strategies, that is enough for now. For a person of my vintage (fifty-three) the situation is weird because the accumulated preconceptions of a lifetime say that this is not how it was supposed to be. We were supposed to get a different future from the one in which we now live.

What happened?

It is perhaps ironic to have a chapter entitled 'The Rise of the Walls' in which the first subheading is 'The Fall of the Wall'. The fact is that, in the long view of history, people build walls for one reason and then tear them down for another only to build new ones again, and so on and so on. There is, in other words, a cycle of guardedness that is written on the landscape in the form of forts and barriers built on the rubble of earlier forts and barriers.

It would be possible, therefore, to start answering the question above from very far back in time indeed. After all, the art of fortification had already reached a high state of development many thousands of years ago, and remnants of powerful military works dating back to the remotest periods of history can still be seen today in Asia Minor, Greece, in the basins of the Tigris and Euphrates, and the Nile valley. That would, however, make for a very long book. Let us then start our story a little less far back in time and closer to home.

The Fall of the Wall

On 5 March 1946, in a speech at Westminster College in Fulton, Missouri, Winston Churchill famously warned that an 'Iron Curtain' had descended across Europe, from Stettin on the coast of the Baltic Sea to Trieste on the Adriatic.[9] It traced the battle lines as they stood on the date of Germany's surrender in the Second World War on 7 May 1945. On the Western side were those people and places occupied by the armies of the democratic Allies. On the Eastern side were those people and places occupied by the Soviet Army. In the former there was liberation – a genuine return to national self-governance (or, in the two thirds of Germany occupied by Britain, France, and the United

States, the chance of an eventual redemption and return to independence) – whereas in the latter, 'liberation' amounted simply to a switch from Nazi domination to Soviet.

The 'Iron Curtain' was initially one of Churchill's arrestingly perceptive metaphors, a description of an emerging political reality not yet obvious to everyone else; but it was not long before the border between East and West was in fact demarcated by extensive fortifications that could not be missed. Its longest and hardest section was the 1,381km Intra-German Border (IGB) separating the two new countries: the Federal Republic of Germany, created after the amalgamation in 1949 of the sectors of Germany occupied by the Western allies; and the German Democratic Republic, founded a little later on the territory of the Soviet Occupation Zone in the northeast.

By the mid-1970s, throughout its length the IGB featured at least two layers of heavily mined and booby-trapped chain-mesh fencing, a deep concrete-lined anti-vehicle ditch, hundreds of guard towers, piers for floodlights by the thousands, and a lighter fence studded with electronic sensors to detect potential crossers. Where towns and villages were bisected by or abutted on the border, they were further enclosed by concrete walls.[10]

The most famous of these concrete walls was, of course, in Berlin, the historic German capital. In fact, Berlin was nowhere near the IGB; it was located 100 miles inside East Germany. However, because the city had been split between the occupying powers, it too had a West and an East fraction under effectively different political control – a microcosm of divided Germany. To say that this arrangement of sovereignty was a complex point of friction in the early Cold War would be a dramatic understatement.

Nonetheless, although the 'Iron Curtain' was effectively closely guarded everywhere else on its length, for many years it was still possible for people to cross it freely between East and West Berlin. That was until the early morning of Sunday, 13 August 1961, when East Germany unleashed a well-planned surprise called Operation Rose in which, over the space of a few hours, an improvised 'border closure' was erected through the middle of the great city.

At first, the Wall was hardly any sort of wall at all, just a jury-rigged mishmash of concertina and barbed-wire, with a few expedient walls mortared together here and there out of whatever materials were easily at hand – bricks, rubble, concrete blocks, and so on. The East German government that erected it called it the 'Anti-Fascist Protection Wall'. However, its object was not military defence but the completion of the *de facto* imprisonment of its own population against the possibility of their flight to the greater freedom and prosperity available in the West – a problem that had plagued the East German economy since its founding just over a decade earlier.'[11]

Better than a war

There is little doubt that the Wall and the IGB were effective in slowing the flight to the West, ultimately bringing it to a nearly complete halt. On the first day the Wall went up twenty-eight people escaped from East to West Berlin, the next day there were forty-one, but after that the number of escapees dwindled to a trickle. By the mid-1970s it had become extremely risky to attempt escape. The most viable means became to tunnel under the Wall, but that took great bravery as the chances of detection were high and the number of successful underground escapees was low.[12]

If the Cold War had an epicentre, it was the Wall in Berlin. It was certainly the scene of some of its most powerful rhetoric, such was its unmistakable symbolic power. The ideological struggle between East and West was concentrated there, materialized in concrete and wire, guard towers and floodlights. On 26 June 1963, in his famous 'Ich bin ein Berliner' speech, President John F. Kennedy put it this way: 'While the wall is the most obvious and vivid demonstration of the failures of the Communist system, for all the world to see, we take no satisfaction in it, for it is, as your mayor has said, an offence not only against history but an offence against humanity.'[13] He went on to declare that Berlin was 'a defended island of freedom'. In truth, though, it seems that Kennedy extemporized the most memorable parts of his speech, his emotions carried away by the power of the scene, the vast crowd he was addressing, the stark brutality of the Wall itself.

Privately, however, in the Cabinet offices and War Rooms of the major powers on *both* sides of the Cold War divide, leaders and advisors were quietly relieved about the Wall, or at any rate ambivalent about it. As Kennedy observed to his advisor on national security affairs Walt W. Rostow, the Wall was 'not a very nice solution, but [it was] a hell of a lot better than a war'.[14]

From the Berlin Blockade in 1948, when Stalin first attempted to force the West out of Berlin by laying economic siege to the city (a gambit successfully countered by the Berlin Airlift), through to 1963 when Kennedy visited, Berlin was a potential flashpoint of a Third World War which everyone feared.

The Wall solved that problem by cushioning a point of maximum pressure between the Cold War blocs like the cartilage in a knee joint. Yes, it horrified and offended the West, particularly West Germans; even worse it effectively sentenced millions of East Germans to life imprisonment in a police state. But for a long time it worked and, frankly, people got used to it.

Endgame

By the time another American President, Ronald Reagan, arrived in Berlin in June 1987 to give a speech (ostensibly on the 750th anniversary of the city), the Wall was nearly impregnable. Almost no one escaped over it – few even tried, as any attempt was so dangerous and so unlikely to succeed. 'General Secretary Gorbachev', Reagan cried before the Brandenburg Gate, 'if you seek peace, if you seek prosperity for the Soviet Union and Eastern Europe, if you seek liberalisation, come here to this gate. Mr Gorbachev open this gate. Mr Gorbachev . . . Mr Gorbachev, tear down this wall!'[15] It was an astonishing demand at the time because the Wall had become something of an established fact of life, not liked but accepted and usually ignored. With the wisdom of hindsight, however, one can detect signs that it was not an absolute impossibility that it could fall, that the Wall might not endure much longer.

Certainly, it was telling when in July 1989 Gorbachev informed the world at a speech to the Council of Europe in Strasbourg that the Soviet Union now ruled out the use of 'all military force, by an alliance against another alliance, *inside alliances* or wherever it may be'.[16] The message: if East Germany was going to continue to keep its population immured, then that decision would be down to its own regime, which would have to use its own resources to enforce it; the USSR had no longer the appetite to put down popular revolts amongst the populations of its Warsaw Pact 'allies' as it had done in the past.

But East Germany was by then bankrupt in almost every way, politically moribund, its leadership physically and morally decrepit, and literally out of money. What it had left, in theory, was brute force. The question was, would it use it? Thankfully, as it happened, the answer was no. That fact was wildly apparent the first time I personally encountered the Wall, in the early morning of 10 November 1989, which I suppose technically was the day after it 'fell'.

The event of the Wall's demise had started to kick off on the evening of 9 November when at 10:42 p.m. the West German ARD television channel led its late-night news programme with the announcement that, 'This ninth of November is a historic day: the GDR has announced that its borders are open to everyone, with immediate effect, and the gates of the Wall stand wide open.'[17] By 11:30 p.m. the first group of East Berliners had pushed aside the gates at Bornholmer Strasse and in the hours soon afterwards thousands more people swarmed through the checkpoints everywhere else along the course of the Wall. Without being too picky, if you were to have to point a finger at a single time and place that the Cold War ended then there in Berlin on that day would be a good choice – all that history concentrated on one object.

I remember it well despite the haze of alcohol combined with a euphoric natural buzz which befuddled me and almost everyone else who was there. My being there was coincidental. I was a twenty-year-old university student and army reservist on a gap-year backpacking trip at the time, touring fortifications and battlefields, fittingly. The day before I had been on the other side of the country scrambling around Ehrenbreitstein, a marvellous nineteenth-century fortress overlooking the town of Koblenz on the Rhine River.

I caught a ride to Berlin about midday with two German girls who were also heading there because the 'something-big-is-happening' vibe that had been emanating from the city all that autumn just felt like it was coming to a head. We drove all day and night in a growing convoy of people headed the same way.

By the time I finally saw it, though, there was nothing jury-rigged about the Wall at all. In fact, it was marvellous – positively state-of-the-art as walls go. Grenzwall 75, as this (the fourth) generation of the Wall was called, after the year of its design, was a testament to the validity of the stereotype of quality German engineering and workmanship.[18] The face it presented to the West, on which side it was heavily graffitied, was actually just the last of the approximately 100-metre-wide complex of barriers that made up the whole border fortification, but it is what most people remember as the Wall.

It was made up of thousands of prefabricated concrete sections – each 3.6m high, 1.2m wide, and resting on an L-shaped platform base of 1.6m depth. Tongue and groove seams at the sides of every slab joined them together snugly while at the top a horizontal steel reinforcing bar welded them securely into a continuous whole. The result was a uniform barrier 22cm thick at the base tapering to 12cm at the top, a more than adequate prophylactic against penetration by people or vehicles. Atop all these elements a circular concrete pipe 30cm in diameter with a 14cm slot cut along its length was cemented into place – a final measure to prevent runaways getting any grip on it in a potential escalade.

Estimates vary of the number of people directly killed trying to get past the Wall in Berlin or the IGB generally in the years of its existence. According to the German Federal Prosecutor's Office, eighty-six people died, whereas another working group reckoned that there were over 200 deaths.[19] Even the higher number ought to give pause to people who argue that 'walls don't work', because the facts are otherwise.

One generation ago, Europe was physically divided by a wall on one side of which were tens of millions of people who desperately wanted to get to the other side. And yet, except in triflingly small numbers, they did not, because the most likely result of trying to was death. What did not work was Soviet communism and the permanent political and economic domination of much of Eastern Europe by the Kremlin in Moscow. The Wall, on the other hand, performed just fine.

The thing is that an objectively very strong wall can be completely useless while a relatively jury-rigged and expedient one can be quite effective. This signals the possibility that the power and meaning behind any given fortification are not strictly written in the walls themselves; they lie in the strategic intent and will behind the construction. For comparison – according to the International Organization for Migration, a United Nations affiliated group – the currently spottily guarded US–Mexico border is the 'deadliest land crossing in the world', with, in 2022, an estimated 853 migrant deaths.[20]

The Future that Failed

The best word I can think of to describe the end of the Cold War that I saw is 'surreal'. The Wall did not literally 'come down' or 'fall' that day, as we tend now to memorialize it – that came a bit later. It was still very much a physical presence when I saw it, but it was a dead fortification nonetheless, non-functional, a relic portending a doom that had been miraculously avoided – it might as well have literally fallen over. A fortification that is not defended is just a wall, not a Wall. It is an inert pile of rock, you might say, easily passed over or around or through as the case may be. As is true generally in war, the moral force, the will to act, to pull or not to pull the trigger, is the vitalizing ingredient – and that was now gone.

I particularly recall the neat seams between the slabs of the Wall, because that was where the concrete was weak enough that a couple of hours of enthusiastic chipping and hammering was sufficient to make a hole in it big enough to put one's head through to peer into the deep security zone on the eastern side where the once fearsome guard towers, floodlights, and attack dog runs were located. It was an unprepossessing, grey, and anti-climactic vision. I glimpsed an awkward looking East German border guard on the other side – obviously at a total loss as to what he was meant to be doing there now; he was armed with an AK-74 assault rifle, not that it made any difference by then. Rather more memorable was the jubilant half-naked drunken man I saw riding a ten-speed bicycle along the top of the Wall, balanced somehow on the ribbon-wide flat section that hours before had marked the hardest, deadliest divide on the planet. Perhaps he was a circus performer, for sure he had excellent balance. In any case, it was clear that the Cold War was over.

Coincidentally, as noted earlier, 1989 was the bicentenary of the French Revolution and the BBC Reith Lecture series that year, given by Jacques Darras, was supposed to address that momentous subject and reflect on its meaning and import in the long view. Inevitably, though, the lectures were influenced by contemporaneous events, and it is interesting to read them now for the picture they give of erudite scholarly opinion at the time – which was certainly a more sober view of events than my own.

Darras astutely contrasted the apparent triumph of liberal democracy in Europe, the metaphorical tearing down of the 'Iron Curtain', with the then-recent forcible extinguishment of the democratic spark in China, where in August 1989 hundreds of democratic protesters in Beijing's Tiananmen Square were literally torn to shreds under tank tracks just outside the red-painted walls of the Forbidden City.

It was a reminder, he pointed out, that history does not work in a single 'progressivist' direction, it is not driving towards a particular objective; it is quite possible to go back – freedoms can be lost as well as won, walls can come down and go back up again. Still, with the end of the Cold War, what he optimistically saw coming for Europe at any rate, and what he admittedly longed for, was an increasingly united continent: a 'Europe without walls' growing beyond and away from the destructive nationalisms of its past towards a harmonious shared future.[21]

Other scholars went further, applying a similarly rosy perspective to the whole globe, supposing, in the words of the American political scientist Francis Fukuyama, an 'end of history ... the universalization of Western liberal democracy as the final form of human government'.[22]

If the immediate post-Cold War era had a *zeitgeist*, it was 'globalization', a system of thought concerning the shape of a 'new world order' comprised of several elements that came to totally dominate thinking on the world's political economy. Stemming partly from the freeing up of global politics with the end of the ideological conflict, and partly by advances in information technology, globalization was supposed to represent the growing *interdependence* and *interpenetration* of all human life, as well as the increasing *integration* of world governance.

It is usually conceived as primarily an economic affair, for good reason – the transnationalization of finance, the deregulation of markets, and the free movement of labour and goods are processes at its heart. In 1997, Alan Greenspan, then Chair of the United States Federal Reserve, put it this way:

> As a result of very rapid increases in telecommunications and computer-based technologies and products, a dramatic expansion in cross-border financial flows and within countries has emerged. The pace has become truly remarkable. These technology-based developments have so expanded the breadth and depth of markets that governments, even reluctant ones, increasingly have felt they have had little alternative but to deregulate and free up internal credit and financial markets.[23]

In other words, at enormous speed, information technology was driving changes in transnational commerce which national governments were powerless to resist even if they wanted to.

First cracks?

Some scholars and activists worried that globalization was drawing the whole world into a form of closeness that, notwithstanding its putative economic benefits, would have serious negative effects. The philosopher John Ralston Saul, an early and trenchant critic of the process, summed globalization up as having 'some remarkable successes, some disturbing failures and a collection of what might best be called running sores'.[24]

Integrating distinctive societies into one universal conglomeration for the purposes of efficient economic production might serve wealth creation in the aggregate, but it also tends to reduce people to the status of crass consumers. The withering of the powers of the nation-state relative to those of supra-national institutions might serve the free movement of capital and labour, but it also tends to separate national 'democratic' decision-makers from any meaningful control by their voters.

Places which had been insulated from the effects of war by distance were now exposed to serious violence at home in the form of 'super-empowered' terrorism, often emanating from the second and third generation of immigrant diasporas alienated from and resentful of their new titular nationhood. For my part, the moment of understanding that things had gone quite fundamentally wrong in a way that it would take generations to correct, if they are correctable at all, came on the morning of 7 July 2005.

On that day London was the target of four coordinated suicide bombings aimed at its transportation infrastructure. Three detonations occurred on London Underground carriages and one on a bus in Tavistock Square. Fifty-two people were killed, and 700 others were injured. I was on the Tube at the time, commuting like millions of other Londoners, but, thankfully, not in one of the exploded trains.

Shortly after the attacks I was asked by a BBC journalist for a quote on what was going on and what I thought it meant. Since I was staring at the BBC News homepage at the time trying to figure that very thing out, the absurd circularity of the situation caused me to politely put the phone down and resolve never to do 'hot takes' on spectacular events of the day.

If I could go back in time and answer the journalist's question with the benefit of many more years of reasoning and evidence, I would like to have remarked that, in their words and deeds, the 7/7 bombers were explicitly rejecting the supposed processes of the globalization of society. As one of them put it in his martyrdom video:

> I and thousands like me are forsaking everything for what we believe. Our driving motivation doesn't come from tangible commodities that this world has to offer. Our religion is Islam – obedience to the one true God, Allah, and following the footsteps of the final prophet and messenger Muhammad . . . This is how our ethical stances are dictated.[25]

In other words, I might have explained that the attack in London was another shot against the pretension of Western universalism embedded in the globalization narrative; that it was conducted by Islamic radicals who had very different and compelling views on the salience of space and place, the direction of history, and the sources of power in our world.

Overall, though, the elites reckoned globalization to be a desirable thing – on balance a positive development in human history. The British Prime Minister Tony Blair seemed to revel in its ineluctability:

'I hear people say we have to stop and debate globalization. You might as well debate whether autumn should follow summer', he told the Labour Party annual conference in 2005.[26] The 7/7 bombers would have begged to differ, and to judge from where we stand now, they had a strong argument.

Flat and fluid, not fortified

In fields beyond politics, such as business management, there was a similar proliferation of popular 'strategies' for the decentralization of industries to better exploit the benefits of global networks and information technology. Hierarchies needed to be 'flattened' to liberate the 'creative power of chaos' in networked organizations. To the adage 'knowledge is power' a new codicil was added: that the best knowledge is not hidden away but held openly at the 'edge' of an organization, where it can be shared, contributed to, and most adroitly acted upon.[27]

As often happens, ideas which took hold first in industry began to be reflected in the military. Soon after the proclamation of an 'information revolution' transforming global economics, the major armed forces of the world also began to perceive their own technology-driven 'revolution in military affairs' (RMA).[28]

A seminal essay on a vision of future war called 'network-centric warfare', written in the late 1990s at the height of the 'dot.com' boom, began with this essential proposition:

> Arising from fundamental changes in American society and business, military operations increasingly will capitalize on the advances and advantages of information technology. Here at the end of a millennium we are driven to a new era in warfare. Society has changed. The underlying economics and technologies have changed. American business has changed. We should be surprised and shocked if America's military did not.[29]

In essence, the world's best armies reckoned that mastering the benefits of information technology would enable them to fight fast and light, to win wars cheaply, quickly, and decisively. In this they took their cues from industry, with its mantras about the profit-maximizing virtues of 'just-in-time' supply chains, 'off-shoring', and 'flattening'. The metaphors popularly used to describe what was happening show the basic ideas underlying these interrelated developments in such different realms, from politics to social life, business, and military affairs.

One of the most popular metaphors was coined by the *New York Times* columnist Thomas Friedman in his best-selling book *The World is Flat: A Brief History of the Twenty-First Century*, published in 2005.[30] The central theme of his analysis, which also began with the fall of the Berlin Wall, was how digitalization was connecting the world's 'knowledge pools' and resources, enabling frictionless flows of goods, people, and ideas on a global scale, largely for the better.

To flatten something is to smooth it, to remove barriers to movement across its surface. A synonym of flattening in the context of civil and military architecture is 'razing' or 'slighting' – the deliberate destruction of the elements of a fortification that make it functional, such as removing its walls and destroying its towers or filling in its ditch. One of the main reasons so many castles and forts of Europe survive now only as decorous ruins is that, as part of the centralization of state power in the sixteenth and seventeenth centuries, kings tended to preventatively destroy such potential points of resistance to their power by ambitious lesser nobles.

That is to say, there was at least one period of 'flattening' in European history before our own times, a period marked quite literally by a modernizing power dynamic that required the levelling of many of the mighty fortresses we associate with the mediaeval era.

That fact is important when we consider another influential metaphor for globalization, that of the sociologist Zygmunt Bauman who in the late 1990s coined the term 'liquid modernity' (sometimes 'late modernity') to describe the current human condition as he saw it. Our situation, he believed, had become defined by the properties of a fluid – above all by an extraordinary openness and mobility we easily associate with 'lightness'.[31] These properties also became the leitmotif of defence 'transformation' in the post-Cold War era, suggesting that Bauman's ideas had a broad currency.

The fall of the Wall, in this view, symbolized the emergence of a new world which was to be profoundly untrammelled, integrative, interdependent, connected, fast moving, and ever changing, a world which flowed around or dissolved obstacles.

As opposed to the 'heavy' modernity of the past where power existed in place, where tangible physical stuff mattered, in liquid modernity, Bauman argued, power was 'exterritorial . . . no longer bound, not even slowed down, by the resistance of space'.[32] This was an extraordinarily consequential claim, if true, and certainly he was onto something – it does seem to explain a great deal about the behaviour of governments, corporations, armies, and powerful groups and individuals over the last few decades.

According to this thesis, a world organized in such a manner and operating in accordance with such principles would look physically different than in the past in some obvious ways. 'For power to be free to flow', Bauman wrote,

> the world must be free of fences, barriers, fortified borders, and checkpoints. Any dense and tight network of social bonds, and particularly a territorially rooted tight network, is an obstacle to be cleared out of the way. Global powers are bent on dismantling such networks for the sake of their continuous and growing fluidity, that principal source of their strength and the warrant of their invincibility.[33]

Globalization, in effect, was supposed to be a process that would manifest in a global *razing*. Either by deliberate effect, as the conscious policy of powerful people and groups in government and industry, or as a natural expression of the network spirit of our connected age – by the will of the people to communicate, share, and move ever more quickly and in increasing volume – the long age of the wall, of barriers, of all sorts of impediment to *flows* was over.

A new age had dawned, in which heavy fortifications rooted in a physical place would be out of place – if not altogether superfluous then tangential to the exercise of real power. For power-holders, being able to 'travel light' was vital; holding on to things once deemed attractive for their reliability and solidity – 'for their heavy weight, substantiality and unyielding power of resistance' – was out of fashion.[34] When the Wall fell all the walls fell, supposedly.

Strategic Stratigraphy

'The reports of my death are greatly exaggerated', remarked Mark Twain on a visit to London in 1897, when he was informed by a reporter that an American newspaper had printed his obituary. Likewise with the above predictions, we must observe from our perspective twenty years later that the death of physical stuff in general and of walls specifically has been greatly exaggerated.

The Berlin Wall is now almost all gone, it is true – just a few fragments of it remain in place here and there. The infamous 'Checkpoint Charlie' crossing point between East and West is preserved as a museum, along with a large section of Grenzwall 75 that was relocated there for posterity. The fortifications of the IGB have been removed and it is now a bucolic nature park, no more than a few hundred metres wide but over a thousand kilometres long, weaving its way through the centre of Europe.[35]

Practically everywhere else, though, walls are very much back in style.

When archaeologists examine a site, literally digging through its layers, they are studying the 'cultural stratigraphy' of a place. The artefacts they find, and the order in which they are layered, can tell the story of the peoples who lived there – who they were, where they came from, how they lived, where they went, and so on. Clearly, fortifications leave significant traces on the landscape.

Even simple things like digging ditches or erecting a wooden palisade can leave marks on the landscape detectable by aerial photography thousands of years later. During a drought in the summer of 2018, for example, the Royal Commission on the Ancient and Historical Monuments of Wales conducted an aerial reconnaissance that discovered two previously unknown Roman marching camps, three auxiliary forts, and other buildings of the Romano-British period, possibly including a previously unknown coastal fort near Kidwelly.[36]

Uncovering and explaining layers of fortifications, I would propose, reveals a strategic stratigraphy. In the case of the Welsh example, the evidence of the discovered forts may lead to a better understanding of Roman strategies of conquest and pacification, and, ultimately, of their withdrawal from Britain. My point, however, is not so much archaeological as it is contemporary. We are now adding our own layer of strategic stratigraphy, one which I would suggest is especially extensive.

How do we explain the existence, in what so many presuppose is a radically connected age, of a powerful fortification *zeitgeist* that appears at odds with the precept of openness?

A pub in rural Buckinghamshire, England, might not seem the most auspicious place to begin to answer that question. In fact, though, it is a fitting place to start. The village of Medmenham lies three miles west of the town of Marlow alongside the Thames River, just below a sharp break in the Chiltern Hills in a nationally designated Area of Outstanding Natural Beauty. The village focus is the church of St Peter and Paul, dating to the sixth century, although the current structure is primarily twelfth century. The Dog and Badger pub, which claims to be 500 years old, is just across the road. The village is a picture postcard of an English country idyll.

Its relevance to the present study lies in the fact that even here most of the landscape and major structures have been shaped to a surprising extent by war and the threat of violence. The pub itself is late mediaeval and robustly built; not fortified as such, but with walls thick and strong enough to have captured a Civil War era cannonball presumably fired in a nearby skirmish, which was discovered during reconstruction some years ago. Even more significant is the hill fort located just fifty metres to the east along the high embankment behind the pub across a narrow lane. Encompassing seventeen acres within a still imposing ditch and berm enceinte, 'Medmenham Camp', as it is known, is one of several such sites established across the Chiltern Hills during the Late Bronze Age and Iron Age. The hill fort's construction and commanding position over the Thames valley demonstrates a need for defence perceived by the inhabitants of this area going back into prehistory.

In fact, most of what we know of the history of this pastoral place has been far from pacific. A thousand years ago this was the borderland between the Saxon Kingdom of Wessex and the Viking Daneland to the north. Raids and skirmishes were endemic up and down this valley, which is why another Iron Age fort just a mile down the road is called 'Danesfield Camp', though it pre-dates the Vikings considerably.

During the Second World War, Danesfield House, a grand country house built in the late nineteenth century inside the ramparts of the fort, was the headquarters of the RAF Central Interpretation Unit – an intelligence group that specialized in the analysis of photographic reconnaissance, which informed nearly every Allied military operation of the war. Some of its most important work included identifying the precise type and location of the German 'Atlantic Wall' fortifications ahead of the D-Day landings, as well as the hidden firing points of V-1 and V-2 rockets, so that they could be plastered by aerial bombing.

It was presumably the nearby RAF base that German aircraft were aiming at when they dropped a bomb on the crossroads between the Dog and Badger and St Peter and Paul church just across the way. The blast blew out the stained-glass windows on one side of the church and sprayed it with fragments, but otherwise left it undamaged. Whether that was the first time this church had seen war is unknown; but the place is certainly no stranger to pandemonium.

In short, even this apparently peaceful place has been at times a contested borderland, a site of active conflict, and most recently near the epicentre of planning for the largest siege operation in human history – and all that history is visible in traces on the landscape and the structures upon it, if you know what you are looking at. An appreciation of the depth of strategic stratigraphy even in such unlikely places as this pervades this book.

Strategy on the ground

There is one other element which makes Medmenham a bit more special than most: the village was for a while the home of the British strategist Basil Liddell Hart. A plain black headstone marks his grave in the churchyard. Liddell Hart was always keen to stress that battle was but one of the aspects of strategic thinking, which must be understood to encompass a wider range of issues, including notably economics.

One of his most famous interpreters and admirers was the historian Paul Kennedy, who presented himself one morning in October 1966 at the door of States House, Liddell Hart's home in Medmenham, to be his research assistant working on a history of the Second World War.[37] Kennedy went on to develop the notion of 'grand strategy', a concept distinguished by a focus on the strategic importance of long-term policies in peacetime – not just wartime.[38]

In summary of this chapter, then, we might say the following. For one, right now the world is experiencing an intensive period of 'wallification' (to coin a term), surprising not only in its scale but also because its development is so contrary to post-Cold War expectations. For another, while its causes are many and should not be oversimplified, which is why we will discuss them further, one overarching driver is a reaction to the violent rejection of the supposed triumph of liberal democratic capitalism intrinsic to the idea of globalization.

There are many ways to try to explain what is happening and why. The one that I have chosen, however, is to look for instances of contemporary fortification wherever and in whatever forms they might appear and then place them in historical context, with a view to teasing out their meaning and importance in terms of strategic theory.[39] This approach is based, in turn, upon two ideas.

First, the proper study of strategy encompasses a great deal more than military matters in or near to wartime. I do not suggest that this book is a work of grand strategy. In fact, nearly all the things I will talk about in subsequent chapters have far more the character of bottom-up than top-down strategies. There is a strategic logic to them, but the word 'grand' does not seem the most appropriate description for what seems a much more organic and distributed set of activities.

Second, what we are studying is best explained by locating it in a historical context that can help us illuminate the present. The Earth is a kind of palimpsest upon which history is written in the physical forms of the structures that we build – and we are still inscribing that history today because, as we have seen, history did not end.

2

Civilization, War, and Guardedness

In a recent history of civilization as seen through the prism of walls, historian and archaeologist David Frye concluded: 'In the early years of the new millennium, the world entered its Second Age of Walls. Few of us even noticed. It all happened quickly, like a worldwide Barbed Wire Sunday, but drawing far less interest from Western observers than the earlier walling of Berlin.'[1] Clearly, I share the apprehension that our age is dominated by walls – securitized architecture more precisely – and the feeling that this is a surprising thing. It occurred somehow in full view, while at the same time without much remark until quite recently. But if this is a 'second age of walls', then when did the 'first age' end? For that matter, when did it start? Neither of these hypothetical points in time are at all clear.

Perhaps we should say that war, civilization, and guardedness have always gone together. In that sense, there has only been one 'age of walls' and we are still in it. However, their forms and primary purposes are highly mutable. In some periods these forms have been overt, and their strategic function has been at the centre of obvious national policy. In other periods, the forms have been less visible, and fortifications have been seemingly distant from the strategic mainstream; indeed, in the last century they went literally and metaphorically underground.

In the twentieth century the world whipsawed between extremes in how fortification stood in relation to strategic and military theory and practice. The story of the coming into and going out of fashion of fortification over the last 100 years is complicated and will be treated in some detail further on. For the time being, let us stick with the more abstract idea of 'ages of history' and the ways in which our current posture of guardedness reflects and is shaped by the character of this age.

The character of war at any given place and time in history is influenced by the dominant societal assemblage in all its intertwined aspects – cultural, political, economic, and technological. This is what makes a given period an 'age' that is distinctive from the times preceding and following it. There are as many ways to divide history by period as there are valid perspectives on human affairs. There are also many conceptual frames which might be applied, from the theological to the technological.[2] A list of how various disciplines and points of view have contrasted one age with another would be long and superfluous.

In the study of war, a common perspective is some variant of the 'wave theory' proposed in the 1970s and 1980s by the futurist Alvin Toffler. In this view, the primary independent variable is the dominant means of economic production in a society; hence the agricultural age (first wave) was followed by the industrial age (second wave), and we are now in, or on the cusp of, an information age (third wave).[3] The dependent variable is military practice: agricultural societies fight wars with agricultural tools and in accordance with agricultural needs, whereas industrial societies fight industrial wars dominated by industrial tools and needs, and so on.

A related more recent proposition involves waves of industrialization, including the 'fourth wave' – supposedly an era of ubiquitous computing and cyber-physical systems in which we are now enmeshed.[4] It follows that an information society, such as ours, will fight information wars dominated by strategic communications and computer network (i.e., cyber) attacks.

Variants of the wave theory more focused upon technology and war divide history differently. Van Creveld, for instance, supposed a long 'Age of Tools' (muscle-powered weapons) lasting up until 1500, after which followed the 'Age of Machines' (gunpowder weapons and other more complex military devices) up to about 1830, then an 'Age of Systems' (a response fundamentally to science and industrialization) which carried on up to 1945, at which point dawned an 'Age of Automation' dominated by computing – an age in which we are still.[5]

My aim is not to provide my own interpretation of the history of warfare through the ages. I generally accept and find useful how it has been periodized by others, and agree that probably in my lifetime, in the West at any rate, we have moved from one age to another, usually referred to as a post-modern 'information age'.[6] As I have in turn labelled this the 'Guarded Age', on account of its surprisingly heavily fortified character, it is useful to consider the paradigmatic aspects of warfare now coming into being.

In a nutshell, I propose that at the level of whole-societal confrontation the character of guarded age warfare is dominated by two, at first glance contradictory, aspects: firstly by the weaponization of ideas – an area in which the West is at a surprisingly marked disadvantage due, amongst other reasons, to the critical tunnelling out of its own cultural myths; and secondly, at the level of physical combat, by a shift away from 'manoeuvre' towards a much more positional form of warfare I would describe as network-enabled attrition – an area in which the West is also at a disadvantage on account of the diminishment of its relative industrial power.

Guarded Age Warfare

War is the sustained and coordinated use of violence between political entities.[7] It has several 'natural' attributes that exist no matter what era in history or place in the world we observe it. It causes pain and destroys value. War is not made on a lifeless entity but against a thinking opponent – one who probably wishes to win as badly as you do and will pursue its own strategies every bit as imaginatively. It is chancy. The outcome of any given action is never completely predictable.

War*fare*, by contrast, is the *conduct* of war, which varies enormously. New techniques for applying force are constantly being invented. As soon as a tactic is employed by one belligerent, the other side begins to learn the technique and to adapt counters to it. Moreover, things which are not in themselves weapons are constantly used to serve military purposes. Humans are very imaginative in weaponizing things.

Indeed, human inventiveness in non-military fields often has a bigger impact on warfare than the improvement of old weapons or even the invention of new ones. The railroad revolutionized military logistics – a key factor in the success of Prussia in the Franco-Prussian War, for instance. Telecommunications is the central requirement of mobile combined arms operations – there would have been no 'blitzkrieg' without radios. For the present study, our main concern is the contribution of architecture, which currently is very lively.

The wars of agrarian societies have distinctively rural qualities: campaigns conform with the needs of the growing season, weapons tend to resemble agricultural implements, there is a heavy use of animals, the rank structure reflects class structure, with the land-owning nobility providing officers while soldiers are drawn from the peasantry, and so on. Likewise, the wars of industrial societies reflect the strengths and preoccupations of factory managers and state technocrats: standardization of weapons, mechanization, mass mobilization, and the 'rational' application of science to military problems, for example.

Amongst the consequences of the industrial revolution, some suggest, is the dawning of an Anthropocene era in which human activity is shaping the global environment more than natural processes. This has obviously had a gigantic impact on the character of warfare. There were plenty of hints of the magnitude of the change through the nineteenth century. Whether the American Civil War or the Franco-Prussian War, the Boer War, or the Russo-Japanese War, we saw the signs of a leap in the scale of warfare and the lethality of weapons brought about by industry. The First World War, however, drove the lesson home unambiguously.[8]

It is impossible to do justice to these developments in a paragraph or two. We must be content with a few overarching observations about the effect on warfare of the change from one age to another. Three things are particularly pertinent, providing insight on what might be happening in our own time.

First, the patterns of the old paradigm are not fully erased or replaced by those of the new one. Instead, there is a blend of the two in which the importance of old things sometimes re-emerges in ways that are quite shocking.[9] Second, although there are few transitions of 'ages' from which to draw firm conclusions, it seems the pace of change is accelerating. The agrarian age lasted a very long time – effectively from the beginnings of civilization up to a couple of hundred years ago. The industrial age, in comparison, is a blip in time. Third, change from one age to another seems to coincide with large and jarring changes in the international order.

Looking at recent technologies, we may ask what happens to warfare when digital computing, microelectronics, and high-speed, high-density communications are applied to it. The general qualities of the information age might be said to be something like the following.

First, there is a high degree of *intangibility* of value in the larger economy. 'Knowledge' industries create wealth not by making things per se but by creating ideas which may lead to physical products (often made elsewhere) or may remain ideas perfectly saleable as such, i.e., financial services, entertainment, and so on. Second, there is a massive increase in the *portability* of information, which practically everyone now can share in volumes and at a speed and reach that would have astonished the most powerful governments a generation ago – this being the main reason it is now phenomenally difficult to keep secrets. Third, there is a dramatic leap in the *scalability* of certain types of inventions – specifically the sorts of ideas noted above – which can go from fringe to mainstream in a matter of days or hours.[10]

Changes in the military sphere have followed similar patterns and reflect the same sort of language. The phrase 'know yourself and know your enemy and you shall never know defeat' – attributed to Sun Tzu but undoubtedly a truism always recognized – seemed to be massively affirmed by digital technologies like advanced communications, GPS navigation, powerful sensors, and precision-attack weapons. For a general to be able to see his enemy's forces before they could see his, to know in real time the whereabouts of everything meaningful on the battlefield, and to be able to strike accurately anything observed, would give him an Olympian advantage. The supposed effect known as the RMA, mentioned earlier, was extremely popular in military circles in the 1990s and into the early 2000s.

When it comes to the fluidity and volatility of the information environment, some analysts concluded that a new era of warfare had dawned in which the importance of the virtual domain – the perception of conflict – superseded the physical.[11] Similarly, others supposed that in such communications-dominant times as these, 'soft power' – the ability of a country to attract and persuade people towards adopting its point of view or agenda through the desirability of its culture and way of life – had become as useful as, or even more useful than, coercion through 'hard power', i.e., the threat of physical violence.[12]

In general terms, the beliefs such terms reflected were in accordance with a larger apprehension that a new age had arrived, resonantly described as a 'new world order', one which was distinctively unipolar, with the United States unambiguously at its head. Of course, that was not the end of the story at all, as we discussed in the last chapter. As with the transition from one age to another in previous times, what appears to be the direction of benefit initially has the potential to whip drastically in the opposite direction as other powers adjust to the 'new normal'.

Fortification in Modern Warfare

On the eve of the First World War all the major European powers subscribed largely to a national security strategy based on grand fortifications. Whole countries were armoured by parallel lines of fortresses along their frontiers, while important cities and communications centres were similarly fortified. The greatest of these defensive complexes, such as the Belgian fortresses of the Meuse Valley or those of the French at Verdun – both built to ward off German attack on likely invasion routes – were potent symbols of national pride, and the military engineers who designed them, Generals Henri Alexis Brialmont and Séré de Rivières respectively, were well known public figures.[13]

But the credibility of such strategies was badly shaken by the two world wars. In the first few weeks of the First World War, forts which were thought impregnable were blasted into submission by specialist German siege artillery like the 42cm Krupp artillery piece, whose 1,600lb shells cracked open the concrete shells of the Belgian forts. It took the Germans just four days and two giant howitzers to subdue one of the strongest fortress systems in Europe.[14]

On the other hand, while the rapid destruction of Belgium's impressive fortresses strikingly illustrated the power of modern weaponry, it did not presage the dawning of a new, fluid style of mobile warfare. The result was quite the opposite, as field fortifications like the continuous trench lines of the First World War's Western Front came to dominate the battlefield at an unprecedented scale and intensity.[15] It is not surprising, therefore, that in the interwar period Belgium, the Netherlands, and particularly France, took the lesson that permanent, sophisticated, large-scale fortifications were the way to go in future.

Unfortunately for them, the highly expensive and impressive permanent fortifications they built served them poorly. In 1940 the German invasion of France and the Low Countries was barely slowed by Belgium's Fort Eben Emael, said to be the strongest fortress in the world and the linchpin of Allied defences in the West. It was captured in half an hour by specially trained and equipped German paratroopers who landed on its roof in gliders and demolished its defences with shaped explosive charges, which were at that time a technological innovation.[16]

Even more famously, France's Maginot Line – a mighty network of underground fortresses built in the 1930s, connected by underground electric railways, each hewn out of the rock and lined with steel-reinforced cement, buried beyond the deepest penetrating power of the guns and bombs of the time, and big enough to house, supply, and maintain a garrison of up to 1,200 men serving dozens of artillery pieces and machine guns in armoured steel cupolas – impeded German operations hardly at all.[17] It was simply outflanked by an armoured thrust through the Ardennes Forest and Belgium which had been opened up by the fall of Eben Emael.

The true picture is more mixed than the description above might suggest. A fairer assessment would note that some fortifications, both fixed and field, gave good service throughout the world wars. The nineteenth-century German fortifications around Metz, built upon the work of Séré de Rivières when the area was a French province, held up General Patton's US Third Army from September to December of 1944 with savage fighting.[18] Meanwhile, Japanese fortifications of the Pacific Islands proved ingenious and extremely tough to defeat for American forces.[19] Moreover, the maligned Maginot Line failed because it was bypassed. In the few instances it was fought over, its powers of resistance, even with low-quality garrison troops, was very high.[20]

By and large, however, the power of mobile operations in the Second World War overshadowed the role of fortifications in the estimations of military science. For example, Colonel Trevor N. Dupuy's summation of the inventions and refinements of tactics and techniques in land warfare to emerge from the war includes 'vastly improved mobile ordnance, fast tanks and tank destroyers, and other cross-country vehicles [which] combined to produce a doctrine of mobile warfare at speeds heretofore impossible', but not a word about fortification.[21]

Retrograde and redundant?

After the war, the power of nuclear weapons massively added to a growing perception of the futility of fortification. The aforementioned Liddell Hart, arguably Britain's most famous modern military thinker, and certainly one of its most imaginative, when asked in the 1950s to write an essay on war in the nuclear era, prescribed a massive civil defence programme that recollected the ravings of the artilleryman in H.G. Wells' *The War of the Worlds*, in which he imagined a world safe from surface devastation – underground: 'Under the great cities, a series of air-conditioned honeycomb towns might radiate from the underground railways, which could serve their present purpose of intercommunication. Provincial centres would also be provided with a low-level layer where work and life would carry on.'[22]

In his diary, however, he admitted that halfway through writing the essay he had considered 'that the only sensible advice was to tell people either "to put their heads in the gas oven" or to emigrate'.[23] Many people and groups, sometimes on a national level, invested in fallout bunkers and other defensive measures against nuclear war. No one placed great stock in their efficacy, however, and by the 1970s and 1980s it had mostly become a niche activity. A partial exception is Switzerland, which has historically maintained a high level of civil defence spending, including the mandating of bombproof shelters in residential homes.

By the mid-1970s, one well-regarded survey of the history of fortification described it as a 'redundant science'.[24] Even now, authors wishing to describe something in strategic affairs as hidebound, retrograde, and/or doomed to failure are wont to invoke the Maginot Line or to decry a 'fortress mentality'. For example, a former Obama-era White House official criticized the Trump administration's ban on some foreign travel into the United States during the Covid-19 crisis as 'his Maginot Line, the false sense of security that in fact left us hugely vulnerable to attack'.[25]

The fact is that nowadays the study of fortification as a pertinent issue of *contemporary* strategic and military affairs is anaemic. The last work on fortification as an active subject of military affairs with significant prospects *for the future* was written over a century ago by the British military engineer Sir George Sydenham Clarke. Even then, he pointed out that there was no 'school of thought regarding fortification', that elementary principles were still 'floating in solution', and that no 'consensus of mature opinion' had been attained.[26]

It is largely agreed in the field that the 'modern system' of warfare – to use the term coined by the American military analyst Stephen Biddle – evolved as an answer to one question: how to conduct meaningful military operations in the face of the radically lethal firepower created by industrial societies? Its elements at the tactical level include cover, concealment, dispersion, suppression, small unit manoeuvre, and combined arms action; at the operational level it combines depth, reserves, and differential concentration.

It does not include static defences – indeed, it presupposes that static fortifications have been fatally vulnerable for over a century. As Biddle put it:

> While survival on the attack was especially problematic (how could one cross the fire-swept ground to advance on the enemy?), survival on the defence was no trivial matter either. Defenders could dig into the ground for protection, but even thoroughly dug static positions could be blasted out by the new artillery given time.[27]

The extant literature on military affairs going back at least to the 1980s, and the championing of 'manoeuvre warfare' as opposed to supposedly retrograde 'attritional warfare', has been very clear on the point. Movement is good; non-movement, static positionality – fortification, in other words – is not good.

Overall, the modern warfare literature does not so much disparage fortification as ignore it. For example, in *The Art of Manoeuvre*, an important albeit specialist work, discussion of the subject is confined to an appendix on military engineers, in which it states:

> friendly obstacles [forts] serve mostly to fix the friendly force in place and do little to delay the enemy. The creation of complex obstacles [i.e., fortresses] often exhausts the defenders, and instead of focussing on defeating the enemy the friendly force gets distracted by its perceived need to defend the obstacle. This is an outgrowth of methodical battle.[28]

It is perhaps no surprise, then, that there is no recent work on strategy that really discusses fortification, since that has been the pattern for several generations of scholars and practitioners.

But this habit of mind is all wrong when it comes to the present day. An educated military man of the seventeenth or eighteenth century would have been familiar with a wide range of military treatises and tactical manuals on fortification. If you look at the current curricula of the staff colleges of the Western world, however, the subject barely registers – and if it does then it is principally as a matter of historical interest.

My argument is not that fortifications have been ill-served in twentieth-century military history, though I think some revision is in order. It is that if you pay attention to what is done rather than said, it is apparent that contemporary warfare is exceedingly positional in character and increasingly fixed around fortified strategic complexes of great size, complexity, and engineering ambition – all requiring significant expense and ingenuity.

The issue is that contemporary military practice is dominated by fortifications and siegecraft in ways that reflect the positional warfare of the more obviously castellated times of the past, but practitioners and theorists barely talk about it. Before I go on to provide specific examples, there is another element that helps explain and contextualize the fortification *zeitgeist* that I have supposed is coming to dominate military affairs, and civil life more generally.

Culture and Strategic Choice

War, like any other sphere of social interaction, is influenced by the developments of mankind (for good or ill) in all fields of life, including culture; it is a microcosm of society's attitudes, preoccupations, anxieties, and assumptions. Mobile warfare was not only a military technique, an invention of a genius commander like Napoleon, for example, or Guderian, Montgomery, or Zhukov, nor just an outgrowth of the technological developments of the new industrial age. It was also a form of war that suited the modernist 'world view' that came into dominance in the nineteenth century.

That world view, especially of Euro-Atlantic society, was highly mechanistic, optimistic, and bold. The basic argument at its root was that while religion and faith had in the past failed to create a worldly paradise, henceforth logic, applied science and technology could. The West, particularly, was at that time culturally and politically ambitious, believed strongly in the superiority (i.e., universality) of its values, and reckoned that war could (indeed, should) rationally be applied to their advancement. The hubristic overreach of these ideas, and the dehumanizing false equivalence of the assumption at their heart – that human existence could and ought to operate like a machine, that society was scientifically perfectible – have caused terrible consequences.

This was not obvious at the time, however. The philosopher Isaiah Berlin was amongst the first to remark on the bitter fruit of this essentially optimistic outlook:

> One belief, more than any other, is responsible for the slaughter of individuals on the altars of the great historical ideals ... This is the belief that somewhere, in the past or in the future, in divine revelation or in the mind of an individual thinker, in the pronouncements of history or science, or in the simple heart of an uncorrupted good man, there is a final solution.[29]

In effect, the modern age put Western civilization in a conundrum. Science and engineering produced dazzling technologies in every field, from the generation of energy to the velocity of communications, the power of computing, the speed of mobility, and, of course, the invention of ever more powerful weapons. But the problems of the world increased at the same rate. War between great powers grew steadily less plausible as a rational act as the destructive power of weapons increased – the exploding of the atomic bombs on Japanese cities in 1945 marking the tipping point. The decisiveness of 'small wars' also receded as 'the rest' gradually developed war strategies and techniques to defeat the West. The world wars shattered the old empires of Europe, raising up two non-European superpowers in their place – subsequently reduced to one, the United States, which now awkwardly faces its own sunset. Meanwhile, the Holocaust blackened the modern West's self-perception of moral confidence.

The result, I would argue, was the growth of a pervasive mood of defeated expectation and frustration at the failure to create 'utopia' that started amongst an educated elite – most clearly in the arts. Consider, for example, the famously apocalyptic poem 'The Second Coming', by the Irish poet W.B. Yeats. Written in 1919 in the shadow of the First World War, at the beginning of the Irish War of Independence (which led, in turn, to the Irish Civil War), and at the highpoint of the global influenza epidemic (which looked likely to kill Yeats's then pregnant wife), it is not surprisingly gloomy. He predicts anarchy followed by apocalypse, while famously 'The best lack all conviction, while the worst / Are full of passionate intensity.' Or the bleak pessimism of T.S. Eliot's 'The Wasteland', written in 1921 – also in the shadow of the war, and while Eliot was on the verge of a nervous breakdown – which paints a picture of nothing so much as a culture in disarray.

What began, however, as a mood among the elite in the early part of the twentieth century has in the early twenty-first become a general Western cultural milieu of shame, recrimination, and repudiation of the past combined with apprehension of the future.[30]

Character of war

Students of war who focus on the specifics of combat, the characteristics of this or that weapon system, or the impact of some new technology, often push aside the indeterminacies of culture. As a result, they sometimes miss the forest for the trees. The strategies conceived and chosen by an expansive, optimistic, and confident civilization will differ from those that occur to an introverted, pessimistic, and self-doubting one, even if the technologies available to both are the same.

This should not be too controversial. It is what Clausewitz was getting at when he wrote that 'Every age has its own kind of war, its own limiting conditions, and its own peculiar preoccupations. It follows that the events of every age must be judged in the light of its own peculiarities.'[31] My proposition is that whatever the 'peculiar preoccupations' may be specifically, generally we may take them as expressing the mood of a culture.

The most salient peculiarities of war today, at least as practised by the West, are its status quo orientation and the risk aversion of major national statesmen and commanders. Christopher Coker summarized the situation adroitly:

> What has changed in recent years is that, for all the talk of human rights and global governance and global civil society, the West is much more circumspect in its use of force: war is about interests, not values. Military force is now applied largely to one end, and one end only – managing the wild zones, the *zones grises*, the fragile states and failing societies from which the main threats it faces now emanate. War has been scaled down, as too has our strategic ambition; the West is no longer in the business of building a New World Order but managing the Global Disorder instead. Even in the US the neo-conservatives, the last knights who are willing to venture out to remake the world in their own image, have come to recognise that it is a hopeless task to make war on inhumanity. The task is to mitigate it. The task, as Condoleezza Rice says, is to make the world not perfect but a little safer.[32]

Whether or not one sees this state of affairs as regrettable is a matter of perspective. There is inevitably a certain amount of low dishonesty about it, insofar as politicians still feel compelled to characterize small wars that are essentially about system maintenance and risk management as value-driven conflicts that must be won. The strategically modest, managerial use of force in the pursuit of a little more safety is a recipe for a series of seemingly endless wars. On the other hand, as Isaiah Berlin warned, the pursuit of the perfect peace is a road paved in crimson.

Technology is a background factor to these developments. Obviously, the shift from a predominantly industrial societal model characterized by mass standardization, centralization, and top-down hierarchies to a post-industrial one characterized by brands, informationalization, and networks changes a great deal about how we humans do things, while not necessarily changing what we do or want to do. Nor does it push in one direction only; rather, it seems to push in several contradictory ways simultaneously.

Network society/risk society

Grand theories of the supposed 'network society' are often oversimplified in popular culture as well as in academia. The best authors on the subject, however, were aware that the increasing integration of global affairs was accompanied by a heightening of divisions that portended a dark future. In the words of Manuel Castells, for example, while the global elite might retrench into 'immaterial palaces' made from communications networks, the experience of normal people 'would remain confined to multiple segregated locales, subdued in their existence and fragmented in their consciousness. With no Winter Palace to be seized, outbursts of revolt may implode, transformed into everyday senseless violence.'[33] If we accept as broadly correct the picture of the culture of 'late modernity' or 'network society' that has been painted, then what strategic behaviour ought we to expect? What are its predominant anxieties and how might the people seek to alleviate them?

First, there is the status-quo-maintenance orientation of the elite, which seeks to keep things as much as possible as they are. This does not necessarily mean they act defensively and not offensively. The difference lies in what we might call 'positive' and 'negative' strategies. A positive strategy proceeds from the question 'how do I produce the thing in the world that I want?', whereas a negative strategy works from the opposite 'how do I prevent the thing in the world that I fear?' The latter calculation may well result in offensive action, but more typically manifests in retrenchment and shoring up. In contemporary military jargon, such operations are referred to as 'stabilization', as though the problem at hand was a bad case of subsidence or erosion, which is not a bad metaphor.

Second, there is the related matter of risk aversion, which, combined with the prevalence of negative strategies, manifests in an infirmity of will and a consequent reluctance to accept losses. Thus, to the primary question 'how do I prevent this thing which I fear happening?' is added a secondary rider: 'what is the least cost that I must pay?' These questions are not wrong per se – there is nothing intrinsically incorrect about maximizing efficiency, nor is maintaining the status quo necessarily immoral. That depends on the status quo. It evinces, however, a dispassionate, bordering-on-inglorious concept of warfare that reflects the desire to hunker down and limit exposure.

In nearly all the instances of contemporary fortification discussed in this book we will find that insurance costs, and regulations authored or lobbied into existence by the insurance industry, figure directly or indirectly in the reasons for their development. There can be no surer sign of a society's acute orientation around the mitigation of risk.

Third, there is a pervasive cultural gloom-cum-apprehension of doom, the loudest signals of which we may perceive in the burgeoning industry of post-apocalypticism. At the individual, family, group, and increasingly also corporate levels, the question is not so much 'how do I forestall the thing that I fear?' (because the thing seems inevitable or at any rate is out of one's hands) but 'what must I do to survive, or suffer less, because of that thing happening?' The result is a range of resilience-boosting behaviours, from 'doomsday prepping' to new patterns of business investment in fortified infrastructures, to the premium calculations of insurance actuarial tables.

In the following chapter we shall look at specific contemporary military fortifications. For each of them there will be sound tactical and strategic reasons for why, where, and in what form they were constructed. Let's not forget, though, that beyond those proximate reasons there are deeper causes. Strategy is embedded in a culture, and will be coloured by the apprehensions, mindsets, preoccupations, and moods of that culture.

3

Contemporary Military Fortification

What is a fortification? Probably every person to whom this simple question is posed will think for a moment that the answer is easy. Probably as a child you made a fort yourself – out of snow, or sticks, or sofa cushions. Indeed, if you are the type of person that I think will be reading this book you probably made a lot of forts. You may know the difference between a cavalier and a caponier, have opinions on the angle of glacis plates, or even preferences for Moorish machicolations over European ones. None of that is necessary, however. Everyone knows what a fort is from normal life experience. That's enough for a start.

As a human being, you know there is a primal urge for safety and security that enclosure behind secure walls, even in play, helps to satisfy. Belongingness is another fundamental need. That is why it is likely your childhood fort-building was a team effort. You, along with a few trusted friends, your 'tribe', as it were, faced off against the kids from the next block, or whoever was your 'enemy'. Probably, your fort symbolized your group, being the 'home base' and where you hung your flag. At any rate, it represented more than a set of walls, whatever they were made from.

Normal life has also taught you most of the essential tactical principles of fortification. The wall of a good fort, its 'curtain', is resistant to the weapons most likely to be aimed against it – whether snowballs or cannonballs. It ought to have some form of obstruction around it, a ditch is ideal, that slows attackers down where they are most vulnerable to your fire. Moreover, it has positions, call them 'bastions', to fire from that are relatively protected from return in kind. Height is a major advantage because it increases the power and range of defensive weapons.

You may well grasp some important strategic principles too. Your fort needs to be in the right place. An undefended fort is no good at all, so it needs a garrison. Economy matters. In other words: a finished fort is better than an unfinished one, so build it as well as you can as fast as you can out of whatever you have that is good enough. On the other hand, symbolism matters too: your tribe's fort shows other tribes your power, so ideally it should be cool.

In short, you already know some important things about fortification, but when it comes down to it, walls have a complexity belied by their apparent simplicity.

This is obvious when you think of the incredibly wide range of structures to which the word 'fortress' has been applied. Fortifications can be continental in scale, like the 'Atlantic Wall' constructed by the Germans to defend against an Allied amphibious reinvasion of occupied Europe during the Second World War.[1] Or they can be much more localized. For example, for 2,000 years there has been a fort of one sort or another on a particular rock spur in the Aosta Valley in northern Italy, guarding the historic route between Italy and France. Currently, it is a powerful nineteenth-century construction, Forte di Bard, which has been recently reconstructed.[2]

They can be visually impressive and dominate a landscape with battlemented walls and turrets perched on rocky hilltops, like the mediaeval Cathar castles of the Languedoc region of France, or Neuschwanstein Castle in Bavaria, said to have inspired the Cinderella castle of the Disneyland theme parks.[3] Or, like the fortresses of the Maginot Line, they can disappear beneath the landscape entirely, with no part of the structure appearing above the surface except armoured cupolas for guns and observation – and even these may be designed to rise only to fire before dropping back into safety.[4]

They can be made of dirt, grass turf, wood, brick, stone, concrete, iron, steel, or some combination of them all. Indeed, with a small amount of abstraction of the concept, they may be made of far less tangible stuff. The Israeli 'Iron Dome' national air defence system is made of radar beams and interceptor missiles – a 'wall' in the sky, in effect.[5] In the latter part of the Cold War, Soviet ballistic missile submarines operated out of naval 'bastions', areas of the sea partially enclosed by friendly shoreline, defended by naval mines, monitored by sensors, and heavily patrolled by surface, submarine, and air forces – a 'wall' in the water, in effect.[6]

Nowadays, very highly secured computer systems are protected by digital 'firewalls' and the most critical of them are 'air-gapped', i.e., physically disconnected from other systems as though by an impassable moat.[7]

Less obvious, but even more important, consider the diverse strategic purposes that fortifications have been built to serve. In the following pages I have aggregated some of these purposes in three specific categories – pacification, consolidation, and separation – using exemplary types of fortresses that seem to me particularly relevant now. First, let us continue with a more conceptual discussion of the purposes and forms of military fortification.

Why Fortify?

At first glance, fortifications are the physical expression of mankind's fear of being attacked, losing one's life or property, or otherwise suffering harm. Yet, noting the sheer variety of how strong structures are employed to achieve this or that end, one's first impression soon looks inadequate. Just as a boxer blocks a blow in order to counterpunch, in warfare one defends against attack in order to be able to deliver strikes in return – they are two sides of the same coin, making it generally fruitless to define this or that piece of technology as defensive or offensive.

In a basic tactical sense, one fortifies (etymologically 'to make strong') places where a combination of terrain and the available materials make it simultaneously imperative and dangerous for one's enemy to attack. Field Marshal Helmuth Graf von Moltke, one of the more famously offence-minded commanders of history, put it this way:

> Skilful leadership will in many cases succeed in selecting defensive positions which are strategically of such an offensive nature that the opponent will be forced to attack them. We will take the tactical offensive only after casualties, loss of cohesion, and exhaustion have weakened him. Thus, is the strategic offensive united with tactical defence.[8]

Consider another distinction between tactics and strategy – it is possible to defend in one realm while attacking in another, indeed that is something of an ideal. An enemy force may be held in place by a fortification, allowing one's own mobile forces to hit them on a flank. Likewise, the defeat of a fortress in one theatre of war might drastically affect campaigns in more distant theatres, as for instance with the

Royal Navy's destruction of Russian naval forts in the Baltic Sea during the misnamed 'Crimean War' (1853–56), which signalled the potential vulnerability of St Petersburg to naval attack, thus swinging Russian opinion on the war decisively.[9]

More generally, fortification is often essential to prevent the escalation of a conflict, deterring by denial. A potential enemy faced by a strong fortress may well conclude that an attack would be fruitless. For a powerful, albeit fictionalized illustration of this effect, think of the scene in the German war film *Das Boot*, when the crew of the titular submarine are told they must go to the Mediterranean via the Straits of Gibraltar, straight through the defences of the fortress – effectively, they reckon this to be a death sentence.[10]

Offence and defence

On a grand scale, naval fortresses, especially the globe-spanning chain of them constructed for the Royal Navy at the height of the British Empire, are quintessentially strategic in the sense of being guarded and vital logistical hubs of profound importance in peace and in war. In the east, Hong Kong and Singapore, and in the West, Malta, Gibraltar, Bermuda, and Halifax, were all intensively fortified 'critical nodes' of imperial power – unfortunately in the case of the first two not well enough, particularly against land attack, as they fell to the Imperial Japanese Army at the beginning of the Second World War. One reason the British 'ruled the waves' was because they were good at identifying the best strategic locations and making them their own.[11]

A fortified strategic defence is seemingly typical of empires that have reached their apogee and ceased expanding. Hadrian's Wall and the Roman Limes through Germany between the Rhine and the Danube are well-known, and still visible, examples of this strategic logic. The collection of linear barriers that make up China's Great Wall, constructed over centuries, arose out of similar conditions.[12]

What tends to escape popular recognition is just how many societies have built such fortifications, and how frequently and for how long they have done so. Archaeologists have identified hundreds of pre-modern linear barriers ranging from dozens to hundreds of miles in length.[13] The boundaries in Western and Central Asia between steppe peoples and settled populations are especially littered with the colossal wrecks of forgotten walls.[14]

Against this, we find examples of the exact opposite dynamic: the prolific use of fortifications by expansive empires. The Russian

Empire's phenomenally ambitious and rapid conquest of Siberia from the seventeenth century onwards was based upon the construction of innumerable small wooden forts known as '*ostrogs*' at successive strategic points of control such as river crossings, many of which are now Siberian cities.[15] Likewise, the American conquest of the Western plains proceeded via the establishment of hundreds of fortified outposts, from Fort Apache in Arizona to Fort Zarah in Kansas, with several dozen of them living on in the names of towns and cities.[16]

Sea power was integral to European global imperial conquest, particularly following the invention of the steamship.[17] The ships needed coastal forts, however, to provide a base of supply and point of trade as well as physical security in an environment where they often did not have clear local military superiority.[18] The pattern, therefore, was usually to establish a landing at a good harbour, ideally with good access to inland waterways or paths to the interior, then to create a permanent fortification as a guard against any native attempts to push them back into the sea.

For example, the 1511 Portuguese conquest of Melaka, an important spice-trading port in Malaysia, was accomplished in the words of its commander, Afonso de Albuquerque, by these means:

> with great haste by day, and the use of torches by night, [having gained a lodgement, we were] intent on building a castle of timber, with many large trees for the interior and a goodly quantity of cannon, and in a month it had been made strong; and as soon as it had been made secure, we prepared one out of stone which we built by dismantling the houses of the Moors, the mosques and other of their buildings. We erected it with great hardship bearing the stones on our backs; and each one of us was day-labourer, mason, and stone-cutter.[19]

That is why from the first days of European global maritime expansion their forts began to dot the coastlines of the world from the Indo-Pacific to the Americas and Africa. Many of these are still around, for instance along the desert coast of Morocco, where there are several superb and important examples.[20] The large and well-preserved Portuguese fortress at Essaouira was established in the fifteenth century in the same place where it is thought Phoenician traders of the seventh century BCE also set up a defended trading post for the same reasons. The town is now a popular surfing destination and the fortress well known.[21]

Four hundred miles further south in the little coastal town of Tarfaya may be found the much smaller and more isolated Casa del Mar, a fortified trading post built in 1882 for British traders to facilitate business with merchants from distant African lands.[22] In its own way, this humble outpost is important because it represents a type of fortification notable for its ubiquity. Up until quite modern times a substantial fraction of global trade was conducted through such fortified coastal entrepots (also often known as 'factories'), from York Factory on the frozen shores of Hudson's Bay to Elmina Castle in Ghana, also built by the Portuguese and supposedly the oldest European building south of the Sahara.[23]

The literature generally tends to define a fortification simply as a tool of defence, and the opposite of manoeuvre. As the *Oxford Companion to Military History* puts it, fortifications 'still represent, as they always have, the endless duel between attack and defence, between immobility and manoeuvre'.[24] From a relatively functional perspective, the *Land Forces Encyclopaedia* states four straightforward purposes of fortification: blockade of access, protection against enemy weapons, improvement of the effect of defensive weapons, and use as observation platforms.[25]

My point is that such definitions, while narrowly correct, are inadequate. The history of war shows that fortifications may be harnessed as easily to an offensive strategy as to a defensive one. They do not represent the opposite of movement, rather they frequently enable it – tactically and strategically. They are the preeminent tool for pacification of conquered territories long after the main battles between opposing field forces have occurred. Furthermore, more general history tells us that fortification has been a central aspect of civilian commerce.

Fortified Strategic Complexes

In short, to understand the important and growing role played by fortification in guarded age warfare we need to go further than the existing strategic studies literature which addresses the topic either peremptorily, or narrowly tactically, or as something of historical interest rather than being immediately relevant. For an example of the latter, Beatrice Heuser's exhaustive study of the evolution of strategy characterizes the science of fortification as 'not obsolete' but 'overtaken' by technical changes.[26] This is wrong, for as we shall see, contemporary fortification is in fact in a period of extensive and ingenious technical innovation.

Fortification, moreover, is at the core of contemporary conflict – not at its boundaries, not a historical concern, but an increasingly vital aspect of war and warfare.[27] Indeed, fortifications are at the forefront of the military efforts of a range of major and minor states to serve national policy – a phenomenon which I suggest is somewhat recognized (as the constructions are usually hard to miss) but poorly understood.[28]

We need, therefore, to re-examine some common assumptions about fortification in order to better illuminate what is going on. I suggest we look at fortresses less as singular military structures with a primarily defensive role and more as 'fortified strategic complexes' – an assemblage of structures, almost always part of a network, with a range of functions including profoundly important symbolic and offensive ones.

To be precise, a fortified strategic complex is an assemblage of military and civil engineering and, increasingly, electronic surveillance systems designed to shape a conflict or security condition by altering, regulating, and monitoring movement in an area over an extended period. Although in the pages that follow immediately I shall focus upon examples of fortified strategic in-military use, it is important to reiterate that the application of fortification strategies in the civilian sphere is even more widespread.

To summarize the preceding discussion, I adopt this approach to understanding contemporary fortifications for several reasons. For a start, while resistance to attack is obviously a primary quality of a fortification, that is far from the only pertinent design consideration. It is striking how often fortresses incorporate design features that weaken their defensive capability. A surprising thing about Renaissance city fortifications, for instance, is how often security was compromised by the design of magnificent gateways owing more to fashion in urban design than military defence.[29] Many castles of the late Middle Ages also sacrificed strength in favour of comforts such as glazed windows, fireplaces, and latrines which, being built into the walls, thus weakened them.[30]

Mobility and money

Likewise, while fortifications are often situated in naturally inaccessible terrain, the better to resist attack, we just as often find them in places that are far from ideal defensively. While popular perceptions of mediaeval castles, for example, are usually formed by their supposed military significance, their defining feature was, rather, that they served a variety of social needs.[31] We may surmise, therefore, that the design and siting of fortifications reflects more than military considerations. Commercial needs, political context, and even cultural aesthetics can and often do supersede tactical exigency in deciding where and in what form they are employed.

Furthermore, while fortifications as fixed structures are themselves immobile, their role in operations is very often to act as a base of mobility for one's own forces while at the same time restricting or channelling the movement of one's enemy. Again, to take the mediaeval castle as an example, its primary function was to dominate the surrounding area by acting as a secure base for patrolling, not as a refuge for its garrison.[32] In other words, fortifications are in no way antithetical to manoeuvre.

Quite the opposite is the case. The construction of a fortification may well constitute a 'manoeuvre' insofar as its intended effect is to dislocate an opponent and to stymie their strategies. To give a contemporary example, the T-Wall barrier built during the 2008 Battle of Sadr City, Iraq was described by one analyst as being the 'equivalent of a Roman siege engine' aimed at forcing the insurgent militiamen to face American military firepower head on.[33] From all of this, we may surmise that the utility of fortifications in war and warfare is more flexible than might be supposed from their superficial simplicity.

3.1 Sadr City
A concrete T-Wall in the Shiite enclave of Sadr City, Baghdad, Iraq (June 2008). The March 2008 Battle of Sadr City was a noteworthy example of the tactical use of expedient fortifications in urban counter-insurgency.
Source: Sgt. Philip Klein, 2008, US Army.

Finally, while we often judge the quality of this or that fortification as a singular construction, fortification as a strategy really comes to the fore when the fortresses are seen as comprising parts of a larger network.[34] Thus, the appropriate frame of reference for answering the perennial question 'do walls work?' is strategic; we should be precise about what policy objective they work (or fail to work) for and judge them on that basis.

Indeed, it is not too much of a stretch to suggest that fortifications are quintessentially strategic. Obvious hints towards this quality would include their cost and durability as well as their significant peacetime importance. While expedient and cheap fortifications abound, serious fortifications have often consumed a high fraction of national expenditure over a period of many years.

Hadrian's Wall or China's Great Wall spring to mind as well-known examples, but there are plenty of others. England's Edward I nearly bankrupted the country with an extensive castle-building programme in Wales, which produced major new fortresses from 1277 onwards at Caernarfon, Conwy, Harlech, and Beaumaris – all, not incidentally, coastal castles that could be supplied by sea.[35] Ultimately, though, it worked to pacify Wales. While Edward I fought in three theatres of war – France, Scotland, and Wales – only in the latter was he ultimately successful.[36]

In more recent times, the Maginot Line, the poster child of expensive modern fortifications, required 3.75 million tonnes of reinforced concrete, for example. In comparison, the German Atlantic Wall, built against the threat of Allied cross-Channel invasion, consumed 17 million tonnes. Even that huge sum, though, is exceeded by an order of magnitude by the 200 million tonnes planned for the defences of Germany against aerial bombardment during the Second World War – an amount that would have equalled that of *all* civilian construction for the previous twenty years.[37]

In contemporary terms, the relative levels of societal investment in fortified strategic complexes such as those described above equal or exceed that which a government today might consider when investing in something like a fleet of nuclear submarines or a continental anti-ballistic missile system.

The point is not simply that fortification strategies are much more complicated than is commonly credited, but that they also remain highly relevant. Let us look now at some examples.

3.2 The fort at Menaka
The 17 Parachute Engineers Regiment which built this base at Menaka clearly meant it to be appreciated from above – to judge from the proud tag in the top right corner!
Source: Armée Française.

Hesco Empire

In January 2021 it was reported that French forces fighting Islamist rebels in Mali had constructed two new forts, one at Labbezanga, a small riverport village on the Niger River, and the other at Menaka, a town about 200 kilometres away, also near the Niger border.[38] Normally, the addition of two forts to the world's existing stockpile of fortified outposts in far-off dusty places would not be newsworthy. What was eye-catching about these forts was that, in an obvious nod to the seventeenth-century French military engineer Sebastian Le Prestre de Vauban, they had been constructed in a 'star fortress' pattern.

We shall return in the next chapter to the subject of star fortresses in some detail. For the time being the important point is that although it has been well over two centuries since the peak of their construction, such was the scale of their building and their intrinsic durability, the global landscape is still littered with their remains. They are in many ways the archetypal imperial fort – an architectural embodiment of centuries of Western military predominance.

At the southern end of Hudson's Bay in northern Canada, for example, may be found the Prince of Wales Fort, built by the Hudson's Bay Trading Company from 1731 to 1771 to protect their trading interests. It is a superb albeit small example of the type. Briefly captured by a French naval force in 1782, who slighted it, it is today in perfect repair.[39] Located just short of the Arctic Circle on the edge of a vast, treeless, frozen emptiness, at the end of a tenuous supply link to civilization, it is not too far a stretch to compare it to the International Space Station – except it had to be a fortified 'star fort' instead of just an outpost in the stars. My guess is that if we build a base on the Moon it will be fortified.

By contrast, tropical Sri Lanka's Jaffna Fort, which is about of the same size and vintage, located about 400 kilometres north of the capital Colombo, has been the scene of active fighting right up to recent times. Tamil Tigers militants fighting the Sri Lankan Army laid siege to it in 1990 for three months and then again for fifty days in 1995. In both battles, dozens of troops were killed in vicious close-quarter fighting, as well as by mines and aerial bombing.[40] Since the crushing of the rebels in 2009, the battered fort has been rebuilt as an upmarket hotel (a recurrent fate of iconic structures, as we shall see), with the assistance of the Dutch government.[41]

Many star forts today remain in more gentle military use: as barracks, such as Fort George near Inverness, Scotland, now home of the Black Watch battalion of the Royal Regiment of Scotland; or as headquarters, such as the Kastellet in Copenhagen, Denmark, now mostly used as a place for high-level diplomatic functions hosted by the ministry of defence; or as residences of high officials, such as The Citadel in Quebec City, now home to the Lieutenant Governor of the province. But mostly, like Neuf-Brisach in France, or Bourtange in the Netherlands, they have peacefully blended into a placid semi-urban scene popular with tourists.

It is doubtful, though, that tourists will be flocking to the two new fortresses in Mali to admire their aesthetic qualities. Indeed, aside from their basic star shape, pleasing from the air, they share little else in common with the grand Renaissance gun fortresses – not least, the surface-mounted structures lack the thick glacis which is a defining feature of the gun fort. This is no surprise, since they were not designed to defeat siege artillery but to act as a base of operations against different sorts of threats.

That does not make them unimportant. Nor does the adaptation of the forts to local materials and threat conditions mark a notable break with the past. After all, in the seventeenth and eighteenth centuries, the 'stockade forts' of New France in North America also usually had a star pattern but, unlike the powerful variants needed for warfare in Europe, they were made of local wood. Even when they were built of stone, such as Fort Chartres on the shores of the Mississippi River in Illinois, they lacked the glacis and ditch necessary for protection against artillery. As the Indians the fortress-builders were fighting lacked such weapons, big-gun-resistant defences were unnecessary.[42]

The same is the case in Mali today. The rebels, comprised initially of mainly Tuareg tribesmen but later joined by militants linked to Al-Qaeda and Islamic State, lack heavy artillery, relying primarily on light weapons and heavy-machine-gun-armed civilian pickup trucks.[43] The contemporary star forts of Mali are worth a closer look not for their seemingly antique morphology but because they are fine examples of a military architecture that is incredibly current, widespread, and surprisingly little remarked upon. The trick is to observe what they are built from rather than their shape. The latter is essentially an incidental quality, in this case a bit of a fashion statement. The former is quite a lot more interesting.

Lego of war

What if Ikea and Lego combined their respective design skills in furniture and toys to make mass-market kits for building life-size forts? You might expect the result would be something of utilitarian design, available in a range of standardized, modular, and interlocking shapes, flat-packable for easy shipping, durable and reusable, while also being relatively cheap. The user could combine these pieces in whatever forms their imagination desired. Such a product exists. It's called 'Hesco Bastion', or more commonly simply 'Hesco', and it is to the War on Terror what the Huey helicopter was to the Vietnam War – the practically ever-present backdrop to a million war photos.

Manufactured by a British company based in Bradford, Hesco is essentially a gabion – a large basket filled with earth and stone – a very old piece of military technology. Think of it as a big building block or a giant sandbag. In the old days these were constructed out of wicker and used to provide protection from enemy gunfire during sieges. The modern version invented by British entrepreneur Jimi Heselden, initially as an anti-erosion barrier (for which it is still in wide civilian use), is made of hinged wire-mesh panels with a sturdy geotextile lining.

Easy to ship and set up, given an adequate supply of local dirt a handful of soldiers with a front-end loader can stack them into a workable fortress in a few hours. Hesco is a commendable piece of modern design, rather like Mies van der Rohe's famous 'Barcelona' chair – a reinvention of an old and familiar thing in a new and current way.[44] The

3.3 Hesco barrier
An American soldier holds his helmet above the Hesco barrier at Combat Outpost Mushan, Pajwai District, Afghanistan in an attempt to draw out gunfire, February 2014.
Source: Sgt. Harold Flynn, 2014, US Army.

Hesco company is currently owned by Praesidiad, a market-leading Belgian manufacturer of force protection and perimeter defence systems including 'Guardiar' and 'Betafence'.[45]

It is hard to judge the total size of this industry. The global perimeter security market was valued at $59 billion in 2021, but 'barrier systems' such as Hesco account for only a fraction of that admittedly large number.[46] It is clearly a thriving industry, however, to judge from the efforts of the company to fight off the intrusion into its business by cheaper Chinese-made knockoffs.[47] In August 2021, Hesco and Maccaferri Inc., a historic Italian gabion manufacturer dating back to before the First World War, were awarded a $500 million contract by the American military for an 'Expeditionary Barrier System'.[48]

Clearly, what Hesco lacks in grandeur it makes up for in utility. Under fire, loose-packed earth has huge damage resistance and as opposed to more solid constructions, which often shatter and spall dangerous fragments, it tends after a hit to just slump back into its original shape. The forms in which Hesco forts can be built are as varied as the combination of imagination, tactical exigency, and cost allows. In open terrain like that of Mali, where there is no extra cost of preparing the already flat ground, engineers can let inspiration run riot and build star shapes if they want. The forms may change radically, but the functions remain largely the same.

Cantons and Marching Forts

More congested or contorted landscapes would produce smaller and less permanent forts that trace the terrain in irregular shapes, rather like Iron Age hill forts, as at Combat Outpost Restrepo in Afghanistan's Korengal Valley, a fort described as 'the most dangerous place on Earth' by the soldiers posted there.[49] The technical term for such a fort is a 'marching camp', usually a field expedient castle built by a military force on the move when forced to halt by darkness or fatigue in uncontrolled territory. However, they can be more permanent and serve purposes beyond resting up in safety.

Roman legions were famed for their prolific construction of marching camps, many traces of which are still visible. Fort-building was central to the Roman strategy of pacification of conquered territories. They provided a small garrison in hostile territory with stout enough defences for some resistance, often while maintaining supply lines for more mobile elements. Over time, marching camps could acquire a degree of permanency.[50]

Since Roman times, the use of fortified strategic complexes – networks of forts – for pacification has been repeated over and over. The Normans, for instance, built no less than a thousand motte and bailey castles to quell the Saxons. According to the *Anglo-Saxon Chronicle*, 'They filled the whole land with these castles; and when the castles were built, they filled them with devils and wicked men.'[51] Moreover, as we have seen, the English in Wales, the Russians in Siberia, the Americans on the Western plains, and Europeans generally on a colossal scale from the sea, did the same.

We should not be surprised, then, to observe how neatly Afghanistan's most recent layer of strategic stratigraphy reflects this very old pattern. By 2010 it was reported that Afghanistan had 700 fortified bases and outposts, approximately 300 of them held by the Afghan national army and police – all now abandoned or held by the Taliban.[52]

Despite all the advancements in weapons and transport and communications technology that have occurred over centuries, NATO troops in Afghanistan very largely occupied the same places to do the same things as armies of the distant past. Overlooking every major road juncture, constricted transport route, and population centre was a forti-

3.4 ANP headquarters
An Afghan National Police compound featuring a concrete enceinte, guard towers, and armoured gate and vehicle inspection area. In this case, unusually, there seems to be no use of Hesco barriers.
Source: US Army Corps of Engineers.

fied installation. The distance between them: approximately one day's march – a density of about one strongpoint for every twenty to twenty-five square kilometres. Their position: basically, where Alexander the Great located his forts. Their function: the same – observation, reporting, communications repeating, and overlapping patrolling.

Combat Outpost (COP) Coleman in the eastern Kunar province was built around a nineteenth-century British border fortress, while COP Castle (the hint is in the name) in Helmand province incorporated a twelfth-century castle once besieged by Genghis Khan's army. Near Qalat City in Zabul province, soldiers at Forward Operating Base (FOB) Langman and Apache guarding Highway 1 (which runs along the old Silk Road) were looked over by a fortress built by the army of Alexander the Great.

Marines based at Fort Barcha in Garmsir district, Helmand, renamed their decomposing mudbrick outpost 'Castle Greyskull'. It had been occupied previously by the Soviets, who extensively tunnelled out and added to a pre-existing fortress of uncertain vintage. A full list of such examples would be very long.[53] Where these structures differed marginally from their predecessors was in the profligate employment of Hesco bastion, i.e., a moderate difference in form, not function.

Hesco is by no means the only significant military engineering product in increasingly wide use. The sector is burgeoning with other reinvented fortification technologies. One of the most interesting is essentially a portable marching fort. Developed by Kenno, a Finnish manufacturer of laser-welded steel-sandwich components, in cooperation with the Finnish army, the 'Balpro' system is a surface-mounted, reusable, modular marching fort, with armoured walls and turrets, that can be carried on a flatbed trailer and assembled by a small team in a few hours.[54]

Although its intended application is a bit obscure, Balpro would seem ideal in an urban warfare context, where the ability to rapidly and securely occupy key points in a city without damaging local infrastructure is desirable. Since Balpro requires no digging in, which tends to damage buried utilities common in urban environments, it could be very useful. In short, the system looks like a mobile version of the heavily armoured police stations the Royal Ulster Constabulary operated in Crossmaglen, Northern Ireland until very recently.[55]

Another interesting development is the assortment of concrete T-Walls (originally a highway safety device) that have been adapted to protect against low-trajectory weapons and blasts. While also frequently used in base building, their most remarkable recent employment is in urban counter-insurgency. Repurposed as barriers separating warring neighbourhoods, in which role they are dubbed 'peace walls', they proved highly useful in reducing violence in Baghdad in 2008.[56] Unfortunately, as may be seen in Belfast, where the British started employing them nearly fifty years ago, they tend to become permanent.[57]

In Afghanistan, however, also noteworthy there was the handful of very large fortified bases. The biggest of these were Bagram, near Kabul, Kandahar airbase, which I described at the beginning of this book, and also Britain's Camp Bastion in Helmand province. About the size of the city of Reading, Camp Bastion was 'home' to up to 30,000 people by 2012. One of its most important facilities was a large field hospital, one of whose doctors captured better than any others the character of the place:

> In a faraway land where the rains are dry and the trees blue and the air bittersweet, and where ants are like dogs and birdsong is not, there life goes for a song – everyone dies young. Safeguarding its sandy southern

perimeter was, until recently, a coalition of The Free sandbagged in a ghetto the size of a small city. Camp Bastion was the hub in an operation designed to secure for others the freedoms they would have wished for themselves had they been less primitive.[58]

Again, the appropriate technical term for Camp Bastion is a 'canton', meaning a long-term base for the quartering of military troops and civilian officials. The permanent military installations of the British Raj were referred to as such and many of these came to have extensive administrative and leisure facilities. Indeed, by the late nineteenth century, life for British officials and their families in the cantons was highly agreeable and stylish.[59]

Body language

Camp Bastion was never so luxurious. Located in the middle of mostly flat and featureless desert, its armoured watchtowers provided excellent visibility. It was ringed by a nine-metre-high fence, coils of wire, ditches, and blast walls. Thermal imaging cameras, motion sensors, and

3.5 Qalat's tea house
The walls of the Alexandrian fortress in Qalat, Zabul province now shelter a glass tea house, built by American soldiers in a goodwill gesture aimed at increasing the city's appeal to tourism, and, much more usefully, two substantial cellular phone towers.
Source: Staff Sgt. Manuel J. Martinez, 2010, US Air Force.

radar monitored movement around it both on the ground and in the air. Besides the hospital and other logistical facilities, the base housed two airfields capable of handling 600 planes a day. It was supremely well-fortified and aptly named.

The problem with it, as I observed earlier about the 'body language' of the Kandahar base, was not that it was a fortress, but that it was shabby. Its obviously temporary quality – containing nothing that could not either be packed in a transport or abandoned without much regret – was unmistakable. As a result, it projected timidity rather than strength, lack of will rather than durability, and an ever-present urgency to leave.[60]

The peculiarly jury-rigged character of the fortified posture of the International Security Assistance Force (ISAF) in Afghanistan was partly its undoing. The cantons of the Raj are mostly still in use by the Indian Army and much admired as comfortable and prestigious places to live.[61] Of Camp Bastion, on the other hand, there is now nothing but 'fluttering tents and old signage' suggesting that a base had once been there.[62] A canton is meant to be awesome and harnessed to a long-term plan of governance – in other words a strategy. If it is neither of those things, it is just a big fort buried in the dust.

In the 1930s, during the period of the Mandate in Palestine, the British Imperial Police developed the concept of the 'police fort', more commonly known now as the 'Tegart Fort', after Sir Charles Tegart, the policeman in charge of the effort. These forts provided a secure refuge to police and other officials in the radically insecure environment of the Arab Revolt of 1936–39. They have aptly been described as 'monuments of power, instruments of suppression'.[63] Most of them, like the cantons of the Raj, are still in use as police stations or military barracks, or, in the case of the big police fort at Latrun, Israel, as a museum.

The fortified police compounds of Afghanistan departed from the Tegart fort design considerably. The latter are usually blocky singular structures constructed of reinforced concrete in a brutalist style that might almost be described as Bauhaus – rational, functional, and utilitarian but not wholly unattractive. Those in Afghanistan were largely based upon the hardened perimeter defence of compounds, with boom gates and blast-walled traffic chicanes (for protection against car bombs), watchtowers, ditches, and anti-climb fencing with razor wire, and so on.

They looked, in effect, like highly guarded business parks or light industrial facilities. In principle and function, however, they were quite the same as Tegart's police forts albeit, like the new cantons, less visually impressive. Indeed, also like those cantons, they are now mostly abandoned and looted, collecting dust and falling apart.

The bottom line is that fortified life is not the exception to the rule of contemporary military affairs; it is, rather, the default experience of war, if not always for the locals, then nearly always for foreign troops and diplomats and other officials, most notably police. Most troops on operational deployment, 90 per cent or more, never or very rarely leave them. They arrive by air into a fortified cantonment, or shuttle from one to another marching camp, perform their duties behind a wall, and depart the same way they came without ever having left its confines.

Moreover, although in the previous few pages I have focused primarily on Afghanistan, I do not mean to suggest that there is something Afghan-specific to the fortified character of military operations I have described. Afghanistan is simply a good example of a general phenomenon observable in other theatres of war for all the same reasons.

NGO forts

Indeed, the matter is not even specifically about military usage of fortified strategic complexes. Outside of a handful of big national armies, the largest consumer of Hesco is the United Nations, which employs it to defend its many vulnerable diplomatic and humanitarian installations scattered across the world. According to the latest available accounts of the United Nations Procurement Division, in 2013–14 alone it purchased around $75 million worth of Hesco gabions, security barriers, and prefabricated fortifications.[64]

The compound of the United Nations Multidimensional Integrated Stabilization Mission in Mali (MINUSMA), for instance, headquartered in Bamako, differs little from Camp Bastion. With its decorative fountain, it shows a slightly greater concern with aesthetics and monumentality, but it too is surrounded by Hesco barriers stacked several metres high, plus coils of razor wire and fence, and a series of ditches. At the heart of the base is a command centre topped by a mast on which is mounted a high-resolution thermal camera. Radar also guards the perimeter.

It is, in a word, a fortress, and a powerful one. Foreign visitors, journalists, and diplomats who go there have no more freedom of movement than I did when I visited Afghanistan a decade ago and was stuck in Kandahar musing on the shore of the Poo Pond. They rarely leave the fort, other than to shuttle under heavy guard to another protected installation and back again. To be on UN deployment is to be protected behind significant and costly barriers.

As another example, consider the Dahab refugee camp in Kenya, also a highly defended installation. While the perimeter is demarcated by fences and Hesco bastion, the main defences are in the central quarters, which are particularly heavily guarded. In the case of an attack on the larger camp, humanitarian workers and volunteers can retreat to heavily armoured refuges where they are secure against light weapons for long enough, in theory, to be rescued by a quick-reaction military force.

Hesco, amongst other manufactures, is a notable provider of such fortlets. Usually referred to as 'safe havens', they come in a range of designs, normally with a very strong ballistic-resistant door protected by a blast-barrier. Typically, they are rated by an estimate of the number of hours it would take a determined attacker with small arms to break in. The longer the expected arrival time of quick-reaction forces to rescue personnel barricaded inside, the stronger the bunker needs to be built.[65]

Here again the primary driver is insurance. Doctors, for example, or other highly qualified specialists, often donate their time and expertise to worthy projects. Insuring them against death and injury, however, is extremely costly – a cost only brought down to manageable levels by convincing insurance providers of the existence of adequate levels of physical protection, i.e., largely speaking, fortification.

Let us turn now to a different sort of fortification, increasingly paradigmatic of this guarded age.

Great Walls

As impressive as the number of fortified installations in Afghanistan might be, it is well exceeded by neighbouring Pakistan, which by the end of 2021 was supposed to have built (or recommissioned) as many as 1,000 forts and border posts along its border with Afghanistan.[66] The forts are but one part of a fortified strategic complex that includes approximately 1,500 miles of dual chain link and barbed wire fencing, plus a 400-mile-long, eleven-foot-deep and fourteen-foot-wide ditch, combined with an array of cameras and other electronic sensors, built at a reported cost of $500 million.[67]

Interestingly, many of these fortresses are based upon the old frontier forts of the British Empire, built for exactly the same reason, with new ones built in a style reflecting those old patterns. The red brick police fort at Lwara in north Waziristan, for example, is built as a square keep with machicolation on its parapet and corner turrets. As the general in charge of the area's defences told a reporter, testifying to the scale of construction and the belief in its efficacy: 'At Lwara ... Afghan and NATO forces had only six posts compared with his 36. Pakistan will soon put up 14 km (8 miles) of fencing across the plain and into the hills to stop militants sneaking past at night. Fencing is going to help.'[68]

The Afghanistan–Pakistan region is impressively heavily fortified but similar levels of effort are observable elsewhere in the world too, as we shall see further on. Colloquially, such constructions are referred to simply as 'walls', 'great walls', or sometimes, in allusion to Churchill's dire warnings of the Cold War, as 'Iron Curtains' descending again on the landscape of human geography. The technically correct term is 'peripheral linear barrier', which refers to their distinguishing feature – a relative lack of depth in comparison to their extensive length – as well as to their normal location on the edge of a given polity.

Much attention has been paid to such continuous frontier fortifications since the 2016 election of Donald Trump on a campaign promise to extend and reinforce the walls on the US–Mexico border. The contentious politics on this issue have focused largely on migration policy rather than military affairs. This is not surprising. After all, a great many of the thousands of linear barriers built since the dawn of civilization had as their essential purpose the prevention of migration, specifically of nomadic peoples and their flocks through places of settled agriculture.

These linear barriers were immensely strategically meaningful and consequential – and very expensive. While they did not necessarily represent a reaction to an overtly military threat, it is difficult to categorize in this area. When it comes down to it, the strategy they serve is keeping an unwanted population out of the territory of those who build the walls.

The Romans illustrate this logic, which is surprisingly current in application. Until their empire began to stagnate and then contract, the Romans pursued a predictable and effective strategy. Where their armies encountered lands and people they could conquer and considered to be worth conquering, they did so brutally and relentlessly. Where they encountered opponents whom they could not conquer but with whom they could treat, i.e., come to agreements to which both sides would hold (more or less), they made lasting political arrangements. Where the empire abutted on people they could not conquer but who lacked the political order to make meaningful treaties, they built walls.[69]

In short, many of the peripheral linear barriers observable today have little or nothing to do with military defence against a conventional invasion or incursion – a case in point being America's Mexican border. Likewise with Europe's anti-migration barriers, which are hardly less extensive than President Trump's proposed wall. They have had mixed success, though their symbolic power as a rebuke of borderlessness, a central idea of globalization, is great.

Nevertheless, it is equally the case that some of these huge linear barriers are objects of substantial and creative *military* engineering serving the national security strategies of at least a dozen nation-states around the globe today. What has been happening for decades, although rapidly hastening in recent years, is fortification on a scale that exceeds by an order of magnitude the famous efforts of the Roman Emperor Hadrian in north Britain, and rivals that of the Great Wall of China – and nearly all of that in the space of a generation or two.

Perhaps the best known is Morocco's Western Sahara Wall, often referred to as the 'Sand Wall'.[70] The appellation is not surprising as the vast majority of its 1,600-mile length consists of sand berms and ditches, similar in form to the ancient Offa's Dyke in Britain or the traces of the Roman Limes still detectable across Germany between the Rhine and Danube rivers. It is also somewhat misleading as to the degree of effort and sophistication involved in its construction.

Dotted with relentless regularity every three to five miles along the Sand Wall are sited forts manned by as many as 100,000 Moroccan soldiers in total. The gaps in many places are covered by high fences, several layers of barbed wire, a range of electronic surveillance devices, and approximately 7 million land mines. By any measure this is a serious work of fortification that has occupied the bulk of national military effort for the last thirty years. Moroccan engineers have been incredibly busy and creative.

The same might be said of India. It is sometimes claimed that so vast is the Great Wall of China it is visible from space with the naked eye. This is untrue. Alas, linear fortifications, while often very long, are relatively thin, which is why they often lack resilience against high-intensity threats. As it happens, though, the fortification of the border between India and Pakistan can be seen from orbit, at least at night, because approximately two-thirds of its 2,000-mile length are constantly floodlit at enormous cost.[71]

The 3,000-mile India–Bangladesh border has also been progressively fortified in a multi-decade project first proposed by Prime Minister Indira Gandhi in the early 1980s a few years before she was assassinated.[72] Although primarily an anti-migration barrier, it is heavily policed – between 2001 and 2010, Indian security forces are estimated to have shot 900 Bangladeshis crossing the frontier. Casualty figures for the most recent decade are not available.

The number of such barriers in the world today varies according to how and what one counts.[73] A few, such as that between South Africa and Mozambique, are rudimentary and effectively now derelict for lack of money, though the perceived need for them has not diminished.[74] Some, such as that between Kenya and Somalia, are seemingly half-built or mired in delay.[75] The so-called 'European Rampart' on Ukraine's border with Russia, once scheduled for completion in 2025, a decade after works began, is unlikely now ever to be built.[76]

Others, such as the North and South Korean DMZ, are thoroughly militarized to the point of practical impregnability outside of a major war that would engulf the whole region.[77] Indubitably there are a great many of them, on all continents barring Australia and Antarctica. In recent years, among the largest and most technically sophisticated have been built in the Middle East, amongst others by Turkey on its border with Syria, and by Saudi Arabia initially on its border with Iraq and now along the Yemeni border as well.[78]

For many years the literature on this subject has been dominated by the Israeli security barrier completed in 2006, which separates its claimed territories from those governed by Palestinian authorities in the Gaza Strip and the West Bank. From the perspective of 2023, however, Israel's great wall is neither particularly large nor technically impressive.

The state of the art at present is probably Saudi Arabia's 900km barrier on its border with Iraq, built by the Munich-based company Airbus Defence and Security, and the similarly long one constructed on the border with Yemen. For the Iraq 'wall' alone, in addition to the physical barriers (secure fences and walls), embankments and ditches, the contract included forty blast-resistant watchtowers, seven command-and-control centres, thirty-eight communication towers, thirty-two military response stations and other facilities, plus radars and detection devices, and 1,450km of fibre-optic cable.[79]

Continuous frontier fortifications of great scale are clearly back in style. There are two significant and related points here. First, national linear peripheral barriers are truly big business. The investment in the works described is hard to estimate because it rarely appears as one budget line in national defence accounts, but is spread across a range of public works covered by different ministries. We know, however, from the public estimates of US–Mexico border installations, that it is measured in the billions.

Second, these are serious works of military engineering. Even those structures aimed solely at preventing unarmed civilians from crossing borders illegally are impressively complex and powerful. The Spanish enclaves of Ceuta and Melilla in North Africa have in recent years witnessed quasi-mediaeval battles in which large and well-organized groups of migrants have accomplished several escalades in the face of increasingly overmatched resistance by border guards.[80] Walls intended as barriers against armed infiltration, such as Israel's West Bank and Gaza fortifications, or even more so those of Saudi Arabia and Turkey, are truly powerful military assets integrated in national security strategies.

Here we might pause to observe another awkwardly uncomfortable fact. Popularly, border fortifications are characterized as white elephants – expensive and not very useful.[81] Reality would suggest otherwise: they are effective enough for what their designers and funders require of them – a plausible means of achieving a separation of people. Moreover, relative to the opportunity cost of not having them, they are perceived to be affordable. There is hardly any other way to interpret the fact of their adoption on such scales and with such great enthusiasm and skill by so many different countries.

Grand Strategic Fortifications

As observed earlier, on the eve of the First World War all the major European powers subscribed largely to a national security strategy based on fortifications.[82] Powerful fortresses lined their frontiers:

> Northern France and Belgium were studded with fortresses, strategically placed above rivers that an invading army would have to cross – especially the long, winding Franco-German Meuse – and their names again and again come up in military history, as far back as the Middle Ages: Liege, Namur, Mauberge, Dinant, Verdun, Toulon, Antwerp. They were expensive and contained thousands of guns.[83]

The strategic logic: territory-wise, what you own is what you can hold and that means fortification. The term I would employ to describe this sort of fortified strategic complex is 'grand strategic fortification', whose distinguishing characteristic is the very long-term integration of networks of hardened structures, extensive and expensive, with the accomplishment of national territorial ambitions.

Once again, grand strategic fortifications are back in use in a very serious way. For coming on two decades, China has been building artificial islands in the South China Sea through massive dredging of sand piled over existing natural shallow reefs. Though it once promised not to fortify them it has done so extensively, with particularly powerful installations now at the Fiery Cross, Mischief, and Subi reefs in the Spratlys as well as on Woody Island in the Paracels. There are additionally many smaller fortified islands each proclaiming and backing up China's territorial claims.[84]

That this chain of fortifications is at sea on islands not created by nature is testament to China's ambition and capacity for engineering mega-projects. The strategic logic, however, is no different from that which motivated the construction of great belts of fortresses through

3.6 The West Bank 'separation fence'
Through most of its length, the Israeli 'separation fence' on the West Bank is just a very robust fence laced with sensors and various anti-intrusion measures. In densely populated, more heavily contested areas, such as pictured here in Bethlehem, the walls are made of interlocking concrete slabs topped by wire and interspersed with armoured watchtowers and steel rolling gates.
Source: Garry Walsh, 2012, Wikimedia Commons. CC BY 2.0.

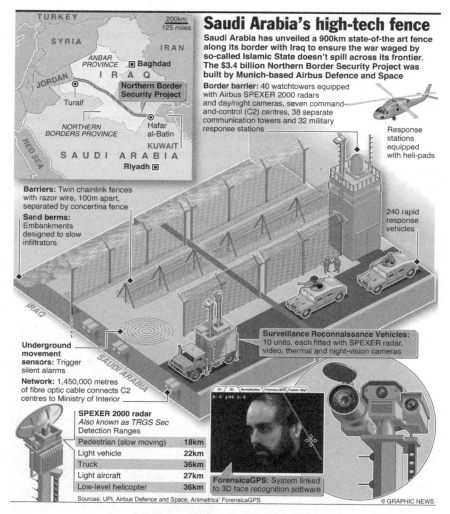

3.7 Saudi Arabia's high-tech fence
Linear peripheral barriers are frequently erected as anti-migration measures. Often though, as with the Saudi 'great wall' on its northern border, they can be very heavily guarded military fortifications. Its multi-layered quality is reminiscent of the layered defences of Byzantine Constantinople.
Source: GRAPHIC NEWS.

Europe over a century ago. Indubitably, these are fortresses: in place of great guns, they deploy anti-ship missiles and military-grade runways; in place of a glacis, they depend upon powerful radars, surface-to-air missiles, and point-defence artillery; in place of casements, they feature protected magazines and armoured missile and aircraft shelters.

One might suggest, too, that Russia today, for all its overt belligerency, is pursuing essentially a fortification strategy. Secure behind its Kaliningrad bastion projecting into central Europe, protected by batteries of hypersonic missiles capable of threatening deep civil and military targets in the West with powerful conventional strikes in minutes, it has the wherewithal to meddle in the affairs of its close neighbours without too great a fear of retaliation.

Ultimately, there is no such thing as an impregnable fortress – nor are fortified strategic complexes by any means a sure thing. Chance being a fundamental feature of war, we should be very surprised at the suggestion of anything like surety. In the case of a power consolidating territorial control, a fortification strategy simply increases the cost to any potential attacker. It remains to be seen whether China's 'Great Wall at Sea' will deter or defeat any challenges to its claims. It does not seem, though, a desperate gamble or a forlorn hope. For the time being no one seems at all eager to test it.[85]

The ongoing war between Russia and Ukraine, which began in the spring of 2022, has put into sharp focus some matters which were long present but only dimly perceived. On a strategic level, from the perspective of a Westerner speaking to a Western audience, the picture is extremely alarming. The antecedents of the conflict date back to the invasion of Crimea in 2014, or even earlier depending on where you wish to pick up the story of confrontation between the two, in which the West is thoroughly imbricated, tracing back to the dissolution of the USSR thirty years ago.

It has evolved rapidly into a proxy war between NATO and Russia. It has also accelerated the emergence of a Eurasian economic and military compact between China and Russia that is without doubt, strategically speaking, the most globally consequential thing to have happened since the end of the Cold War.

Meanwhile, the collapse in Western 'soft power', especially the perception of the West as a neutral steward of a universally beneficial, rules-based economic order, has been precipitate. Its efforts to economically isolate Russia from the world have rebounded severely on its own economic well-being in ways that were conceivable but highly implausible before the war.

Industrial warfare

At the same time, sticking to more military matters, the character of the war in Ukraine is striking. High-tech conventional warfare between 'peer-competitors' was meant to be 'rapid and decisive', in contrast with past patterns of non-digitalized, industrial warfare, as well as more recent experience of asymmetric counter-insurgencies. Instead, in the words of the respected military analyst Dave Johnson, what Russia has done in Ukraine is

> what they've always done: rely heavily on massive firepower and a very slow, incremental attrition manoeuvre. You just grind, and what you're betting is that you have more staying power than the adversary does, not just in people, but in munitions ... When Russians set their mind on something and pile on, it's very hard to stop.[86]

The situation on the ground is clearly subject to change. The fact is, though, that here we are, fifty years or so into the information age, looking at an industrial war conducted along a front of more than 1,500 miles, crisscrossed by trenches and fortifications of a scale, depth and intricacy that would not have shamed the experienced engineers from the latter days of the First World War.

Ukraine has shown astonishing military resilience, probably signalling the superiority of defence over offence under current technological conditions. Nevertheless, Russia is likely still winning inexorably on account primarily of its superiority in the kind of military muscle that was supposed by now to be obsolete.

In the end, wherever the new line between East and West is redrawn – a line that the end of the Cold War was supposed to have made meaningless – it is a fair supposition that it will be marked on either side by grand strategic fortifications.

Thus far we have been discussing the use by Western armed forces – primarily in non-Western places – of fortified strategic complexes for a variety of strategic purposes including the pacification of occupied populations, the physical strengthening of existing territorial boundaries, and the consolidation of new territorial ambitions. The latter is more the preoccupation of anti-status-quo powers such as Russia and China, but in any case it involves extensive fortification and provokes, in turn, even more military fortification.

As I have pointed out, such operations have a strongly positional and fortified character – an expression, I would argue of a culturally determined strategic default setting towards guardedness that is born out of an acutely sensitive appreciation of risk. This is at odds with the way that military theorists tend to talk about how warfare ought to be – but it is the way that warfare actually is now.

We will next consider the adoption of fortification strategies in the civilian sphere in the context of Western society. The connection between these two categories, or milieus, of conflict is both consequential and worrisome. Much of what we have discussed so far in terms of tactics, techniques, and technologies was developed for operations in the context of war 'over there', but it has been reapplied very significantly on our own streets 'back home'.

Most of the story that follows, though not quite all, centres upon the urban environment. In the next chapter, therefore, we shall focus specifically on the long history of the co-evolution of war and the city as seen in the shape of the latter's interior and exterior structures and layout.

4

Storming the City

If we are to understand the myriad techniques and devices that secure urban environments today, it is useful to look at past practices. As I shall show in this chapter, today's problems are not categorically new. They are more complex, and contemporary cities are very much bigger than cities of the past, but the problems are not new as such, so it is useful to see how they were solved under simpler and smaller-scale conditions. At the very least, applied history helps us to focus on the right questions. Moreover, understanding how we got to our present condition is the best foundation for any informed guess about the future.

War and the city go back a long way. Indeed, if you think of the one as organized political violence of a certain scale and the other as the major unit of settlement of an organized political community of a certain scale, then it might be said they have a common origin: civilization – a word which not incidentally has the same Latin root as city.[1] Over time, neither has remained the same; rather, each has altered in reaction to the other. We can observe this co-development through the annals of military history as well as through the study of the changing morphology of the city.

Fortification has been a primary feature of urban design from the very beginning, manifested with great variety – a fact which we may observe easily in old cities like Rome, Vienna, Jerusalem, or Istanbul which exhibit a deep strategic stratigraphy – as we earlier called the layering of new fortifications atop old ones – creating a palimpsest of past and present wars comprised of landscape and architecture.

In 1875, the French military engineer E. Viollet-Le-Duc wrote a wonderfully idiosyncratic novel-cum-history of fortification called the *Annals of a Fortress*. In it he tells a story whose main actor is not a person but an imaginary spur of land in Burgundy which he named La Roche Pont. He described fortification after fortification being built there over a span of 2,000 years, each different from the one before it, through a competitive cycle of offensive and defensive techniques and technologies. The story ends with the Franco-Prussian War 1870–71, when the fortress was again under siege.

In the introduction to the English edition, the fortress historian Christopher Duffy says it would be a 'worthy enterprise' for someone to write a sequel taking the tale up to the present time.[2] That is the spirit of this chapter, if not its exact design. My intent here is to trace the urban form, its external contour as well as its internal configuration, generally over time. I will cover some of the same ground as Viollet-Le-Duc – alas not in the form of a novel, nor with reference to a single specific location – but bringing the story up to date.

Fortification of Early Cities

Let us start with the remains of Catal Huyuk in Turkish Anatolia, a city of as many as 10,000 people dating back approximately 9,000 years – one of the oldest human settlements known to archaeology. It has a curious, almost hive-like, clustered form that entirely lacks streets. The houses also lack windows and doors and are built on top of one another in a solid mass, with entrances via ladders through the roof. In that sense, it is a primitive city, lacking all the parts of settled living as we know it – differentiated structures, streets, public squares, and so on – although its permanent inhabitants showed some diversification of labour and social organization.

It might be argued that Catal Huyuk's protective features were an accidental by-product of its peoples' peculiar building methods rather than an explicit defensive design. It is now widely understood, though, that warfare was endemic in early and pre-civilization times, a reflection of the tension between 'hunter-gatherer' peoples and those who had taken up settled farming.[3] In this light, it is unlikely that the fortified quality of Catal Huyuk was coincidental.

From the outside, the continuous and unbroken outward-facing walls of the windowless houses on the city periphery would have been an effective defence: a city wall, in effect, with a parapet comprised of the roofs of the houses from which missiles could be launched. A challenging place to attack for nomads lacking siege weapons. In fact, handling an enemy who fights from the rooftops and windows of solidly built, closely packed houses looking down on narrow alleys is still a significant challenge to modern armies.

Jericho in the Palestinian West Bank, a still-inhabited city dating back as far as 11,000 years, is more unambiguously fortified. Its walls, parts of which may be seen today, were already 6,500 years old when, as the Bible (Joshua 6:5) famously describes, they were brought down by the trumpets of the Israelites. Leaving aside the actualities of Jericho's fall to Israel, the main purpose of its walls, obviously, was to prevent enemies from easily entering the city. To get past a wall you must go over, through, or under it, all requiring effort and time, during which you may be exposed to the weapons of the defenders. Walls slow attackers down and make it easier for defenders to stop them – the foundational principles of military fortification.

To appreciate the look and feel of the earliest fortified cities one of the best places to visit today is the citadel in present-day Erbil, capital of Iraqi Kurdistan. Since 2014 it has been a UNESCO world heritage site and is currently being restored. It combines three important elements that are highly symptomatic (if not axiomatic) of the type.

First, it tops a large mound that varies in height from twenty-five to thirty metres, effectively occupying a natural defensive landscape feature. Second, it has a continuous town 'wall' tracing the edge of the mound, made up of the reinforced and windowless rear faces of the outermost houses. Third, it has a jam-packed interior of mud-brick buildings arranged in an organic jumble looming over narrow, winding streets. The latter warren-like character is typical of the older quarters of Middle Eastern cities but is especially pronounced in Erbil.

An effectively fortified city of this era required walls strong enough to resist penetration by determined enemies equipped with battering rams, picks and siege towers, or mining tools, and high enough to prevent escalade by very bold enemies trying to climb over them as fast as possible. They needed battlements to protect defenders from missiles as well as to permit them to fire their own missiles. Obviously they required a gate to allow passage in and out of the city in normal times, but one that was strong enough to resist being forced open by attackers in wartime.[4] Even today, building walls several metres high and thick, that are durable and stable against the natural elements, let alone against the efforts of powerful enemies to tear them down, is neither easy nor cheap. For early civilizations it must have been very demanding.

Surprisingly, however, so far as we can tell from the archaeology, all these problems were solved by Mesopotamian and ancient Egyptian military engineers – often spectacularly – many thousands of years ago. The Nubian fortifications of Egypt's Middle Kingdom, for instance, achieved a standard that arguably would not be equalled anywhere in Western Europe until the late mediaeval or early modern era.[5]

In other examples, the walls of ancient Ur are reckoned to have had a thickness of up to thirty-four metres, while those of Babylon rose to a height of twenty-five metres and had towers rising a further five metres. Crenelations protected the defenders, while fighting galleries located in projecting towers allowed them to sweep the base of these huge walls laterally with showers of arrows and other missiles. Nearly always, a deep ditch (often water-filled) made approaching the walls even more difficult. Moreover, some cities developed double or even triple circuits of walls. In the largest constructions, these amounted to many miles in total length.[6]

In short, the ancients clearly perceived a necessity to defend settled places almost as soon as they were invented, employing impressive techniques and technologies at what must have been substantial cost. Thousands of years before the invention of the water wheel, for instance, fortification systems were well developed. It is a good question whether the plough, perhaps the quintessential technological artifact of civilization, was invented before the first fortification or after – certainly the two are very close in origin.[7]

With very minor modifications and enhancements, this system of urban defence remained effective up to the fifteenth century CE. I would suggest that the late mediaeval fortification of Constantinople (now Istanbul, Turkey) may be seen in hindsight as its apotheosis. This consisted on its landward side of three integrated defensive layers from the city side outwards – first, a high and thick inner wall punctuated by huge towers every couple of hundred feet, then a terrace below it protected by a lower but still powerful outer wall, then a covered walkway guarded by still another slightly lower outer wall, followed by a sixty-foot-wide and twenty-foot-deep stone-lined moat that was, finally, guarded by a miniature wall.[8] Its downfall, literally, came with the huge and cumbersome direct-fire gunpowder artillery employed by the Turkish warlord Mehmet the Conqueror in his defeat of the city in 1453.

City walls

The effect on urban planning can be assessed first by looking at the outer periphery of the city. I should note, though, that not all ancient cities were fortified. Like modern ones, many were quite open, particularly when they were part of the sovereign territory of militarily dominant or otherwise externally secure powers. The Spartans famously scorned defensive walls as unmanly, in insulting comparison with their enemies the Athenians, who were prolific wall-builders.[9]

The cities of the Roman Empire in its heyday were also generally unfortified, such was the power of its frontier, the vigorousness of its legions, and the intrinsic security of its interior. Only in the later empire do we see cities defended increasingly by circuits of walls, as the defence of the Roman frontier eroded and the power of its mobile armies diminished, exposing the populations of open cities to depredation.

In Britain, the cities of London, Exeter, and Leicester are good examples of late-Roman walling of what had been open cities.[10] 'Urban wallification' seems to have been a strategic choice born of a necessity faced by powers that, if not necessarily in decline, had nonetheless reached the height of their territorial ambitions. They reflect an urge to solidify what has already been gained, and to preserve enclaves of higher material comfort than the wider regions around them, in the most economical possible manner. Note that the sharp rise of urban fortification in the Roman Empire beginning in the third century CE occurred while the building and maintenance of Roman roads, i.e., mobility, went into sharp decline.[11] We will return to this apparent tension of security and mobility in the next chapter because it is still a fundamental problem.

Very typically in history, if not always, securing the city largely consisted of girdling it with protective walls. These were costly to build – indeed, as we observed earlier, history features numerous monarchs and potentates bankrupting their treasuries with fortification-spending. They were also expensive to maintain, so they were frequently allowed to fall into disrepair when there were no obvious threats.

Furthermore, they restricted movement in and out of the city, causing traffic jams and making the number, placement, and design of gates a constant source of friction between military and commercial imperatives. The citadel in Erbil, for example, had just two gates as late as 1944, while archaeologists suggest that ancient Jericho might have had only one.[12] And they obviously limited the construction of new buildings in the city, which usually ended up jammed right against the walls and sometimes boiled over them.[13]

One of the earliest, most widespread, and strictest urban planning regulation was the injunction against infringement on the intramural zone between civilian buildings and the city walls. In practice, nonetheless, from what we can see of the mediaeval era, the rules were frequently broken by all classes – the poor found it convenient to lean their shanties against the city walls, while the rich often exploited the open space to build pleasure gardens and private amenities. In China, where city walls were often spectacularly large, the poor even scooped out caves from them in which to live.[14]

As a result, when a city sensed an imminent attack, there was usually a period of frenetic demolition by its defenders, tearing down buildings near the interior walls to create a fire break, allowing the fortification to function and troops to move. Neighbourhoods outside the walls were also torn down to provide a field of fire and deny shelter to invaders. Materials thus liberated from civil structures would find ready re-use in repairing the walls.[15]

The main point with respect to urban planning and the city form is that *internally* the city from classical to mediaeval times could take a variety of forms without much reference to external threats, except during a crisis when buildings impinging on defences would be razed in a panic.

The shape of early cities as opposed to later ones tends to look relatively organic or natural. That is because walls tended to follow the local topography, notably where high points made defensive walls more effective because of the natural increase in elevation. Iron Age and neolithic hill forts are often called 'trace forts' or 'contour forts' for just this reason, because they trace the high points of the existing landscape. Early fortifications also tended to lack projections, i.e., they were generally circular.

The reason is likely not so much military as economic, as a circular form is the most efficient way to enclose an area with the shortest amount of wall – an important consideration in societies with little material surplus. When you consider, also, that the longer the wall the more soldiers are required to defend it, it is no surprise that the tendency overall was for city walls to be sinuous and as short as possible.

The Gunpowder Revolution

The adaptation of the city (and of war generally) caused by the advent of gunpowder artillery was gradual, involved increasingly large and complex engineering, and had characteristics of extreme economic and political significance. The historian Geoffrey Parker, for instance, has argued that the emergence of hugely expensive artillery-resistant fortifications led to dramatic changes in the size and composition of armies – a 'military revolution' which necessitated, or contributed to, the development of the large centralized administrative apparatus that is the foundation of the modern state.[16] It is difficult to do justice to such a great period of interrelated military and political change in a few lines. If, however, we stick to our focus on fortification and its demands on the urban form, then it is possible perhaps to summarize it without too much offence to nuance.

The basic problem with the arrival of gunpowder artillery was that the soaring walls of mediaeval fortifications following the natural contours of the landscape, while adequate to defend against all but the most determined attacks with muscle- and gravity-powered weapons, could not resist the battering of cannons, particularly once it became possible to cast relatively light and mobile artillery.

The fall of Constantinople's superb mediaeval walls hinted at this emerging reality. Although they did the job, Mehmet's cannons were gigantic, practically immobile, and prone to exploding the operators. The invasion of Italy by Charles VIII of France forty years later, in 1494, made it stupendously obvious that a watershed had been passed. At the beginning of that war, the mediaeval walls of the frontier stronghold Monte San Giovanni, which had once withstood a siege of seven years by mediaeval means, were battered down by Charles VIII's relatively mobile new bronze cannons in just eight hours.[17] The pattern was then repeated on a score of other Italian cities thought previously to be highly defensible.

Gunpowder had a profound impact on the shape of the city but its effects were not immediately felt nor distributed equally. Restoring the viability of defence required significant experimentation and mutation of fortification, initially in Italy as a response to the sharp lesson of the French invasion. Over a period of a couple of centuries, this culminated in the fortification system known as the Italian Style, *trace italienne*, or, more commonly, the 'star' fortress.

As we noted in the last chapter, many examples of these geometrically complex fortifications remain scattered across the globe, especially in Western Europe, so popular and successful had they become. They are often extraordinarily elaborate, as reflected in the terminology developed to describe their parts – bastions, ravelins, lunettes, demi-lunes, tenailles, and so on. But their main features include:

1. A rampart broad enough to provide a firing platform for defending artillery, low enough to be difficult for attacking artillery to target it, and thick enough to resist those hits which do manage to hit the mark.
2. A combination of ditches, bastions, and walls sufficient to prevent escalade.
3. A conformation of the defences, i.e., the 'trace', which leaves no dead ground around the fortress that would allow an attacker to get close to the rampart without exposure to defensive fire.

The key to the *trace italienne* style is that it is not an organic form following the contours of the natural landscape. It is, instead, highly regular, geometric, and artificial, due to the step change in the effectiveness of artillery that occurred in the early modern era. Whereas in earlier times defensive fortifications generally adapted to the landscape, now, in order to address the capabilities of new weapon systems, the landscape had to be reshaped to meet the needs of the fortification. In simple terms, the edge of fortified cities went from being curvy and irregular following the logic of the ground to being pointy and regular, with the ground reshaped where tactics and weapons characteristics required it.

Fortified cities changed from an amoeboid shape with few or no projections to a regular polygon with several corners or points, in accordance with the size of the area being secured and the configuration of the landscape. Established principles dictated the number of bastions for surrounding a city, and for the arrangement of the fortress's parts, depending on the effective range of defensive artillery.

Bastions and gates

In theory, the more corners, each capped by a bastion (a stable fighting platform from which guns could sweep all approaches to the fortress in a murderous crossfire), and the more regular the shape, the better. In practice, cost considerations tended to reduce the number of bastioned corners and the nature of the ground led to irregularity in shape. In their most developed form, star fortresses possessed astonishing complexity, and we are necessarily cutting corners in our descriptions of it.

For the present analysis, here are some overarching observations. Firstly, notwithstanding the intricacy of the design of these fortress cities, they essentially combined two basic forms: the bastion and the curtain (or wall). Often when architects estimated a price for their work, they simply gave the unit cost of these two elements, leaving it up to whichever potentate was paying to multiply the price by however many units were required to cover a given area. Rather like today's 'hard landscape' designer, of which we will hear more in the next chapters, planners of early modern city defences had a range of relatively standardized products, a set of principles for their use, and a budget.

It is unsurprising that at the dawn of the modern era we see standardization emerging in fortress architecture; the idea of standard measures is an aspect of modernity observable in other fields like commerce, industry, and science.

Secondly, squaring the imperatives of security with aesthetics took on a new angle. Undoubtedly, gunpowder artillery made the high but relatively thin walls of mediaeval fortification militarily obsolete, but high walls remained symbolic of civic pride and identity. Many cities, therefore, kept their old walls and gates long past the point of their military utility because, simply, people and rulers liked them.

A fine example of this are the Aurelian walls of Rome, in use for 1,500 years up to the wars of Italian unification in the 1870s. The Vatican's magnificent Porta Pia, for instance, designed by Michelangelo, is a disaster as a military gate but a triumph as a piece of art. Thankfully, Garibaldi's army declined to smash it when they successfully attacked the city, choosing instead to blow a hole through a more anonymous section of the wall a few tens of metres away.

It is interesting that the fascination of the Baroque period with enormously complex ornamentation governed by simple underlying rules and symmetry, so apparent in civilian architecture like St Paul's Cathedral or in the work of musical composers like Handel and Bach, is also reflected in patterns of military engineering. There is a very definite beauty to star fortresses like Bourtange in the Netherlands or Neuf Brisach in France, rather like a fugue but made out of stone and earth. When seen from above, the city as an object of military pride and political desire is obvious in a way not so apparent from the ground. Viewing this attractive symmetry was, of course, beyond the capabilities of the people who built them, long before the days of aviation.

From the ground, the beauty of the squat walls of such fortresses is distinctly less apparent – if visible at all, as generally their bulk was concealed by a glacis and ditch.[18] Instead, a popular genre of art in the sixteenth and seventeenth centuries was the bird's-eye representation of cities as imagined by artists, collected in illustrated folios and published widely to serve a great public interest in siege and city views.[19] The popularity of such art was presumably connected with the urge of citizens to show off a hugely expensive but practically hard-to-appreciate public architectural accomplishment. In other words, it shows the powerful symbolic investment of people in fortifications even when they cannot see them in their full glory.

Thirdly, the existing problem of limitation to urban growth caused by enclosing city walls became even more acute. By comparison with mediaeval walls, which had a relatively narrow footprint that even then was generally intruded upon by civil construction in peacetime, the defensive works of artillery-resistant fortresses extended much further. Ultimately, the sprawling belts of fortification including the curtain, the ditch, a bewildering variety of attached and detached projections, and a glacis that might cover hundreds of metres, could effectively dwarf the areas it was meant to protect.[20] Even in peacetime no city governor could permit civilian construction on a fortified city's glacis. Indeed, when Napoleon fortified the city of Palmanova in Italy, three nearby villages were razed to the ground to clear fields of fire.[21]

From sinuous to star-shaped

The peripheral shape of the city, what we might call its integument, the 'skin' presented by its exterior walls, became much more geometrically regular and pointy in response to the threat of gunpowder artillery. In addition, cities began to actively shape the landscape around them, rather than being shaped by it. In practical terms, for an artillery fortress, if there was a hill in the way then the hill had to move; if there was a river nearby that could be bent, literally, to defensive use then it would be.

In its fully developed form, the star fortress also had a complicated subsurface defensive complex. Knowing that attackers might seek to undermine a fortress, even before the first row of bricks of the first bastion was laid out, military engineers would have dug out countermines and listening posts projecting out into vulnerable areas. In short, the artillery fortress imposes itself on the landscape in ways that mediaeval and earlier fortification types did not.

Fourthly, artillery-resistant fortresses also made substantially more demands on the configuration of the city *inside* the walls, in ways that potentially seriously impeded its ability to function as a civil enterprise. Why? Imagine an idealized artillery fortress as a star-shaped polygon with eight even sides, the curtain wall, and eight points, each capped by a bastion. Usually, when a city was attacked, enemy operations would be concentrated on one or two bastions rather than all of them at once. Therefore, once the defending commander had determined the point of main enemy attack, he would want to shift his artillery to concentrate at those points of greatest need as quickly as possible.

Now, consider that a heavyweight artillery piece of the early modern era weighed about 15,000 pounds and the means available to shift it were limited to muscle power. It stands to reason that the best arrangement of streets under such conditions would see the main thoroughfares run straight and level from any given bastion directly through the centre of the city to the bastion on the opposite side. The result would be a radial pattern of streets emanating from a central open area, where a command centre could be located, each terminating at a bastion – a highly defended fighting platform where heavy guns were mounted.

From a civil perspective circular and concentric streets are not necessarily a problem for traffic flows and the arrangement of markets, housing, major public buildings and so on. Indeed, many communities have adopted a radial pattern, seeing it as an ideal in conformity with natural forms, i.e., rounded rather than square, and providing a symbol of community in a common core. The first *kibbutzim* planted by Jewish settlers living out a sort of Hebrew communism in mid-twentieth-century Israel had such a design, for example.[22]

The issue is that the gates of a city must be in the walls, not in the bastions. For civil purposes, in relation to the normal flow of people and goods, it makes most sense for streets to terminate in walls with gates, whereas streets that lead directly to bastions are most convenient for the transfer of heavy guns from one place to another. The conflict is obvious. As opposed to a mediaeval city where streets and buildings could take on whatever shape organically suited the needs of civilians so long as they did not interfere with the outer walls, an artillery-resistant city was an integrated fighting machine that made much greater demands on the city as a machine for living.

Economics of fortification

In effect, we have here a perfect instance of a problem which we will consider later in respect of our own streets now – that of an intrinsic contradiction between defensive and economic imperatives. Designers have never completely resolved this issue. The seventeenth-century design of the Italian fortified city Palmanova is a good example of a compromise that didn't work. In that case, three of its six main streets pointed to bastions while three pointed to city gates, leaving six of the city's nine bastions out of communication with the centre. The design proved neither militarily satisfactory (the city was abandoned as a military post in 1866) nor a civic success. Palmanova still exists, but primarily for the entertainment of military architecture enthusiasts.[23]

By the late nineteenth century, advancements in weapons technology – notably the invention of the rifled gun and the explosive shell, which together multiplied the power of artillery many times over – had made traditional fortification methods thoroughly obsolete. Economic and population growth, moreover, massively exacerbated the long-standing problem of corseting cities with continuous walls, although sometimes a lingering benefit of them was the convenience they provided governments when it came to levying customs charges at entry points. For example, the Wall of the Farmers General built in the 1780s around Paris, parts of which still exist, was twenty-four kilometres long and had sixty gates in it, but it had no military function at all, being entirely for the purpose of tax collection – one of several civic annoyances leading up to the French Revolution.[24]

In the 1860s, when the fortifications of Paris were being rethought as part of an extensive civic refurbishment overseen by the Baron Georges-Eugène Haussmann, Prefect of Seine under Napoleon III, it was briefly considered to surround the city at some distance from its periphery with another huge continuous bastioned enceinte wandering over hill and dale. Basically, the old pattern of urban defence would be applied on a stupendous scale to a city that had expanded by that time to an area of 105 square kilometres and over 2 million inhabitants. This plan was abandoned for being either tactically preposterous or far too expensive or both.[25]

As an aside, it is often argued that the true focus of Haussmann's renovation of Paris, which shaped the look of the fashionable inner city today, was on internal security, specifically the fortification of the French government against urban political revolution. Whereas the winding and narrow streets of classical to mediaeval times could be easily barricaded to impede the movement of military forces attempting to restore order, Haussmann's wide and straight boulevards (ironically, a word derived from the Scandic 'bulvark', or English 'bulwark') had the supposed opposite qualities, being too big to barricade and highly convenient for the rapid transfer of troops from their garrisons on the outskirts to hotspots of revolt in the centre.[26]

While this belief would dovetail nicely with the story of the contemporary preoccupation with internal security that interests us in this book, there is no strong evidence that Haussmann had any particular interest in security or designed his streets with counter-revolution in mind. Moreover, if the intent was to stymie political uprising through urban design, it was a failure, as the rebels of the 1871 Commune of Paris took the city easily – though they ultimately failed to defend the streets, despite building extensive and powerful barricades, because the army simply went around them by smashing through the walls of neighbouring buildings instead.[27]

The era of continuous urban enceintes gave way for a time to a transitional arrangement in which cities were ringed at some miles distance by small but powerful fortresses that could protect it, in theory but not always in practice, by covering its approaches with interlocking fields of artillery fire. Superb examples of this are the fortresses of the Meuse River in Belgium, which were built to defend the cities of Liege and Namur, the fortifications around Verdun, France – scene of some of the most savage fighting of the First World War – and the German fortifications of Metz, now a French city.[28]

Within the more distant confines of a ring of forts the city was free to grow again in whatever shape its inhabitants found to be fit and pleasing. Perhaps the best example of this are the stupendous star-pattern fortifications of Vienna that withstood the Ottoman siege of 1683. By the mid-nineteenth century, however, they had become an expensive nuisance, militarily obsolescent but using up valuable real estate. They were demolished in 1857 by imperial decree, making way for today's ring road. Except for the names of subway stations like Schottentor and Stubentor ('tor' means 'gate' in German), which mark the places where city gates once stood, hardly a trace of the walls remains. On a lesser scale, New York City's Wall St also marks the place of a long vanished defensive work.

On one level, the shift from continuous walls to the encirclement of cities by chains of forts is highly discontinuous. The Chinese character for 'city' is an ideogram of a walled enclosure, which shows the semantic and actual overlapping of encircling walls and cities through much of the history of human settlement. The strategic intent remained continuous: to defend cities by keeping the fighting as far as possible from population centres and civilian buildings.

While developments in weapons technology eventually made such efforts fruitless, the late nineteenth century was a transitional period in which it was still remotely plausible to consider the defence of cities against attack by constructing fortification *around* them, using a network of integrated forts to place enemy artillery beyond effective range of the urban centre. This was ultimately a losing game for city defenders, because the technology of attack that was advancing far outstripped the old fortification defences – basically, enceintes could not keep artillery out of range while also being economical.

Death from Above

The advent of aerial bombardment truly sealed the new reality that even the best-defended city could not keep military combat away from civil life when under deliberate attack by a determined enemy. This was the gist of a House of Commons speech in 1932 on future war given by the British politician Stanley Baldwin, in which he memorably declared that the 'bomber will always get through'.

In that he was not perfectly correct: defence against bombing turned out to be quite possible, but Baldwin's apprehension of the arrival of a new 'notion of death and destruction' was spot on:

> What the world suffers from is a sense of fear, a want of confidence; and it is a fear held instinctively and without knowledge, very often. But my own view – and I have slowly and deliberately come to this conclusion – is that there is no one thing that is more responsible for that fear . . . than the fear of the air.[29]

In terms of destruction, the effect upon cities of mass bombing by aircraft hardly requires elaboration. A decade after Baldwin's speech cities were being blasted to smithereens, firstly by Germany in 'the Blitz' against Britain and in return on a gigantic scale upon Germany by British and American bombers. As the RAF Air Marshal Sir Arthur 'Bomber' Harris put it, Germany had sowed the wind and would reap the whirlwind. It is estimated that by 1945 Allied bombing had destroyed 40 per cent of the urban areas of the seventy largest German cities, killing 305,000 civilians.[30]

The adaptation of cities to aerial attack has at times been very extensive but is generally much less obvious than wall and bastion fortification systems for defence against land attack. It took just thirteen years to go from the Wright brothers' first motorized airplane flight at Kitty Hawk, North Carolina to the first civilian air-raid shelter in Cleethorpes, Lincolnshire – where it still serves as a garage. That was built in the summer of 1916 by a local chemist, Joseph Forrester, after German Zeppelin airships bombed the town killing thirty-one soldiers in a nearby barracks. In short, even before heavy fixed-wing aircraft became the main author of strategic bombing, back when hydrogen-filled dirigibles were the state-of-the-art of death-from-above, the city had already begun to adapt.

In the early part of the Second World War the Russian-born aviator, industrialist, and air-power theorist Alexander de Seversky speculated on the impact of air power on the urban form in his book *Victory Through Air Power*, which was so popular that Walt Disney made it into a film in 1943:

> Civilian architecture will inevitably be affected by the air age. Materials for roofing and other purposes will be increasingly selected with reference to resistance against explosive and incendiary bombs. The location of rooms will be conditioned more and more by the bombing potentials. I venture to guess, for instance, that gathering places that do not require daylight – such as motion picture theatres, ballrooms, and banquet halls used largely at night, certain restaurants, and meeting halls – will be built underground as natural air-raid retreats. That tendency, together with advances in air conditioning and ventilation may invert all our architectural concepts; 'skyscrapers' may be built downwards instead of only upwards.[31]

As with many such predictions there is a degree of exaggeration here, a tendency to over-emphasize some perceptible elements of change while underestimating the durability of elements of continuity – notably the strong human tendency to want to live above ground rather than under it. Notwithstanding, de Seversky's predictions are surprisingly accurate.

Underground forts

Take, for instance, the area of London where we started this book, on the Strand near King's College London. Here and there one can still find a few examples of bomb damage such as the holes in the bronze lions at the base of 'Cleopatra's Needle' – a granite Egyptian obelisk removed to Britain in the 1870s, on the edge of the Victoria Embankment – caused by fragments from a German bomb dropped on the street in 1917. Some elements of the response to such attacks, like the Churchill War Rooms on the edge of Whitehall, are relatively obvious and well known.

Others such as the bomb-shelter-cum-ballroom three stories underneath the Savoy Hotel (currently serving as one of the world's best-protected and most expensive conference rooms), in which the London rich held dance parties during the Blitz of 1940–41, are not so visible. The point is that the city responded to a new form of attack with a new form of fortification – the air-defence bunker or bomb shelter – both very rapidly and very extensively.

As a measure of the speed of this development consider that in 1916, in the very early days of aerial bombing, King George V was protected by parking the Royal Train in a railway tunnel, securing the sovereign at the cost of severe disruption to the train network – a distinctive economy and mobility versus security problem. By 1944, in comparison, central London was a veritable honeycomb of bomb-proof bunkers and at least ten miles of tunnels connecting the buildings of the major ministries, command centres, and key communication facilities. In addition, seventy-nine tube stations were converted for night-time use as bomb shelters and eight other stations were designated as 'very deep shelters' – a nice example of the latter being Belsize Park station, where the shaft-head building is still visible.[32]

The very deep shelter at Chancery Lane station, later renamed as the Kingsway Exchange, was transformed into a huge, fortified complex with two parallel tunnels over 350 metres in length. During the Cold War it became the home of a highly secure telephone exchange, and the terminal of the first transatlantic cables. Later, the infamous nuclear 'hotline' connecting the White House and the Kremlin ran through it as well. In the mid-1980s it was the backup site to the main 'Pindar' nuclear command and control bunker now located beneath the Ministry of Defence.

'Kingsway, built to withstand a siege, protects its citizens better than the walls of Troy' is how it was aptly described in the 1969 issue of *The Courier*, the internal newsletter of post office workers (in Britain, until the establishment of British Telecom in 1981, the telephone service was run by the General Post Office).[33]

Such fortifications, being located deep underground, are easily forgotten about even when they are not actually secret. The existence of the Kingsway, for example, was an official secret until 1966 – and not widely known after that. The complex of London's subterranean defensive structures is extensive and largely still in existence, so far as we can tell since visits are discouraged.[34]

The pertinent point is that defence from air attacks has significantly shaped cities, in ways that are very large, but also very easy to miss. London is by no means unique in this respect. Underground Moscow is at least as tunnelled out and probably much more so. One gets a sense of this from places like Bunker-42, a sixty-five-metre-deep nuclear shelter that is now part of the Cold War Museum at Taganskaya Metro station, and which presumably represents a fraction of Soviet underground bunker-building. Similarly, deep beneath the cobbled streets of today's Prague lies 'the metro protective system', a vast complex of Cold War-era nuclear shelters for up to 200,000 people, in addition to hospitals, warehouses, morgues and airlocks – the last very obviously visible while travelling on the underground.[35] One might compile a long list of such structures.

Until recently, a reasonably informed person might have thought the fate of such facilities was either to be sealed up or converted into museums for a curious public, rather like the Churchill War Rooms. Recent events, though, show that the expectations of reasonable people are not always a reliable guide to a messy and volatile reality. For example, a tour guide at the Sonnenberg Tunnel – a vast public nuclear bunker-cum-museum (effectively the centrepiece of a national fortress) outside Lucerne, Switzerland – said in 2022 'I've been getting calls from people asking me, "Can you please tell me where I would have to go if the war in Ukraine gets closer?"'[36]

In German and Austrian cities today there remain many vast concrete *flaktowers* (public air-raid shelters with anti-aircraft installations on top) built at enormous expense by the Third Reich as a defence against Allied bombing. As high as fifty metres and immensely powerful they are, for the most part, too difficult to demolish. The Nazi government was highly sensitive to the intrinsic ugliness of most surface-mounted air-defence bunkers and sought initially at considerable expense to 'soften' their features. Some bunkers were designed to look like churches, others like normal houses with fake dormers and gables, while the Dietel-type bomb shelter was modelled on a neo-Romantic mediaeval gatehouse. As the war progressed, however, architectural adornments of bunkers could not be afforded and they became much more simple and severe in appearance – here again an aesthetics and economics versus security problem.[37]

Two very good examples of the more austere style may be seen in all their incongruousness in the *Augarten,* a delightful baroque garden in the heart of today's Vienna, where one gigantic *flaktower* – thirty metres high with anti-aircraft gundecks jutting from its top – now houses a small café in a tiny section of its bulk. The other bunker, equally large, is nearby, festooned with microwave antennas for mobile phone traffic. The architect who built the towers had planned to finish them with a façade mimicking the style of a Hohenstaufen castle, but wartime austerity cancelled this decorative phase of construction. These concrete monoliths remain brute testaments to the industrial-scale violence of mid-twentieth-century warfare. They could easily last for as long as the pyramids.

The City Itself as Fortress

Obviously, the ideal way to defend a city under modern conditions is to defeat enemy forces in the field in combat as far away as possible from population centres. Failing that, expedient defences, such as hastily dug anti-tank ditches, barricades, bunkers and so on, might serve to halt an attacker on the outskirts of the city. The result, though, is likely to be a siege – a form of warfare that has never gone out of fashion.[38]

For example, I live in an unremarkable medium-sized commuter town outside London which has long been an important node in the transportation network of southern England, being approximately one day's ride by horse from the city centre and having a natural crossing point of the Thames River. Nowadays, a main rail line and a major highway also pass through. Even this place, though, is marked by fortifications of a surprisingly recent vintage. I had long wondered, for example, at the purpose of the circular concrete pit with an iron pillar embedded in its centre on the edge of a wood in my local park. A derelict paddling-pool? Play equipment? Even by the standards of modern public art it is too ugly to be a sculpture. Usually, it is full of beer tins, so it still has some utility to someone.

It turns out to have been the firing point of a 'spigot mortar', a type of British anti-tank weapon invented at the beginning of the Second World War. The whole edge of the park which overlooks a road junction was a prepared anti-tank ambush including at least three other concrete-reinforced positions, one of which – a pillbox with a machine-gun port hidden in a garden wall – still partially remains.

Thankfully, none of these defences – hastily thrown up for fear of German invasion at the beginning of the war – were ever put to the test. Examples can be found all over the country.[39] My point is that the strategy which they served is time-honoured, relevant even in Britain not so long ago and relevant elsewhere to this day. Defensive fortifications like this force an attacker to conduct a series of siege operations, slowing down a military advance on a particularly important objective, like a national capital or other political and economic place of significance.

The basic problem for the attacking army is that it is dangerous to leave behind undefeated strongholds from which defenders can launch attacks on vulnerable supply lines. It is possible sometimes to ignore fortified outposts, to bypass them and carry on directly towards one's main objective, but it is risky. Even if a fortified place can be bypassed – which is not always possible with the way transportation networks are concentrated in built up areas – forces often need to be detached from the main attack to prevent isolated garrisons from making sallies or raids. This weakens and slows down the attack.

A good example showing the longevity of this strategy is the ninth-century Anglo-Saxon shift from undefended *wic* trading sites to fortified urban *burhs* in response to the Viking threat. Ultimately, some thirty of these well-structured urban fortresses formed the framework of the successful defence of proto-England, helping to consolidate the early victories of Alfred the Great. Many of these fortified towns remain, often recognizable by place names ending in 'burgh' or 'bury' (e.g., Shaftesbury), though the palisades have rotted away and the earthworks gently eroded.

That said, the Saxon defences at Wareham were intended to be used as late as 1940 against German invasion – a pillbox (still visible) was installed in the northern wall at the top of the High Street and the western rampart was renovated to act as an anti-tank ditch.[40] In other words, under certain threats, a society whose towns and cities have been relatively open and largely undefended by fixed fortifications can rapidly swing in the opposite direction and back again. It is no surprise that at the time of writing similar structures are being built around Kiev.

This anecdote on the longevity of some fortifications aside, by the mid-twentieth century war and the city had developed a macabre and ironic relationship. On the one hand, the very old strategy of employing cities as fortified bulwarks against major attacks continued (as it does today, as has been seen most recently in the grinding attritional fighting between Russia and Ukraine in the towns and villages of the Donbas region). This power of obliterated cities to continue to resist is not a new development in history, but many of its greatest examples, such as the 1936 siege of Madrid, or the battles for Leningrad, Stalingrad, Warsaw, and others during the Second World War, are relatively recent. It was this quality of resistance that led Hitler to declare city after city 'fortresses' against the twin advances of the Allied powers – Britain and the United States from the West and the Soviet Union from the East.[41]

On the other hand, the irony of being designated a 'fortress city' was that, as weapons technology made external fortification futile, the city had to be fortified with the fabric of the city itself. The city then became both a prize and its own battlespace.[42] If the enemy could not be stopped at the outskirts, they would have to be fought within the city itself. This concept of the modern open city, no longer encircled by continuous ramparts or rings of mutually supporting artillery forts, but as essentially a fortress composed of civilian rubble assembled in place as the battle proceeds, is still the current state of the art.

Resilience of cities

In the West after the end of the Cold War, and the consequent diminishment of the threat of major war, this has seemed increasingly irrelevant. Examples of urban warfare elsewhere in the world have been plentiful, of course, but not until recently has the problem seemed directly relevant to the populations of cities at home or so close by. Through to the end of the Cold War, however, NATO considered the ability to use urban areas of Germany for defence against Soviet military power, particularly its large, armoured formations, as one of its relatively few conventional advantages.

People forgot that, as it was put in a mid-1970s study of the defence of Europe against the Warsaw Pact, 'developed areas archipelagoed in depth over Western Europe represent an extensive fortified area that is particularly suited for defence against armour heavy attackers while maintaining economy of force'.[43] What was true before may well be true in the future, even if we in the West got out of the habit, for a while, of thinking about our own cities this way.

The effect upon the urban environment of fighting with modern weapons should be obvious. A machine gun's bullets alone will pulverize brick and concrete like a jackhammer, incendiary rounds will burn anything inflammable, while the effect of explosive shells and bombs on buildings and infrastructure needs little elaboration.[44] Likewise, the vulnerability of people when military operations and civil life are entangled is extreme.

Any amount of serious combat in a built-up area will rapidly reduce it to smouldering heaps of wreckage, which is why the Red Cross has called for increasing international legal restrictions on the use of explosive weapons in urban environments.[45] While this is desirable from a humanitarian perspective, from a dispassionate practical perspective its chances of success are slim. To take a current example, the fighting in the Donbas region today is unequivocally an artillery war fought on both sides by generals who look at urban areas as fortresses to be defended or reduced by cannonade and siege.

With respect to how high-intensity combat affects the shape of a city, note two counter-intuitive things. First, paradoxically, given the vulnerability of structures to fighting, many modern buildings – in terms of their utility in combat – can be quite resilient. As UK tactical doctrine on urban warfare states:

> Corners of buildings or parts of floors may collapse but the core of the building will retain its strength. Even though modern buildings may burn easily, they often retain their structural integrity and remain standing. Once high-rise buildings burn out, they are still useful for combat purpose and are almost impossible to damage further.[46]

In short, for the purposes of defending an urban area it can be easier to do so *after* it has been turned into rubble. Military history, as we have seen, is clear on this matter.[47]

The pattern of modern urban warfare tends to see civilian structures hastily fortified, then blasted to smithereens. Then, as often as not, the rubble is refortified by the survivors or by reinforcements, and the fighting continues. This miasmic quality of urban warfare is why generals have a somewhat schizophrenic attitude towards it, for the most part wanting to avoid it wherever possible, while also seeing in it a plausible means of strategic defence against a more powerful attacker.

The truth is unpleasant and not often openly confronted: it turns out that under modern conditions sometimes the ideal place to preserve your military power is by embedding it deeply in civilian architecture. This is obviously an inversion of natural human sensibility, not to mention the laws of war, which seek to limit the intermingling of military force and civil life by insisting on the protected status of civilian objects. It is also nonetheless the implacable logic that commanders trying to win wars are drawn into.

Scenes of smashed cities evoke in people feelings of horror and fascination, whether the imagined scene of destruction in Picasso's famous painting of the bombing of Guernica, or photographs of the obliterated homes, torched schools and offices, shattered churches, and so on of many other wrecked cities. Perhaps because we regard cities as quasi-living things, we are particularly shocked by their destruction, akin to homicide, even genocide or 'urbicide' as some scholars have put it.[48] Perhaps too the speed with which combat turns the ordered regularity of the built environment into a bloody shambles is alarming because it shows the precariousness of civilization.

Plainly, cities are reservoirs of enormous symbolic and actual wealth; naturally, therefore, their destruction causes great pain. Their deliverance from destruction is a great joy, as, for example, in 1944 when Paris, which Hitler had ordered to be razed, was liberated by the Allies undamaged. That it survived intact was due as much to the refusal (at great personal risk) of the German commander, General Choltitz, to carry out an order that would have been an act of infamous vandalism.[49] He ought to be remembered for a courageous omission of duty, allowing the world to retain intact a glorious cultural artifact.

The urge to keep non-combatants and civilian structures away from the fighting can be traced all the way back to the common origin of the city and war. No doubt this is why we might say that preserving Paris was 'civilized', whereas an attack upon a city, whatever the reason, is likely to be described as 'savage' or 'barbarous'.

The truth, unfortunately, is that in the long history of civilization the tendency is for war and the city to increasingly occupy the same place, converging towards one another. The situation recalls the famous quote of an American officer in the Vietnam War: 'It became necessary to destroy the town to save it.'[50]

Slightly tempering that bleak assessment is our second, also rather paradoxical, observation: while cities may be severely damaged with frightening ease, they are also, contrary to the literature which uses this word too incautiously, practically impossible to *kill*. Throughout history, cities have been sacked, burned, bombed, flooded, irradiated, and poisoned, yet have always bounced back because they are astonishingly naturally resilient.[51]

Warsaw, for example, was systematically demolished in three waves of fighting during the Second World War: the 1939 invasion, the Jewish Ghetto uprising in 1943, and the general uprising in 1944 – after which Hitler commanded that particular care be taken to destroy all buildings of cultural, historic, or aesthetic significance. It is a pity for Warsaw that the officer in charge was no Choltitz and the task was undertaken with ruthless efficiency. When the Soviet Army finally occupied the city in January 1945 over 80 per cent of the city's buildings were in ruins. Interestingly, Warsaw was not just rebuilt but, particularly in the Old Town, meticulously reconstructed, if not always entirely convincingly.[52]

More recently, in 2003, the city of Grozny was declared by the United Nations to be the 'most destroyed city' on earth. After two major rounds of savage urban fighting in 1994–96, and again in 1999–2000 when Russian forces finally subdued the capital of breakaway Chechnya, it was reckoned that every one of the city's buildings was battle damaged, nearly all of them to the point of requiring demolition. Twenty years later it is difficult to find any physical mark of the war on the totally rebuilt city.

The City Today and Tomorrow

We have covered much of the history of the attack and defence of cities in search of patterns and trends that can help us better understand our current dilemmas. A summary of some of our findings is useful before offering a final observation that will lead into the following chapter, which focuses more on the contemporary scene.

My first observation is that the shape of the city, both internally and externally on its periphery, is a product of many forces, including economic incentives, political realities, and social pressures – notably population growth. Simple fashion, aesthetics, things which people like and dislike for whatever reason, whether tradition or whimsy, have also played a powerful role. Military science and new weapons and tactics are also important, but military imperatives have not always superseded other considerations shaping the city over time.

People want to be secure. For good reason Maslow's famous 'hierarchy of needs' lists 'safety' as the next most fundamental human requirement after food and shelter. Cities, moreover, are repositories of a society's wealth, culture, and sense of prestige, making them objects of desire to an enemy. They need, therefore, to be defended. They need also to *work* as places to live and generate prosperity – which excessive or badly designed defences can easily impede. This basic strategic tension between imperatives will be explored further in the next chapter.

In simple terms, the edge of the city has gone through a series of transformations. Initially, it was an enclosure formed by some kind of continuous barrier, whether a stand-alone wall or the walls of the outermost buildings, tracing the contours of the local landscape according to its defensive potentialities, following the high points of a natural rise or the banks of a river. The need to adapt to the gunpowder revolution meant that city walls got much lower and thicker, but also straighter, more standardized, and regularly geometric. At the same time, military considerations started to have a greater impact on the internal arrangement of the city's streets. As artillery became more powerful, and the size of cities began to grow, it became impossible to combine continuous walls with economic viability.

After a transitional phase of rings of fortresses without full enclosure of the city, peripheral defence of cities came to be seen as highly militarily improbable. The result by the middle of the twentieth century was a pattern of city defence without enclosure, depending on ad hoc fortifications rather than permanent ones.

There is no single reason for these changes, rather a range of contributory factors. On a basic level, though, the problem is just space. Over time, cities got bigger and bigger, while the range and power of weapons got greater and greater. Inevitably, given the nature of geography, it became impossible to maintain much distinction between the outside of the city where fighting could occur and the inside where it would not. People did not stop fortifying cities. Instead, some fortifications became internalized – sometimes quite literally, with the most secure facilities squirrelled away deep under the city.

Overall, the trend going back over thousands of years, though admittedly static much of the time, is towards increasing demand on the internal configuration of cities for defence and a greater intensity of violence throughout the whole of the urban environment, as combat is diffused from the periphery inwards. In effect, relatively recently there has been a shift in our conception of cities: rather than being incipient fortresses, we assume that, should war occur, they will be destroyed. This is not an unfortunate by-product of combat; it is, rather, the current understanding of how urban warfare ought to be conducted.

Uncomfortable truth

Under conditions of modern warfare, a 'normal' open city may be transformed into a closely guarded one very rapidly by the 'weaponization' of certain sorts of infrastructure that we normally do not see as having a military capacity.

Ring roads, for example, a typical feature of many large cities – Beijing has five of them concentrically, Tokyo has eight, Moscow and London just one apiece but those very heavily developed – are easily militarized. They are intrinsically strong structures, very often elevated, and nearly always walled on either side; they have a limited number of easy-to-control access points, are generally under constant visual surveillance from cameras, and are often overlooked by high buildings; being open spaces lacking cover they constitute a near-perfect killing ground.

It does not take a great deal of imagination to see how a ring road like the M25 London orbital could be as challenging a defensive barrier as the walls of Constantinople. When you consider that a completely incinerated modern concrete and steel apartment complex, let alone a giant heavy industrial facility like the Azovstal steel works in Mariupol, can remain fully structurally intact after an attack, then it is probably obvious that such a place might as well be called a bastion.

It would certainly be an ideal place to locate an artillery battery, with lots of covered firing positions, plenty of underground storage, and even convenient platforms for the location of observers, long-range cameras and so on. The effect on whatever fraction of the civilian population that does not flee such places before combat occurs will be catastrophic. Anything not armoured will be destroyed. The fact that cities almost always bounce back from this sort of battering is cold comfort.

From an urban planning perspective, with one notable exception there are no major cities currently which have incorporated defences against a high-intensity attack by ground forces over a sustained period. The exception is Seoul, South Korea, which because it is located close to the North Korean border (within heavy artillery range), and on a likely invasion route, does possess a range of permanent military engineering works on its periphery and scattered throughout the city. Giant concrete blocks have been cantilevered over major highways where they can be dropped, if necessary, by exploding their supports to create an instant barrier. There are also extensive belts of 'dragon's teeth' anti-tank barriers around the city, including in the river bottoms.

Probably more not to alarm the public than to keep them secret from the enemy, some aspects of Seoul's defensive fortifications are not much talked about – but they are an open secret. These include the militarization of certain residential and other civil buildings, well-described in a local interest piece published in a Canadian newspaper just before the visit of President Trump to North Korea in November 2017:

> If you don't know what you're looking for, the small row of apartment buildings on the southern banks of the Han River are unremarkable mid-rise boxes, built like so many others in the South Korean capital.
>
> But cast your eye up about halfway, and something odd appears: the stairwell windows on the sixth floor are much smaller than those on

other storeys. Look closer and it becomes clear they are fortified as well, tucked into thick walls that overlook a river that, if war breaks out on the Korean peninsula, would provide a key natural barrier to the advance of troops from the north.

Those windows are, in fact, gun ports. Inside, the floors have been reinforced in case one day they need to support soldiers and heavy firearms positioned here to repel invading forces. It is a military installation inside an apartment building, unknown even to most of its residents.[53]

Other defensive innovations in Seoul include not just civil-defence bunkers in dense residential areas but whole apartment complexes in vital areas designed to be easily demolished to create an instant rubble field, i.e., a sort of wall, in the event of an attack. In short, while in the above I may have seemed to be speculating based on historical patterns about alarming things that may someday concern people not currently living under threat, Seoul nevertheless shows that the awful is entirely possible given certain strategic conditions. Indeed, in Ukraine the striking resilience of steel-framed high buildings to battering by heavy shelling has meant that such structures have proved to be highly effective fighting positions. In other words, even seemingly delicate skyscrapers may prove highly redoubtable in military terms.

Let us ponder the validity of our assumptions about the strategic conditions that have shaped our cities today. Has anything important changed? In my view, the answer is yes, substantially. Taking the long view, we might observe that the last two centuries of war, from Napoleon onwards, have been atypical. Certainly, with respect to the city form, the unguarded and unwalled openness of the city is historically unusual. Extremely open cities have existed throughout history, but they were associated with militarily vigorous, socially confident, politically ambitious civilizations, which at the present time the West is not.

The current wall-less-ness of our cities is based upon three factors. The first and most important is a perception of the absence of the threat of major war. For nearly a generation since the end of the Cold War it has been supposed that major interstate conventional wars, wars of territorial conquest specifically, are obsolescent.

Then there is the long-standing problem of the vertical dimension of attack upon cities, whether by the firing of artillery or aerial bombardment by aircraft. When it comes down to it, can you fortify the sky? If so, can whatever it is you come up with be defined as some sort of architecture? Finally, the sheer size of cities and the mobility requirements of the broader global political economy in which they are embedded make the idea of corseting them with barriers sound preposterous.

None of these assumptions are secure. As of 2022, major wars over territory are decidedly a live factor in international affairs. As for the fortification of the sky, at the time of writing even the severely denuded Ukrainian air-defence system – based upon thirty-year-old Soviet missiles – can prevent Russian aircraft from operating freely at any height above the ground that exposes them to radar detection.

More advanced systems, soon to include new forms of directed-energy weapons, will make air war even more difficult. As for whether you can fortify the sky and call it architecture, the designation of the highly effective Israeli anti-missile system 'Iron Dome' would seem to make the answer a definite yes. Iron Dome, it is said, 'securitises the atmosphere as an impenetrable semi-sphere that encapsulates urban space'.[54]

Finally, in the aftermath of the Covid lockdowns in which barriers to mobility shot back into use on every level – from interstate to intrastate at regional and municipal levels, and even at the individual household level – it is hard to escape the conclusion that, whatever the global political economy is now based upon, it is not untrammelled openness.

Which raises the intriguing question: could urban enceintes make a come back? If so, what would they look like? For now, I would argue that, historically, a preference of statesmen and commanders for fortification strategies has been the norm in European military history. If this seems a controversial assertion it is because we are only now emerging from an atypical two-century-long period. In other words, if there is a contemporary turn towards fortification, it would be a regression to a norm, not a departure from one.

In what follows, we will see how new forms of fortification typify the urban space. They do not look like the fortifications of the past, but they are, indubitably, fortified strategic complexes. However, they are not military in their nature. As we have seen in this chapter, the distinction between military and civil fortification is highly ambiguous. There are both military and civil imperatives. At times, practice favours one of these imperatives over the other, for multiple tactical and cultural reasons. At present, civil fortification is favoured – a topic that is the main preoccupation of the following chapters.

5

Securing the City

We have looked at how the techniques and technology of attack and defence throughout history have shaped the way cities look and work, externally and internally. I have deliberately taken a sweeping approach, choosing illustrations widely in search of big trends and general lessons. Now, we shall concentrate on the present and recent past and on more specific principles in order to structure the case studies in the following chapter.

The main thrust of this chapter is that fortification at its root always reflects a trade-off – an inherent tension or 'tug-of-war' between two or more significant human desires. Always present is the desire for security. Fundamentally, any fortress is a physical manifestation of the primitive psychological state which is the human fear of being attacked. That perfectly normal urge for security – relief from fear – is set against other heartfelt desires such as the wish to live in an environment that is attractive and welcoming as opposed to one that is ugly and foreboding. Likewise, the powerful urge to be free, both as an individual and as part of some affinity group (family, tribe, or nation), can be seriously impinged upon by efforts justified in the name of security. Nowhere is this more obvious than with surveillance, always an intrinsic element of fortified strategic complexes.

If there is a single takeaway from this chapter, it is that walls are not simple. The superficial crudity of walls, howsoever formed – slabs of concrete, bricks piled on bricks – belies a deep strategic complexity. A wall is rarely just a wall; for that matter, there are a great many 'walls' you would not recognize as walls because they are designed to blend in and not stand out, even in plain sight.

The seemingly simple question, 'do walls work?' leads to more subtle questions: What are the walls supposed to be doing? How are they doing it? To what ends and for whose benefit? These are the questions which animate this chapter. We shall try to answer them by direct observation of what we can readily see on our streets and in our buildings both private and public. A bit of theory will help to simplify some things which are intrinsically complex.

It is worth stipulating that the walls under consideration mean different things to different people: how one views a specific wall depends a lot on which side one is on.

Many experts cited in this chapter are in the fortification business, which, as we shall see, is growing massively and profitably. They are, overall, quite positive about it. My own subjective feelings are a mix of fascination with the strategies and ingenious technologies involved and an apprehension of dread that they are a sign of things going wrong with our society. One of the most penetrating philosophical treatments of the subject put it this way:

> walls today represent power, but they also represent isolation, security, but at the same time fear. They are a second-best solution to the problems of our societies. They have always been a second-best solution; one might speak of an ideal society, one of peace and freedom, as a society without any walls other than that minimum needed for shelter and privacy: without boundary walls. But we have come to accept this second-best solution as the best we can do. We accept walls that divide people and rigidify the relations among them as inevitable. They pervade our cities, they are visible (or block our sight) wherever we look, they symbolize status, rank, and power (or its lack). They are taken for granted and accepted as desirable, in one form or another, by everyone.[1]

One need not be a neo-Marxist intellectual to agree with nearly all of that, as I do. Where I differ slightly is in thinking that all solutions in which there is a degree of trade-off between points of view involve, by definition, some sort of compromise, which is to say they are second-best at best. Neither do I believe in the possibility of an ideal society – in this world, it seems to me, 'good enough' is an achievable and admirable aim.

What follows is a description of urban civilization as it is, which unfortunately to my mind is still some way off from being good enough.

As a reader your opinion may well differ. Bottom line: I think there is no ideal solution to the problems being addressed here, and no simple answers will be provided. My intention is to tell a story about how our cities are made up of a great many 'solutions' dreamed up over the years and expressed in physical forms – occasionally good, often bad, sometimes good enough.

Let us start with our first and arguably oldest 'tug-of-war' – the tension hinted at in the previous chapter between defensive and economic ambitions.

Security and Mobility

Urban geographers tell us that to understand cities we must see them not just as places in space but as interconnected systems of networks and flows.[2] A city is by necessity penetrated by channels of rapid communication and transportation that support its primary function – the generation of wealth, or power – through the concentration of people in a particular place for industry and commerce. For a city to work it must have motion; rather like an organism, it requires circulation in order to live.[3]

Cities, moreover, are increasingly connected to each other as nodes in larger global networks of flows of goods, people, and ideas.[4] In 2015, the UK government published a national security strategy which had, as its subtitle suggested, two priorities: security and prosperity. The then Prime Minister David Cameron wrote in the foreword to it that Britain needed 'the sea lanes to stay open and the arteries of global commerce to remain free flowing'.[5] For an island nation such as Britain this focus on the sea is not surprising.

My point is that the streets of a city like London are a continuous part of that same global arterial system. Indeed, data scientists have shown that London is in many ways the overwhelming centre of the global corporate elites, and has been for about two centuries.[6] The management consultancy firm Kearney has a long-running 'global cities' index (London, New York, Paris, and Tokyo are usually at the top) which ranks them on their ability to sustainably attract capital, people, and ideas through an 'abundant and constant connectivity' with the rest of the world.[7]

Here, then, is the primary problem: how do you secure a place which relies upon abundant and constant flows for prosperity? Lewis Mumford, the great historian of cities and civilization, put it this way: 'human life swings between two poles: movement and settlement . . .

At every level of life, one trades mobility for security.'[8] Logically, this 'trade' cannot be all or nothing. Too little security can allow violence that will strangle normal civil life; too much security can crush the mobility on which normal civil life depends. There must be a balance. What is it and how is it achieved?

This problem is most obvious in cities at war, but it remains a pertinent factor in the architecture and planning of all cities even in nominal peacetime. Furthermore, cities depend not just upon mobility in the present; they are also in motion over time. This is often hard to observe because we tend to keep the same names for things such as buildings, streets, and neighbourhoods – which have been changing since long before any of us stepped into the flow of the world.[9] In other words, there is an evolutionary quality to cities, a pliability and mutability, that is at odds with our subjective human experience of them as hard, relatively unchanging and static places.

Flows

A good place to observe this is from the traffic island in the middle of the Strand in London, where it meets with the eastern end of the Aldwych. Indeed, the name 'the Strand', which means 'shore', is a nice example of the above point about continuity and change. The shore of the Thames River is nowhere near here anymore, having been covered over by the Embankment 150 years ago, yet we still call it that.

Anyway, imagine you are standing just by the William Gladstone Memorial watching the stream of cars and buses. Perhaps the riverine appellation still applies. It is obviously still a place of flows par excellence – the Victorian statesman Gladstone, four times elected prime minister, was, fittingly, a champion of free trade and what we might now call an 'open' society at the height of the British empire.

The Strand is also one of London's oldest and most iconic streets. Traffic has moved past this place in a continuous stream for about 2,000 years, since Roman times when it was the start of the road to Bath, a route still in existence, though now the road is much larger and known more prosaically as the 'M4 corridor'.

The Strand is an 'artery' in the sense that it connects three major 'organs' of British power: the City of London, Fleet Street, and Whitehall. So closely are each of these districts associated with a particular activity that in common speech they are metonyms, respectively, for banking, media, and government. Consider then that alongside the visible stream of vehicle traffic on the surface there is another even

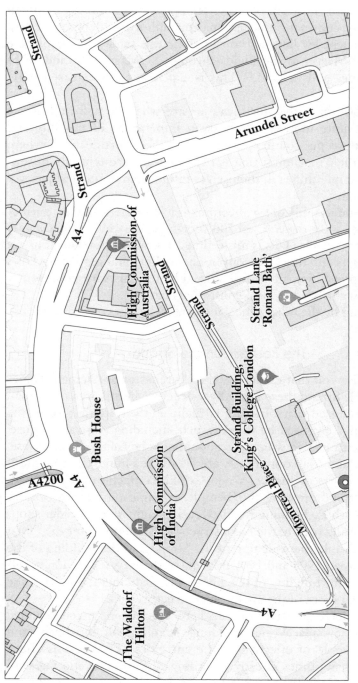

5.1 The Fortress on the Strand

'The Fortress on the Strand' is a pedestrian zone covering two blocks of the Strand taking in all the buildings south of the Aldwych Crescent. It is guarded on its periphery by a series of heavy duty 'hostile vehicle mitigation' systems including bollards and planters. It is also heavily surveilled by CCTV cameras.

more vital stream: a torrent of money and power and influence, unseen but effectively conveying the national metaphorical lifeblood. There is even an ancient ley line said to run along this same route, from the church of St Martin-in-the-Fields through St Mary le Strand to St Clement Danes and beyond.[10] This is a place of power based upon movement.

My proposition is that fortifications are what we will find at the intersection, quite literally, of the twin imperatives of mobility and security. If it seems counter-intuitive to expect fortifications where flows are at their maximum that is because walls are typically misunderstood as simple things in themselves rather than as integral parts of complex systems.

It is common to think of fortifications as just barriers, the less permeable the better – like the colossal 700-foot-high 'ice wall' in the *Game of Thrones* fantasy novels. This is misleading. In practice, fortifications are less like barriers and more like valves, channelling and regulating flows rather than preventing them full stop. Their forms vary enormously depending on a myriad of local contextual factors.

So, standing by the Gladstone Memorial, what do you see here?

The Fortress on the Strand

It may surprise you that except for the churches of St Clement Danes and St Mary le Strand there is hardly a structure in this area older than a couple of hundred years. Indeed, virtually all the important ones, the grand buildings enclosed by the Aldwych, including Australia House, the classical entrance to which you should now be facing, Bush House, India House, and Marconi House, are less than a hundred years old.[11] The Royal Courts of Justice, a neo-Gothic confection on the north side of the Strand opposite the Temple, is a mid-nineteenth-century construction, whose building required razing eight acres of older shops and houses dating back to the reconstruction of London after the Great Fire in 1666, while the widening of the Strand and the building of the Aldwych between 1900 and 1905 was one of the largest London developments since the building of the Thames Embankment, requiring the erasure of even more of the area's older structures.

In short, much of what you see here are ancient names applied to relatively new places and buildings standing on the burnt and demolished rubble of effectively different cities. The area has been transformed many times already according to the wants and needs of previous generations, most recently out of the desire for great buildings more commensurate with the stature of the British Empire at its height, and to alleviate traffic congestion. It is being transformed again today in a major redevelopment whose aim, in the words of Westminster City Council, is 'transforming this historic gateway to the West End into a world-class and contemporary traffic-free public space'.[12]

The most noteworthy aspect of the redevelopment is the pedestrianization of the Strand from Surrey Street to Wellington St, turning the formerly busy road into a fully enclosed 'park' centred on the church of St Mary le Strand. The stated rationale has been relief of traffic congestion, better air quality, and conformity with general fashion. Another reason for the redevelopment, not stated but clearly implied in the design and construction of the whole fortified strategic complex, is the increase of security through an interlocking matrix of defensive 'hard landscaping', surveillance systems, and what we might call 'bunkerized' architecture.

It does not look like a fortress in the traditional sense, because, as we have seen with the problem of flows, there are two competing imperatives at work – in this case security and aesthetics. The grandeur of the urban scenery of the Aldwych crescent as seen from either St Clement Danes or the intersection with Wellington Street is practically unsurpassed in the world. Hundred-foot-high, Portland-stone-fronted, classically embellished buildings line its whole length. Bush House, at its centre – for many years the home of the BBC World Service, and now part of King's College London – is styled deliberately as a statement. It is a gargantuan Romanesque temple with huge columns topped by a pediment and an impressive statue bearing the inscription 'to the friendship of English-speaking peoples'. When finished in 1929, it was reputed to be the most expensive building in the world.

Aesthetics

In other words, this is more than a street; as Westminster City Council rightly boasts, it is a symbol of global stature and ambition. Here, then, is an example of the second general problem: how do you secure a place meant to symbolize a given civilization's artistic and philosophical creativity? It is an old challenge. Aristotle, quoted by Mumford, said that 'men come together in cities in order to live; they remain together in order to live the good life'.[13] But cities have grown in scale and complexity, along with the means of attacking them. Too little security may imperil our lives, but too much security can destroy the experience of living well. If you accept that the city is more than a 'machine for living' – that it is also a 'crucible of culture' – then you need to confront the idea that securing it has an aesthetic dimension beyond the mechanical.[14]

You can't make structures overtly stronger – more resilient and defensible – without diminishing their other desirable qualities. This is most easily visible in the architecture of older cities walled primarily on the outside against external attack. The design of city gates, for instance, to welcome visitors in style and provide a tangible symbol of a city's wealth and creativity, often conflicted with the needs of defence – a tension frequently resolved in favour of fashion over function.[15]

It is more difficult to see when city walls are internalized throughout the urban landscape as they are nowadays. It remains a practically ubiquitous trade-off, a 'second-best solution', negotiated and manifested in fortified architecture and urban planning.

Where you are now on the forecourt of St Clement Danes (on which the Gladstone Memorial is sited) is a good place to observe two deceptively humble elements of this defensive system. First, there is the attractive long, gently curving planter/bench seating located immediately in front of you on the kerb, mirrored in another planter across the street in front of Australia House. Both are constructed of brushed off-white concrete reinforced by a dense internal lattice of interwoven two-inch steel rebars and backed by a buttressed steel plate which in turn is bolted into another concrete mass buried to a depth of about six feet. A well in the centre, varying from about two to eight feet in width, is filled with earth, ostensibly to accommodate several trees. Aside from being pretty, these add further useful mass to the obstacle.

Second, there is the row of 'traffic' bollards on either side of the planter that continue around the perimeter of the fortified strategic complex. Bollards are of course a common part of the contemporary streetscape, safely separating normal pedestrian and vehicle traffic. These ones, though, are not normal in that sense.

They are 'RhinoGuard 75/40 Shallow-Mount' bollards manufactured by the UK-based hard-landscaping firm Marshalls, designed for places like this where it is difficult to dig deeply due to the complexity and density of underground utilities.[16] They are extremely robust, with a hardened steel core hidden under the decorative stainless-steel outer sleeve. This in turn is mounted in a roughly 1 × 1.3 metre rectangular double-layered steel baseplate mounted in concrete lying beneath the street surface. The total weight, which is 560 kilograms, not counting the concrete (about half that of a small car), gives an approximate sense of its strength.

In the language of contemporary site security planners, both the planters and the bollards are 'Impact Rated Hostile Vehicle Mitigation' (HVM) measures, or 'defensive street furniture'. In plain English, they are intended not just to stop normal traffic accidents but to impede deliberate attacks upon pedestrians by people in fast-moving heavy vehicles. The category of such fortification products, known as 'hard landscaping', is enormous and diverse.

To give a sense of its scale, the UK Centre for the Protection of National Infrastructure currently lists 435 products from fifty-six different manufacturers.[17] In the language of students of military architecture, they are contemporary examples of two elemental and universal features of fortification: a 'curtain wall', a device designed to prevent an attacker passing through a defended perimeter; and a 'baffled gate', an arrangement of walls that causes an attacker to slow down, usually by turning, at an entrance.[18]

Neither provide any sort of impediment to people on foot, obviously, since their purpose is not to prevent escalade by an assaulting infantry force; it is instead to separate vehicular from pedestrian traffic, like a colander draining pasta, to mitigate the damage of 'hostile vehicle' attacks. It is important to break down this form of attack into two main types that differ greatly in their damage potential.

Ramming and bombing

The first is a ramming attack where the vehicle itself is the weapon. Any place where vehicular and pedestrian traffic is mixed, or a crowd of people is exposed, is a potential target for such attacks. The July 2016 ramming attack in Nice mentioned earlier is a particularly powerful example.[19] Another would be the December 2016 lorry attack on a Christmas market in Berlin.[20] The ideal target is one with a high density of pedestrians canalized in a straight line, and which is free from obstacles, allowing an attacker to get a vehicle up to high speed on a route from which it is difficult for people to escape quickly. The April 2017 Westminster Bridge attack in London was much less deadly than the one in Nice, with only five people killed, but it clearly illustrated the vulnerability of people walking on bridges to ramming attacks.[21] Some of those killed in that attack died not by vehicle impact but by drowning in the Thames into which they had jumped trying to flee.

Ramming attacks are very low-cost and under certain circumstances highly effective. The main challenge is finding a driver willing to mow down potentially dozens of people in cold blood. The weapon itself can be had for the cost of a truck rental. Fortunately, defence against it is relatively straightforward, if costly. Vehicles and pedestrians can be separated from each other with a wide range of barriers.

Moreover, designers can significantly blend such fortifications into the streetscape, making them relatively unobtrusive, even attractive. A good example is Westminster Bridge, which after the attack was lined, as were all the main London bridges, with relatively cheap Temporary Vertical Concrete Barriers (often called 'Jersey barriers', the same T-walls discussed previously, or 'hostile vehicle restraint' systems). These are now being replaced by more attractive 'heritage-style' bollards that do the same job less obtrusively.[22]

Small but sharp elevation changes can achieve the same effect, such as those surrounding the Washington Monument in Washington, DC as part of the security-driven redesign undertaken by the landscape design studio Olin in 2005. In that case, as with Westminster Bridge, Jersey barriers installed in the post-September 11 counter-terrorism panic, were replaced for aesthetic reasons. The result, complemented by long, curving granite benches-cum-walls, is a functional and graceful fortification of an iconic monument that does not overtly look like a fortress.[23]

The second form of attack – the vehicle-borne explosive device, or 'car bomb' – is a vastly more complicated challenge. Explosive weapons cause damage in three primary ways: blast – a wall of highly compressed air moving at supersonic speed; fragmentation – pieces of the bomb and its casing and any other debris propelled outwards by the explosion at high velocity; and extreme heat released in detonation. All are deadly but let us concentrate on blast as it has unusual properties.

When a blast wave hits a building, it wraps around all its surfaces like a fluid for a fraction of a second, engulfing it and exerting pressures to all exposed sides. The forces generated are enormous. The effect upon a structure depends on many factors. In general, though, the bigger the building, the greater the effect, because it is exposed to the blast wave for a longer time. Likewise, the closer it is to the explosion, the greater the damage. Moreover, the wave of overpressure first caused by the explosion is followed by a reverse wave of nearly equal intensity as air rushes back into the vacuum created by the initial blast. In effect, there are two blast waves – or even more, as blast may 'echo' off other structures. All are highly destructive.[24]

It is possible, albeit expensive, to make buildings somewhat blast resistant, but difficult to make them beautiful and functional at the same time. Look at the Admiralty Citadel, for example, the squat concrete Second World War fortress located near Horse Guards Parade in London, built in 1941 to protect the Royal Navy's vital command, communications, and control centre against German bombers.

It is still used by the Ministry of Defence as an intelligence centre. It might easily be mistaken as an early example of brutalist architecture, foreshadowing more famous structures like the Barbican Centre – a grade II listed performing arts centre and apartment complex in central London – but built a decade before that architectural style became common in Britain.[25] Churchill called it a 'monstrosity' but nowadays, being almost entirely covered in creeping ivy, it sort of blends in, as though the peaceful city were slowly digesting a foreign object.[26]

Standoff distance

Unfortunately, little can be done to seriously strengthen many existing buildings, particularly the traditional load-bearing brick and stone ones which so delight tourists in European cities.[27] Major structural modifications, such as adding more mass, or reinforcing supports, are costly, very disruptive of appearance, and ultimately not terribly effective. Moreover, if one considers fragmentation, the problem is even more daunting; a powerful blast wave will propel anything not securely fastened down like a missile, while flying shattered glass has a horrific injury potential.

In the 1998 Nairobi, Kenya bombing of the American embassy, for example, glass fragments whirling in the blast injured many, including eighteen people permanently blinded and a further fifty-seven severely visually impaired (253 people were killed).[28] In that case, the bombers maximized soft-tissue laceration injuries by first detonating a grenade in the street, the sound of which drew people in the surrounding buildings to the windows to see what had happened, before detonating the main explosive – equivalent to about 2,000lbs of TNT.

The result was a charnel house, as described by the US ambassador, who was also injured in the attack:

> I bowed my head, stemming the blood from a gash in my lower lip, and took a few steps forward. I saw the sidewalk littered with glass shards, twisted metal, and puddles of blood. Another step and I came upon the charred remains of what had once been a human being.[29]

The basic problem is simply that most civil structures are designed primarily to resist vertical forces (i.e., the weight of the building itself), not the sharp horizontal (and upward) forces produced by an explosion next to them.

When such structures are hit by a blast wave the load-bearing walls can collapse, causing the structure to 'pancake' on itself. That occurred in the July 1994 bombing attack on the Jewish Community Centre in Buenos Aires, in which eighty-five people were killed, mostly crushed between collapsed floors.[30] Even steel-framed structures may collapse in a similar manner if hit with a powerful enough blast and hot enough fire, as was seen with the Twin Towers in New York City on 11 September 2001.

Contrary to what Hollywood may have taught you, there is little to no shadow for a blast wave. A person on the opposite side of a building or wall from an explosion may be protected from fragments and to some extent also heat, but is not so protected from the blast wave as it flows over and around an obstacle. A bomb equivalent to 5,000lbs of TNT, approximately the size of the April 1995 Oklahoma City bomb, which would fit easily in a common two-axle delivery truck, generates atmospheric overpressure of 2,900 psi at a range of thirty feet and 100 psi at 100 feet.[31]

To put this in perspective, the total disintegration of a human body occurs at pressures above 2,000 psi, and adult human lungs will collapse, possibly fatally, at just thirty to forty psi. Death is certain at over 100 psi but can occur as low as ten psi in children and the elderly.[32]

In short, buildings are very vulnerable to blast and people are even more fragile than buildings. The only reliable way to limit the damage is to maximize the distance from any explosion. As noted above, the drop in severity of blast overpressure is very sharp from thirty feet from the epicentre of the explosion to 100 feet – a few tens of feet can make a big difference in survivability. Therefore, site security design usually focuses on the minimum distance between likely targets and potential explosions, which, as large bombs require some vehicular transport, means restricting road traffic access. This distance is referred to in the literature as 'setback' or 'standoff'.

Cost calculation

Obviously, creating standoff is a severe (and expensive) conundrum in a congested urban environment. Just check local real estate costs. According to the UK Office of National Statistics, the cost of one square metre of property in Westminster in 2022 was £13,135.[33] Prices in the centre of other global cities are comparable. Which brings us back to our humble bollards, elevation changes, and planters for stopping vehicles.

The seventeenth-century French military engineer Marshal Sebastien Le Prestre De Vauban, King Louis XIV's master of fortifications and siegecraft, was greatly admired for his precise calculations based on observation. Whether it was the weight of gunpowder needed to explode a mine of a given depth or the practicable daily rate of advancement of trenchworks in a siege, he had calculated a number based on empirical testing. One suspects therefore that he would have approved of the standardized PAS 68 rating of the RhinoGuard 75/40 shallow-mount protective bollard. It reads as follows:

$$V/7500(N2)/64/90:1.8/0.0$$

This seemingly inscrutable sequence needs a little explaining. PAS 68 is one of the many 'Publicly Available Specifications' overseen by the British Standards Institution (BSI). Although there are other impact ratings such as the IWA 14, which stands for 'International Workshop Agreement' overseen by the International Organization for Standardization (ISO), PAS 68 is one of the most long-standing, influential, and widely recognized. It is relatively easy to interpret once you are familiar with its components.

The V describes the method of test (i.e., the threat) which in this case is a Vehicle. The number 7,500 is the weight of the vehicle in kilograms. The N2 in parentheses refers to the type of vehicle according to another British classification system, in this case a two-axle truck with the cab mounted over the engine. The next number, 64, is the speed in kilometres per hour the vehicle was going when it hit the object being tested (i.e., the defensive bollard). The angle of attack comes next – usually, as here, it is at 90 degrees (i.e., straight on). After that comes a crucial number, in this case 1.8, which is the distance in metres that the load carrying part of the truck passed the rear face of the bollard before coming to a complete stop after impact. The last number is the distance that any debris weighing more than 25kg was dispersed by the impact, in this case zero.[34]

Thus, we may say there is a fortress on the Strand today – a very powerful one, technically rated to stop at least a loaded 7.5 tonne vehicle hitting it at forty miles per hour. It exists because of the fear of two primary types of attack – ramming and, much more powerfully, bombing by a vehicle-borne explosive device. It works by selectively admitting some sorts of traffic while excluding others, thus creating some setback distance to mitigate the damage from an explosion, or ideally to deter an attack by limiting its potential consequences. In strategic studies this is referred to as 'deterrence by denial', which occurs when an unwanted behaviour is curtailed by making the expected benefit to an attacker appear less certain or not worth it.[35] For aesthetic reasons, the fortress is designed to blend into if not actually enhance the existing classical street scene.

At root there is an economic calculation, a morbid assessment of the balance between potential casualties in an attack on a particular place and the costs of blast protection/setback, multiplied by some factor representing aesthetic considerations. In Britain today, police Counter Terrorism Security Advisors (CTSAs) in each regional police force provide help, advice, and guidance on the factors involved in such assessments.[36] In the case of the current Strand redevelopment, that bill amounts to £32 million, according to Westminster Council, for one city block.[37] Not all areas of London, or any other city, are so expensive per square metre of real estate, have such levels of intrinsic vulnerability, or feature such a range of attractive symbolic targets. The number, though, provides a useful measure for guessing at the global scale of investment in such urban fortification efforts.

Panoptic Fortification

Now turn around and have a look at the pretty little church of St Clement Danes, reputedly founded a thousand years ago by the Danes who had conquered much of Britain as far south as London, hence the name. Unhappily, it was completely burned out by an air raid on 10 May 1941 when a German incendiary bomb plunged through its roof leaving only the tower and bare walls standing. It remained in this obliterated state for fifteen more years.

Indeed, in destroyed form the church makes an appearance in George Orwell's dystopian novel *1984*. Its protagonist, Winston Smith, comes across a photo of it in a junk shop and recognizes it as the destroyed building he passes daily on his way to work not realizing it was once a church. He reflects on the way the ruling Party uses even the architecture of the city to serve its version of history.[38] The coincidence of the alignment of this place with a novel warning against the dangers of the surveillance state epitomized by 'Big Brother' will become more important as we continue.

St Clement Danes was eventually rebuilt and reconsecrated in 1958 as the central church of the Royal Air Force. That is why the two other statues you will see either side of the Gladstone Monument portray the RAF's wartime leaders, Arthur 'Bomber' Harris and Hugh Dowding, commanders of Bomber and Fighter Commands, the sword and shield of British air power, respectively. If any place in the world might be described as a temple of 'hard power' it is this one.

Aerial bombardment, however, is an older 'notion of death and destruction' than the one with which we are concerned at present. Our interest now is with the opposite end of the church, facing east, where you will find a small statue of Samuel Johnson, compiler of the first English dictionary, standing before a wall still spattered with German bomb fragment damage.

To your left as you look eastwards are the Royal Courts of Justice. The first thing you may note, now that your eye is getting attuned to hidden fortifications, is the line of stone benches along the busy street in front of the entrance. This is not a place where any normal person would choose to sit for a cigarette or a lunch break, inches from a busy road, but then the 'benches' are not really for sitting on; they are another example of defensive street furniture. More wall than seat, they protect the entrance of the court, which is often crowded with protesters and news crews, from a ramming attack.

Note the little sign attached to the iron railings around the building:

> Public Notice: CCTV images are being recorded within this building for the purpose of public safety.

Much has been written about the burgeoning of counter-terrorism surveillance infrastructure in Britain and many other countries. It has a deep history that it is important to understand.[39]

Designing out terrorism

'Modern' terrorism is not new to London. It can be dated back at least as far as the so-called Dynamite War of 1881–85, when Irish-American Republicans conducted bomb attacks throughout Britain, hitting railways, military barracks, government buildings, a newspaper office, the Tower of London, and the House of Commons.[40] The Anarchists added more attacks, most memorably the (probably accidental) bombing of the Greenwich Royal Observatory in 1894, an event immortalized in Joseph Conrad's novel *The Secret Agent*.[41] The Suffragettes also carried out a number of bomb attacks, especially in London in the area around St Paul's Cathedral and the financial district.[42]

More recently, before the rise of Islamic extremist bombings, the Provisional Irish Republican Army represented the main source of attacks on London in a consciously designed strategy of exerting economic pressure on Britain, targeting mainland financial institutions, to force changes in its policies in Northern Ireland.[43] To that end, in April 1992 a one tonne bomb concealed in a Ford Transit van was exploded outside the Baltic Exchange building, killing three people and wounding ninety-one others. A year later an even more powerful truck bomb, equivalent to 1,200kg of TNT, was detonated at Bishopsgate in the heart of the financial district. As it was a weekend, there were mercifully few casualties – one killed and forty-four injured – but the damage caused was enormous. The economic cost of the two bombings is estimated at about £800 million and £1.45 billion, respectively.[44]

The police had *an* answer to the problem of IRA attacks derived from the experience of securing Belfast, a much smaller but still intense laboratory of counter-terrorism, having been wracked by bombings since the beginning of the Troubles two decades earlier. Locally known as the 'Ring of Steel', it involved the installation of an initially improvised but ultimately highly developed system of barriers and gates encompassing the Belfast city centre. This not only reduced vehicular access but also enabled checks of all pedestrians entering and leaving.[45] Belfast came soon to have the character of a 'besieged citadel'.[46] It was a staggering, if necessary, imposition on the patterns of normal civil life, which reduced a violent threat by, in effect, treating everyone as a suspected terrorist.

The difficulty with applying this solution to London was that interrupting the power flows of the City would be radically more consequential. The police could not set up static checkpoints there without gravely damaging London's reputation as an open global city and therefore its economic prospects – at a time, moreover, when it was vying with Frankfurt, Germany to be the financial centre of Europe. Justifying the Belfast-style locking down of entire sections of the Square Mile was simply beyond political possibility.

If London was to have its own 'Ring of Steel' it would have to be adapted to the local political and economic conditions of a 'global city' and implemented without excessively offending public opinion. It needed to deliver security while fitting in. A tricky problem: how to defend against terrorism without terrorizing citizens and diminishing the city's reputation as a global entrepôt by adopting an urban 'body language' that constantly advertised its vulnerability?

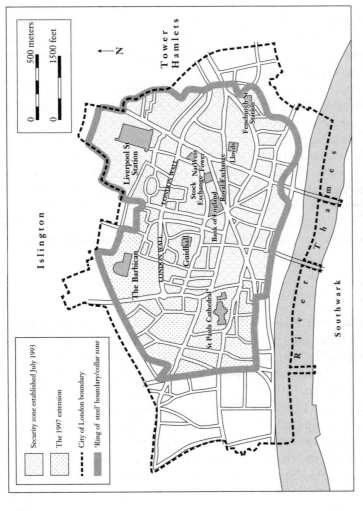

5.2 City of London's 'Ring of Steel'

The 'Ring of Steel' has a distinctively concentric pattern. Having started as a relatively constrained system of defence around the financial centre, it has subsequently expanded into a practically nationwide network of surveillance systems and interconnected barriers.

Source: Reproduced with permission from Stephen Graham (ed.), *Cities, War, and Terrorism: Towards an Urban Geopolitics* (Oxford: Blackwell, 2004), p. 287. Redrawn by Polity. Original drawing by Jon Coaffee.

The first step was semantic – a clever bit of strategic marketing: fortify, or lock down, the City of London but rationalize this in terms of other desirable public goods besides protection of the public against the danger of politically motivated mass murder. As with the current Strand redevelopment, the desirability of restricting vehicle access points to the City with physical barriers was couched in terms of its environmental benefits, i.e., cleaner air and less road congestion. Ultimately the number of physical entrances was reduced by about two-thirds with the remainder becoming heavily guarded.

Another vital element of the ring was the sophisticated network of CCTV cameras deployed at all the remaining entrances to the financial district: unobtrusive, unblinking, electronic sentries. The truly novel innovation, though, was not the cameras per se – people had been remarking on their proliferation in British public spaces since the late 1960s[47] – it was the networked system's ability to generate and process information automatically, by electronically reading a passing vehicle's registration number and feeding that information to a live database. The result: a meticulous 24/7/365 account of who had entered and left the area, as well as the ability to alert police instantly to vehicles of interest.

Wall of data

Known as Automatic Number Plate Recognition (ANPR), the system is surprisingly older than people generally think. It pre-dates the 'Ring of Steel' significantly. The idea of using data to control traffic goes back to a 'pay as you drive' scheme developed by Britain's Road Research Laboratory in the late 1960s – a system later adapted and applied to monitor and enforce London's current congestion charge scheme. That system, however, required the installation of electronic transponders in all registered vehicles, which would be activated by electrical 'checkpoints' installed in the road surface. It was never put into use.[48]

ANPR had the advantage of requiring no such equipment to be installed in private vehicles. Invented in 1976 by the Police Scientific Development Branch, it was first used in 1979, with the first arrest credited to it, over a stolen car, coming in 1981. Its application by the London Metropolitan Police to the Ring of Steel in 1993, however, was a major milestone in its development. Initially, the data generated by ANPR systems was localized to the operating local police force. In this case, the cameras of the Ring of Steel linked back to display screens in Wood Street police station. Then in 1997 the Police National ANPR

Data Centre (NADC) was set up to handle all such data from across the UK.[49]

If you look eastwards along the Strand towards Temple Bar, now marked by a statue of a dragon (curiously known as 'The Griffin') on a pedestal in the middle of the road, you are looking at the boundary of the City of London – indeed, all entrances to it are marked by such ornamental dragons, one of the innumerable quirks of London generally. There was once an elaborate stone gate here designed by Christopher Wren, which was removed in 1878 to relieve traffic congestion; it is now located at Paternoster Square near St Paul's cathedral. But the site has been guarded since at least the Middle Ages – originally probably by a bar or chain, for which reason it is known as the Temple Bar.

Lying roughly midway on the route from the Tower of London to the Palace of Westminster, historically the two main London residences of English monarchs, Temple Bar is still the principal ceremonial entrance to the City. As a visible symbol of its continuing power as a barrier, even today when the King enters the city, he will stop for a quaint ceremony in which the sovereign asks the City of London's mayor and aldermen for permission to enter. The mayor in return hands over a sword as an exhibit of welcome and loyalty.

It is a good place from which to consider the virtual elements of London's bespoke fortified infrastructure. Strictly speaking, the edge of the City of London is not the same as the edge of the Ring of Steel. The 'security zone' first established in 1993 was more tightly constrained, with its centre around the Bank of England one kilometre distant. That was extended again in 1997 to encompass the districts around St Paul's Cathedral and the Barbican, bringing it about 500 metres from St Clement Danes.

There is an obvious concentrically fortified quality to the system as new layers of protection were added to surround existing protected enclosures. From the perspective of 2022, however, it is something of a moot point where the Ring of Steel begins, because in the intervening years the system has grown to be effectively nationwide, albeit particularly dense in this part of London.

Currently, there are about 13,000 ANPR cameras (some mobile) in use nationwide, generating in total 60 million 'read' records daily, which are kept for at least one year.[50] Basic searches of ANPR can help to find specific 'vehicles of interest', a stolen vehicle for example. They can also be used to analyse the movements of specific vehicles over time, for instance to research an alibi. Data can be cross-referenced and integrated with data from other sources to build information and intelligence about movements at a particular place through pattern analysis over time. In effect, the data can tell the location and movements of known vehicles of interest and, through observation, analysis, and correlation of movements in a particular area, potentially generate insight into hitherto unknown threats.

Unblinking sentry

As impressive and unnerving as this capability may seem, it is important to recognize that it is also effectively a fifty-year-old technology. Nowadays, it is trivially easy for a computer to recognize a set of numbers and letters of a standard font and size set against the high contrast background of a number plate. Recognizing *people* just by their faces is a much newer, and much more difficult, accomplishment. Another reason why the Temple Bar is particularly important in our story, therefore, is because it remains a place of experimentation. Not far from here at Oxford Circus is where in 2020 the London Metropolitan Police began the rollout of live facial recognition (LFR) technology.[51]

Basically, LFR does for people what ANPR does for vehicles. Cameras are placed in areas where they can scan the faces of passers-by, which are compared in real time against watchlists of 'individuals of interest' – where there is a supposed match, the system alerts an operator who can visually confirm the match and initiate an appropriate action: apprehension, tailing, etc.

A NATO-funded programme for the Detection of Explosives and Firearms for Counter Terrorism (DEXTER), developed in partnership with Italian and other police forces, has a similar intent and principle. It uses microwave imaging to see through the clothing of individuals, even while they are moving and in a crowd, to automatically detect explosive belts or firearms. Another sensor uses laser spectroscopy to detect traces of explosive residue on skin and clothing. Both are integrated with a data management and communication system that can alert guards to threats in real time. The system was successfully tested at Rome's Anagnina Metro but is not yet operational. Ironically, while such a system obviously intrudes on privacy, it works without invading anyone's normal presumption of anonymity.[52]

That is not the case with retrospective facial recognition (RFR), a further advancement of the London system which specifically allows authorities to check unknown faces against even larger datasets and can be used to create new datasets for correlation analysis. In short, if you travel in Westminster today, from your arrival at Oxford Circus tube station to the time you depart the edge of the system (indeterminate at this time), your biometric data will be collected and analysed with practically every step you take. Moreover, if you go there regularly there will be a record of your pattern of movements that contributes to an overall picture of what is normal on any given day. There is no possibility of anonymity in this case; to be unknown is to invite suspicion.

Indeed, departures from the norm by individuals are in theory and increasingly in practice detectable through machine-learning techniques. Most activities have a 'pattern of life', whether as in nature with the shifting seasonal boundary of glaciers, or the migration of birds, or in things like traffic flows on the motorway. People also exhibit established patterns of life – places travelled, routes taken, and so on – which are visible algorithmically to police counter-terrorism surveillance.[53]

If LFR follows the trajectory of development of ANPR then it is reasonable to suppose that the system will be expanded nationally. Indeed, given that LFR is essentially an information-processing technology that can be harnessed to standard CCTV surveillance cameras, of which there are about 6 million in the UK already (one camera for every ten persons), the expansion of the system could be very large and rapid indeed.[54] How one feels about this may depend upon one's perspective. For people in the industry, such as the managing director of Eagle Eye Networks, a US-based global provider of video surveillance analytics:

> It really is an exciting time. We're watching video surveillance being transitioned from a security system to a core business intelligence system, improving efficiency and effectiveness as well as security. The impact of AI is just starting to be seen in video surveillance – it's 'out of the lab' and in the real world now.[55]

The technology, to my mind, is rather like the Ring of Power in the *Lord of the Rings* novels, which ultimately corrupts its wielder but first ensnares them with the promise of its huge ability to do good. In the words of a report by the UK Information Commissioner's Office, facial recognition technology 'can make aspects of our lives easier, more efficient and more secure' but, it continues with technocratic understatement, in a 'privacy-intrusive' way.[56]

Lest the Tolkien reference seem frivolous, it is worth taking note of two other company names: 'Anduril', a major global security company specializing in the development of automated systems – and also the name of the reforged sword wielded by the hero Aragorn in the fantasy novels; and 'Palantir', arguably the biggest data analytics company in the world – and also the name of the cursed seeing-eye stones in the books. Such coincidences reflect a certain collective wellspring of metaphor, which is why I like the term *zeitgeist* to describe the underlying causes of what is happening.

An analysis of the video analytics industry by Mordor Intelligence – also coincidentally named – reckoned that globally it is rising at a compound annual growth rate of 24.5 per cent, from $1.5 billion in 2020 to a projected $4.1 billion by 2027. 'For analysing threats, recognising, mitigating, and monitoring purposes', China, it is said, is investing particularly heavily in facial recognition capabilities.[57] The danger this poses to civil liberty cannot be ignored. There is a blurred line between securing the population and managing or controlling it. It is quite likely that, in managing our fear of terrorism, we are making the city a more fearful place – more authoritarian and less democratic – while depleting our social capital.[58]

Network of networks

People are therefore quite correct to invoke fears of Big Brother, or Sauron for that matter. The technology is being increasingly adapted by private businesses for their own purposes, largely for marketing and sales research. Just as software can track your viewing habits on the internet and then target you with advertisements, LFR can track you in the real world and combine with electronic billboards (such as those lining the escalators at London Underground stations) to tailor advertisements directly to you.

Private companies are also implementing LFR as a contactless substitute for key card entry to facilities by employees – a development accelerated by the perceived public health need to limit physical contact with shared devices.[59] In short, our near future promises to be one of ubiquitous surveillance, including the tracing and profiling of mobile individuals, which even Orwell did not imagine.[60]

What, though, is the relevance of this to fortification? The answer is that surveillance has always been a part of guarded urban life – partly for security and partly for control, much as today. In its first form, the Ring of Steel very largely overlapped with the old Roman wall of London. There is clearly a difference between a Roman centurion standing at a city gate watching traffic go in and out of the city and a facial recognition camera tracking the faces of people entering and exiting Westminster Station, but it is a difference of degree not of kind: both record traffic, correlate information, and, in accordance with some decision-making algorithm, flag individuals for further investigation.

Likewise, surveillance has always been a main reason for building fortifications. What, after all, is a 'watchtower' but a fortification located where it is convenient to conduct surveillance?

Moreover, such fortifications have generally been built as networks of forts designed to intercommunicate and mutually support one another. Again, while the interconnected 'fortlets' of the Roman Limes that once guarded the frontiers of the empire against German tribal incursion, or the ring of forts around some European cities a century ago, differ from the interconnected surveillance networks now deployed in places like London, it is again a difference in degree and not in kind.

In the professional security industry literature, so-called 'layered security' is frequently invoked as an ideal. Students of fortification might talk instead of 'concentric' fortifications – layers of walls within walls. In the current security context, the quality of being 'layered' refers to a combination of elements including both physical barriers and informational/surveillance-based systems working together in an integrated system.

It is easy to feel overwhelmed by the rapidly changing technologies involved. The chief technology officer for Gallagher – another global integrated security systems company (which, incidentally, provided the access-control system for King's College London's Bush House in the Fortress on the Strand)[61] – put it this way in an industry journal: 'In a world where security threats are evolving daily, so too must our defence. It is no longer possible to view different security technologies in isolation.'[62] He is surely correct that threats and defences 'evolve' in a sort of natural competition, indeed that is a main idea at the heart of these chapters.

Likewise, the injunction to look to the security advantages of *combinations* of systems, rather than individual technologies in isolation, is an idea very much in line with principles of war going back as far as the fifth-century BCE Chinese military philosopher Sun Tzu.[63] It is important not to lose sight of the underlying and mostly unchanging principles.

Modulation of society

To comprehend the character of today's urban fortified complexes one needs to see them as assemblages of varying components – often quite simple – which interact in complex ways. In this case, the job of the camera and its associated networked video analytics system is to record and identify individuals in the flow.

The work of physical structures, the whole physical space of the city including both barriers and thoroughfares, is to channel the flow of people into the range of the system's sensorium and to modulate its speed of passing to a rate that does not exceed the capacity of the whole system to process the data. Together, these create a fortified strategic complex. Public space is made 'guarded space' by exposing every place to the gaze of a surveillance network.

The French philosopher Gilles Deleuze defined these systems of tracking as 'mechanisms of control' which he said produce a 'modulation' of some aspect of society.[64] If we accept these terms, it might be suggested that we seek to control people by channelling their movements across the boundaries of a surveillance system in order to modulate (or 'mitigate', the term usually used in government and industry) the deadly impact of terrorism. In Belfast in the 1970s, people could not but notice that the effort to secure the population proceeded from the logical premise that everyone must be treated as a suspect. Because of the inherent limitations of that system's sensorium, the physical components of the control mechanism had to be more overt. That is no longer the case to the same degree.

Video management systems now can use data in ways that are potentially extremely powerful. The contemporary guarded space tends to emphasize things like centralized control systems, real-time situational awareness, and 'proactive' security which depends on data-analytic technology. These are used to assess some things of genuine commercial interest. In a big shop, for example, recording where people walk ('footfall') and where and for how long they stop ('dwell time') in certain areas can signal to managers the products and displays in which people are particularly interested.

These systems can also signal potential dangers, such as unattended objects that might be bombs, spot weapons, or determine the location of gunfire by the triangulation of concussive sound waves. Increasingly, they can search for individuals in multiple video streams by description (e.g., 'man in orange shirt with cane'), and some products claim to be able to assess a person's mood. This latter technology is known as facial emotion recognition.[65]

How one feels about this depends a lot on where one sits. As the business development manager of 3xLOGIC, a large American company specializing in video management systems, put it:

Today's [systems] have powerful capabilities that allow video to be used much more effectively than in the past. We are also at the beginning of an exciting journey in terms of how AI and machine learning are meshing with human input to increase reliability and effectiveness.[66]

As a commuter into London myself, I begin to interact with a fortified strategic complex that we might call a 'panoptic fortress' from the moment I enter the vision of the camera installed on the forecourt of my local train station, which is operated by the British Transport Police. Between there and the door of my office I will pass through a hundred 'gates' in some concrete 'surveillant assemblage' of walls, passages, entrances, and exits all under the observation of a networked recording apparatus that is increasingly able to interpret and analyse the resulting enormous data flow by computer.[67]

The system knows my 'pattern of life': who I am, where I am and where I've been; it can probably guess where I'm going on any given day based on past patterns; and it might also have a good idea of how happy or grumpy I might be. Whether or not it cares, it may constantly judge the mood of individuals in its algorithmic search for the tell-tale tics and pattern-of-life-out-of-placeness of someone on a mission to explode himself in the rush-hour traffic.

It is important to note that the system as I have described it is neither fully developed nor fully deployed anywhere yet. The designers and engineers involved in creating it frequently stress the difficulties that remain with its application; indeed, the fifty-plus years of effort it has taken to get to where we are now is in a sense heartening. None of the major individual technological elements needs to be invented, however, and the direction of travel is crystal clear – particularly in London where, as we have seen, things are being rolled out quickly in certain places.

There are perfectly good reasons to be concerned with matters of physical security and counter-terrorism. In a negative mood, however, the situation might instead call to mind Max Weber's famous 'iron cage', a metaphor he used to describe what he saw as the increasing control of society through rigid rules and rationalization.[68]

More often, the parallel drawn is to the 'panopticon' of the eighteenth-century English reformer Jeremy Bentham. This was a proposed prison designed to maximize the exposure of inmates to surveillance by building it as a circular structure, something like an inverted colosseum, with a central observation tower allowing guards to see into all the cells.[69]

No human city, and certainly not London, can ever be a true panopticon in this sense because of the absolute jumble of buildings and streets that accumulate organically in any place that humans inhabit for any length of time. It would require both a blank slate and a huge degree of rigidity in planning, although the panopticon/radial design of cities has been a popular utopian ideal and occasionally tried on a small scale.[70]

The fact is that over recent decades, with London as a prime example of an increasingly globalized condition of fear, two things have come to be accepted as foundational to securing civil society, most notably in the West (where it represents a sharp departure from a historical norm of individual liberty and relative openness): every space is susceptible to attack, and every person is a potential attacker.

If this is the case, we would have to watch everyone and fortify everywhere. Many would disagree, vehemently, if they thought about it, or at any rate would consider the countermeasures to the threat to be more injurious to society than the threat itself. But these assumptions are buried in the operating procedures of government, as reflected in legally binding planning regulations and building guidance.

Secured by Design

In Britain today most cities and local authorities now require a counter-terrorism design and access statement in planning applications for all large urban developments. Three main guides have been published by the Home Office and the Office for Communities and Local Government: *Working Together to Protect Crowded Places*; *Crowded Places: The Planning System and Counter-terrorism*; and *Protecting Crowded Places: Design and Technical Issues*.[71]

In these documents planners are enjoined, indeed required, to consider in their building designs a range of matters already touched upon, such as the creation of standoff to mitigate blast effect, laminating window glass to reduce secondary fragmentation, ensuring proper lighting so that CCTV cameras can operate effectively, and so on. Further guidance comes from the Royal Institute of British Architects, the police (especially in the form of the previously noted network of CTSAs), and the British Security Industry Association, amongst others.

In the current jargon of policing and planning this is known as being 'secured by design'.[72] Urban geographers usually locate the origin of this idea not directly in counter-terrorism but in crime control, and particularly in the work of the influential urban planner and architect

Oscar Newman. His interest was in the security of big public housing projects in American cities where it was felt that crime was spiralling out of police control. He came up with the concept of 'defensible space', also known as Crime Prevention Through Environmental Design (CPTED).

This involves an assemblage of 'real and symbolic' barriers and surveillance like that described above, on a smaller scale and in a more domestic setting, with overtones of petty-crime prevention rather than counter-terrorism. The physical layout of a well-designed neighbourhood is meant to enhance the perception of ownership and community, or 'territoriality', among its residents, leading to better security outcomes and thus more agreeable places to live.[73]

The overlap in the industry, and indeed in the general discourse, between crime prevention and counter-terrorism is very pronounced and often confusing. There is a genuine overlap – terror exists as does crime and the systems for preventing/mitigating them are often the same. But terrorism prevention is sometimes described as a rationale for projects that are essentially solely about crime prevention – and vice versa.

As an example, the managing director of Jackson's Fencing – a leading UK maker of perimeter security systems which started in 1947 as a firm supplying timber fencing to the farming community – described a government project in which it was involved in this way:

> [We were] recently commissioned to install a large number of alley gates [of their Barbican design] in Wellingborough and Kettering. The aim of the commission from local government [was] to help the public safety of the local residents and to reduce crime and terror threats on the streets of the county.[74]

Kettering, a market town of 60,000 people in north Northamptonshire, is the second most dangerous medium-sized town in the country as measured by the rate of crime per 1,000 people. It is not, however, a hotbed of terrorism.

In practice, we may observe that over time the idea of 'defensible space' as a zone of essentially participative citizen control of security aimed at crime has taken on an ever more militarized and fortified aspect, which seems to have been far from Newman's intent. Critics often connect this development to structural problems in society, notably class, race, and the supposed contradictions of neoliberal capitalism that are presumed to be its main cause.

Thus, the neo-Marxist scholar David Harvey concludes that 'increasing polarization in the distribution of wealth and power are indelibly etched into the spatial forms of our cities, which increasingly become cities of fortified fragments'.[75] One might debate the conclusion about the cause of this – as a non-Marxist, I am sceptical of the causational account. The observation, though, of both the fragmentation and fortification of society, is a matter of empirical fact.

Others point to the apparent formation of effective 'microstates' – wealthy guarded urban enclaves that live and function differently from the sovereign entity of which they are nominally a part.[76] We will return to this idea with some specific examples in the following chapters. For the time being, I would stipulate that it is not just 'the wealthy' who are locking down in an enclaved manner; guardedness is a posture adopted across the social spectrum, from the literally ironclad ghettos of the poor through the fortified compounds of the middle classes to the guarded aeries of the very rich.

Ultimately, it is hard to gainsay the urban geographer Mike Davis, who wrote in the early 1990s:

> We live in 'fortress cities' brutally divided between 'fortified cells' of affluent society and 'places of terror' where the police battle the criminalized poor. The 'Second Civil War' that began in the long hot summers of the 1960s has been institutionalised into the very structure of urban space . . . In cities like Los Angeles, on the bad edge of postmodernity, one observes an unprecedented tendency to merge urban design, architecture and the police apparatus into a single, comprehensive security effort.[77]

For now, whatever the structural cause, we may simply observe that somewhere along the way, after starting with the concept of 'defensible space', the programme of planning now called 'secured by design' intertwined with a range of what are essentially military planning considerations. Let us now look at specific examples.

6

Hiding in Plain Sight

In the previous chapters we looked at changes in the internal and exterior form of cities in response to security concerns including external conventional military threats and internal terroristic violence – with the latter more pertinent in most places today. I have stressed throughout the continuity of underlying principles of guardedness underlying strategic complexes, despite their widely diverging physical forms.

In the following two chapters we shall look at specific examples: firstly, in this chapter, at changes in (primarily) public architecture; secondly, in the next chapter, at the private architecture of individuals and families, civic associations, and corporations.

Each case shows similar patterns. Looking at historical fortification types, we will see how they are, in fact, exceedingly current, and ought to be viewed as essentially archetypal, significantly consistent in function through time while changing in superficial form.

Unlike military fortified strategic complexes, civilian defences are a product mostly of bottom-up rather than top-down factors. This does not mean they are less strategic. Each are objects of significant engineering skill meant to achieve a recognizable political objective – security – via the physical manipulation, regulation, and monitoring of the built environment and the activities therein.

Citadels

A citadel – literally 'little city' – is a fortress co-located with a town or city, which it is designed to command and control both literally and symbolically. Sometimes located within the confines of the city, it may also be located on its edge, or nearby. Where exactly depends largely on the local topography (e.g., any high ground), as well as the political and military situation.[1] It is a piece of strategic architecture that exists in a political relationship with a given population.

Any urban fortress carries potent political meaning to those who live and work around it, in addition to its military potential vis-à-vis an external power.[2] Historically, citadels have formed the main part of a city's 'sovereign district', a secured area providing, amongst other things, space for the government bureaucracy, treasury and other storehouses, palatial residences for the ruler and his court, and barracks for guards. The design of a citadel is governed by two main considerations: the dignity and grandeur of the ruler, and the concern for their safety.[3]

Designers of citadels have long recognized that they are making a political statement through architecture that requires a delicate balance. The Italian Renaissance architect Leon Battista Alberti advised:

> The Palace of a king should stand in the heart of the city; it should be easy of access, beautifully adorned, and delicate and polite, rather than proud and stately. But a lord should have a castle rather than a palace, and it should stand so that it is out of the city and in it at the same time.[4]

Defence is a function of the citadel but usually not its main reason for being, which is to project and symbolize power. Peking's Forbidden City and the Kremlin in Moscow, or even Windsor Castle – places where the administrative centres and living quarters of the sovereign are tightly sealed within layers of rigid fortification – are citadels which inherited and continue to use the defensive apparatus of previous ages, being fortified in an obvious way.

The fortifications of sovereign districts like London's No. 10 Downing St or the White House in Washington, DC have a distinctively different character. Notably both started out as essentially civilian residences set in a democratic urban milieu which consciously held up accessibility to power centres as symbolic of the equal, accountable, and transparent qualities of the greater polity. Both have been progressively fortified over time, in Britain initially as a response to mortar attacks by the IRA in the 1980s. Efforts to secure the White House have been more recent, more extensive, and considerably more socially traumatic. As a commentary on the wallification of Washington during the Trump presidency (a development which has accelerated) put it:

We all want to believe in the postcard vision of the White House, that you as a citizen can walk past it and see it, that its lawn and greenery and elegance and spaciousness extend to you as a citizen, that the president lives there but he is a citizen just like the rest of us. All of that is somehow denied by building a wall around it.[5]

In effect, people judge the health of their society by changes in public architecture, based both on instinctive response and sound reasoning.

The Kremlin with its crenelated mediaeval walls looks different from the White House with its assemblage of modern ones, but the difference is unimportant. Citadels are not defined by a specific morphology. What truly distinguishes a citadel is its integration with the political life of the population centre it dominates. Nowadays, the contemporary structure that best expresses the multiple contradictory design influences caught between security and openness, the grandeur of the sovereign and the consent of the governed, is the embassy, and specifically those outposts of the global hegemon, American embassies.

Embassies under attack

Embassies are more than places of bureaucratic and diplomatic activity. They are political architecture, symbols of the power and ambition of the nation-states which create them. I will pick up the story where the need for security – expressed in the fortification of embassies – started to supersede the desire to show off to a foreign audience. This development started further back than is generally recognized.

American embassy design immediately after the Second World War, from which the United States emerged as the preeminent Western power, was overtly political and triumphant. It showed a preference for a relatively elevated and isolated position, typical of citadels of the past, and the use of modern materials to 'improve' upon traditional, i.e., local, form. In an accurate albeit loaded term, US embassies were imperialistic, consciously reinterpreting classical architectural features to show off the 'new Rome' – socially progressive, confidently mighty in commerce and technology.

A superb example is the former American embassy in London's Grosvenor Square, built in 1956 to a design by Eero Saarinen, also known for the iconic design of the Washington, DC Metro. The building is a modernist take on a Greek temple, raised from the ground on concrete pillars set in a false podium, surrounded by a dry moat. It is a terrific building in modernist style, but it was not uniformly well-received at the start. 'For all its sham politeness', noted the architecture critic of the *Observer*:

> this building has also to be American, new, crisp, and glamorous. Hence the rather aggressive, staccato modelling of the façade, the perpetual gilding, the costume jewellery [a gigantic American eagle] that overdecks it all. Every detail contradicts the original and overpolite intentions.[6]

By the mid-1960s, the site had become a perennial focus of protest, most famously with the fracas of 17 March 1968 when 10,000 anti-Vietnam War demonstrators battled outside the embassy with 800 police, 117 of whom were injured.[7] The London embassy was not the only one attacked. The American ambassador in Guatemala was assassinated in the street a block from the consulate in August 1968. Between October 1964 and March 1965 other US embassies and consulates were assaulted twenty-five times in Sudan, Bolivia, Bulgaria, Indonesia, Vietnam, the Soviet Union, Czechoslovakia, Panama, Hungary, and Venezuela.[8]

Though the United States was a primary target, by the 1970s analysts perceived a general shift in asymmetric terrorist tactics from airplane hijackings to assault and the attempted seizure of the embassies of many countries. A RAND study documented forty-eight incidents between 1971 and 1980 of seizures or attempted seizures of embassies, consulates, and other diplomatic facilities.[9] The 1979–81 Iran hostage crisis, in which Islamic militants seized sixty-six American citizens at the US embassy in Tehran, holding fifty-two of them hostage for more than a year, was particularly dramatic. In response to these trends, heavy security measures were increasingly adopted, particularly by the United States, as well as countries like Israel, Germany, and the Soviet Union, which transformed their embassies in certain threatened areas into 'virtual fortresses'.[10]

The April 1983 bombing of the US embassy in Beirut, Lebanon, in which seventeen American diplomats and sixty Lebanese employees were killed, was a watershed moment. The problem was twofold. First, the frequency of attacks was rising. Second, they appeared to be shifting from attempts at armed seizure of buildings to large bomb attacks. From a fortification perspective, whereas the former can be dealt with largely by moderate strengthening of structures and stricter access control, defending against blast effect is a more serious problem.

In 1985, the US Department of State commissioned Admiral Bobby Inman to study the issue and develop new planning standards for the security of American embassies. His most far-reaching conclusion was that they ought to be located on sites of at least ten and ideally fifteen acres or more in size to allow something like a 100-foot standoff distance around the main building. Since this posed a huge logistical and financial challenge in most large cities, the logical implication was that embassies would have to be located outside of central cities in suburbs where land was cheaper. Battista Alberti would not have approved.

'Being on the busiest or most fashionable street or corner may have been an asset in earlier days', the report stated, but 'today it is a liability'.[11] As far as security is concerned, it is hard to go against Inman's logic. Consider the current US embassy in Egypt, finished in 1983 at the same time as the Beirut bombings. Set in the centre of political Cairo, a short walk from Tahrir Square, it is an obvious symbol of American presence in the country. But due to the small site, the building is ten stories high (tall for an embassy) and lacks adequate standoff distance. Nowadays, its defence is supplemented by a ring of shabby-looking concrete blast-barriers that run through the surrounding streets, to the annoyance of drivers in an already massively congested city.

The overall impression the Cairo embassy posture conveys is an unbecoming and unconvincing mix of cringing grandiosity. Rather like the eighteenth-century fortification of Palmanova, noted earlier – an ultimately inadequate effort to square ease of transport of goods for commerce with mobility of guns for the military – it is central to the city but neither particularly secure nor particularly symbolic architecturally of a confident great power.

Critics at the time of the Inman report clearly understood the disadvantages of the new security-dominated guidelines, especially the symbolic retreat from power implied by leaving the political centre of capital cities, as well as by the more utilitarian designs in the new buildings. Nonetheless, a contemporaneous National Research Council report approved the new emphasis on security over aesthetics:

> the [United States] places strong emphasis on the aesthetic aspects of embassy buildings. And in the past, such a design emphasis was reasonable. Aesthetic considerations in many instances were permitted to pre-empt security concerns in a world in which the U.S. presence abroad was seldom threatened or challenged. But the recent growth of anti-U.S. terrorism must cause the State Department to re-evaluate its position.[12]

Ultimately, what set most Inman projects apart from previous embassy designs, aside from their remote location away from urban centres, was their colossal size, huge cost and architecturally soulless, squat, boxy banality. Externally, they were isomorphic, so designers were left with little more than playing with surface ornamentation to distinguish them. As one architectural historian put it, 'even top designers cannot do much to make a citadel look inviting'.[13]

The American embassies in Kabul, Afghanistan and Baghdad, Iraq – completed in 2005 and 2007, respectively – are good examples. Both are unambiguously fortified complexes of over fifteen acres, with blast-resistant perimeter walls guarded by watchtowers and high-security gates, armoured glass windows and structurally reinforced buildings. The Kabul embassy cost an estimated $800 million to build; Baghdad's rang in at $600 million – with an operating cost of $1.2 billion annually as of 2008.[14] Interestingly, both were built in the centre of the city, out of alignment with Inman principles – in both cases because local conditions meant that real estate costs were not a decisive factor. Baghdad's Green Zone simply occupied and upgraded the already extensive sovereign district carved out of the city's riverfront by Saddam Hussein.[15]

Likewise, the design of the new American embassy in Ottawa, Canada, completed in 1999, is another interesting example of a departure from Inman principles, but in a less permissive financial context (i.e., greater average real estate cost), which means it has a much smaller footprint. Rather than being located on a large and distant suburban site, it sits beside a busy street in the centre of the city near the Houses of Parliament. The building has minimal standoff on its front, no more than the width of a broad pavement, although it does incorporate blast-resistant walls behind portions of its exposed façade of armoured glass. That it was approved at all is surprising; ironically, the plans were presented to a Canadian panel of architects and planners on 19 April 1995, the day of the Oklahoma City bombings. Ultimately, the perceived low terror risk in Ottawa, as well as the lack of good alternative sites, justified an exception to the normal rules.[16]

Had the decision been taken after the August 1998 bombings of the embassies in Dar es Salaam, Tanzania and Nairobi, Kenya, it is less likely an exception would have been granted. Shattered glass façades and limbless blinded diplomats staggering in the street are not a good look for a superpower. As one diplomat present at the Nairobi bombing put it:

we [had] deemed the threat of terrorism less in Nairobi and East Africa than in other, more turbulent parts of the world. We did not foresee that Middle East terrorists, crazed but hardly foolish, had concluded that as U.S. embassies were increasingly well protected in their own region, they would go after the more vulnerable ones, such as our embassies in East Africa.[17]

He might as well have said Ottawa, where placing a truck bomb alongside the embassy's main entrance would be just as easy.

Embassies as castles

In 1999 the State Department adopted the Standard Embassy Design (SED) programme, which regularized the Inman guidelines that had been spottily adopted. The 11 September 2001 attacks added further impetus to the idea that fortification was not just necessary but necessary *everywhere*.

In the new global-terrorism-dominated paradigm, arguments that SED only made sense if you defined an embassy primarily as a guarded workplace and ignored its symbolic role tended to fall short. By the early 2000s, SED led to a series of new embassies-cum-fortresses, alienated from their local context, and far from local power centres.

The American embassy in Abuja, Nigeria, for example, is a nearly windowless concrete pillbox surrounded by a grubby concrete wall from which protrude stanchions for razor wire. The design, unfortunately, is typical rather than exceptional. Many such were built by the American-based global construction firm BL Harbert International, which specializes in government buildings including both embassies and military barracks – viewing their catalogue, it is difficult to tell them apart.[18] Corporate and concrete, gated and walled, these embassies are undoubtedly fortresses, but at the same time craven, clad in faux ornamentation; they lack the severity, abstraction, and ambition that sometimes redeems in-your-face brutalist architecture.

It is a truism that every action produces a reaction. Eventually, the pendulum swings back. In 2010, then-Senator John Kerry, later Secretary of State, penned an op-ed introducing the Embassy Design and Security Act, decrying the prevailing situation:

> Although this effort [i.e., SED] significantly improved the safety of our diplomats, unique architectural wonders built to last were replaced by a standardized 'embassy in a box'. They are uniform in appearance and

6.1 The American embassy in Beirut
The new American embassy in Beirut is located ten miles outside of the city on its own hilltop, looking for all intents and purposes like a twenty-first-century version of one of the mighty Crusader castles of the Middle East rendered in reinforced concrete and ballistic-resistant glass.
Source: US embassy in Lebanon.

quickly assembled fortresses designed to meet security specifications in one of four sizes – small, medium, large, and extra-large, epitomized by our supersized embassy in Baghdad.[19]

The State Department thus began to steer away from standardized design, adopting the Excellence in Diplomatic Facilities Initiative in 2011. While not a retreat from fortification per se, it represented an intent to build embassies which were both architecturally noteworthy *and* secured by design. Two recent examples, one in London and the other in Beirut, are worth a closer look. Both are located in high threat areas, and both involve leading architects – each solving the basic problem of balancing aesthetics and security in ways that are quite different but also very similar.

The Beirut embassy, designed by the California-based architectural firm Morphosis, is under construction and due to be completed in 2023. At forty-three acres it is a gigantic complex, occupying a whole hilltop, possible because it is located ten miles outside the city. It will cost over $1 billion, largely because of the need for intense security measures, including a long, high perimeter wall. The embassy buildings are partially buried and blend somewhat into the landscape. The State

Department chose the design because it 'didn't look like a fortress', which is, of course, ironic because, while pleasing to the eye, it is more fortified than any of the SED complexes noted above.[20]

It looks like a futuristic version of the mighty thirteenth-century Crusader Castle Krak des Chevaliers, which is also located on its own hilltop in Syria just over the border from Lebanon. The embassy's perimeter walls lack mediaeval crenelations and are narrower and lower but, thanks to reinforced concrete, they are equally powerful. In fact, mediaeval engineers might have envied the design of the embassy's guard towers, which are cantilevered over the walls, presumably for maximum visibility of their base, in a way that could not be done with mortared stones.

Despite efforts over the years, the Saarinen-designed American embassy in London proved impossible to retro-fortify. The Grosvenor Square site was simply too small and in 2016 the embassy was sold to

6.2 The American embassy in London
The new American embassy in London is something of a modern masterpiece of fortified architecture. Although it looks something like a Borg cube out of *Star Trek*, it is effectively a very current take on the concept of the motte and bailey, combined with a range of other low visibility fortification measures.
Source: Copyright Kieran Timberlake.

the Qatari sovereign wealth fund, which is renovating it as a five-star hotel. A new $1-billion embassy designed by the architectural firm Kieran Timberlake was built on a considerably larger site at Nine Elms on the south bank of the Thames, officially opening in 2018.

The architects proudly proclaimed that they were guided by ideas of transparency, openness, and equality, and that their design would achieve the desired level of security while not employing fences or walls. They also said they were inspired by European castles – not by their thick walls but by the way some mediaeval fortresses blended into the landscape.[21] The embassy resembles nothing so much as a Norman motte and bailey castle reinterpreted for the twenty-first century.

The first clue is the 200-foot blast-resistant glass, concrete, and steel cube which makes up the embassy building. Although its façade is sheathed on three sides by a transparent envelope of material described by one architectural magazine as a 'hectic array of meringue-peaked brise-soleil playing off the epigrammatic nature of the glass cube', it is still, fundamentally, a castle donjon. The donjon, moreover, is set on an artificial plinth that sits, in turn, on a natural hill, giving the complex an obvious elevation above the local area.

The second clue is the standoff distance achieved by the site, which by Inman standards is admirable: no unguarded street comes even close to being within 100 feet of the main building. The buffer zone has a series of defensive measures. The northern perimeter is guarded by a yew hedge, which hides PAS 68-rated bollards. After this steel-reinforced hedge, there are two sharp changes of ground level and then a moat, referred to as a 'pond', after which comes the bomb-resistant embassy on its raised plinth, which presents itself as a high wall disguised in part by a decorative waterfall.

To the south, the site is edged by other defensive street furniture, specifically robust 'benches' affixed to a thick slab of concrete that rises to a berm, referred to as a 'meadow', which is supposed to evoke a sense of the rolling American plains. About a third of the way along this feature the ground plummets into a steep ditch. It is labelled as a 'bioswale', a landscape depression usually employed for channelling stormwater runoff, but that also happens to be ideal for trapping a moving vehicle. The whole assemblage is an artful demonstration of the way a twenty-first-century fortress can possess all the essential elements of an eleventh-century one and more without looking (much) like a castle at all.

While this example is quite spectacular, its blending and hiding of defensive architecture is not altogether new. Indeed, a characteristic feature of the awesome country estates dotting the British landscape today, very often built in the place of or incorporating mediaeval fortifications, is that they are surrounded by 'ha-ha' walls. Essentially a wall hidden in a ditch, hence also known as a 'sunken-wall', the traditional ha-ha creates a vertical barrier to movement without impacting visually either the grandeur of the distant manor or the owner's views of his or her gardens, fields, and property.

The innovative thing about the London embassy is its intrinsic blast resistance. Recall our earlier point that the effect of an explosion upon a building depends greatly upon how long it is exposed to a blast wave. The bigger the building, the longer the exposure time. The London embassy is indubitably a large and powerful building, but as the very high-ceilinged main floor lobby shows, something interesting is going on. The overstrength concrete slab making up that ceiling, i.e., the bottom of the huge cube above, is elevated on a thirty-foot-high four-sided colonnade that effectively conveys the combination of transparency, openness, and impact sought by the architects.

More practically, if by some ingenious scheme a bomb were to be exploded in the lobby, much of the power of the blast would be louvred outward away from the building core through the powerful columns – the duration of the pressure upon which would be diminished by their relatively slender form. The suspended slab would absorb both primary blast and secondary fragmentation effects, while the diagrid structure of the building overall would flex, strongly mitigating the potential 'pancaking' effect of blast damage. In short, the embassy represents the cutting edge of the possible with respect to making a building simultaneously blast-resistant, functional, and pleasant to look at.

In both the Beirut and London embassies, contemporary architects confronted the basic problem of security versus aesthetics within a specific political context that is not fundamentally different from those which confronted the architects of citadels in the past. It is therefore not surprising that they came up with dramatic reinterpretations of old forms of fortification. In the case of London, the result is like a castle in the sky – a powerful fortification that defends its inhabitants against the main perceived threat by shielding them in an armoured cube suspended thirty feet above the ground. The design 'DNA' of the Beirut embassy, particularly its hilltop location and terrain-following perimeter wall, clearly evokes old patterns.

Barbicans

In its simplest form a barbican – from the French 'barbacane' and possibly of Persian or Arabic origin – is a reinforced gate of a walled city or castle, typified by strong flanking towers and an overhanging gallery for launching missiles against an enemy trying to breach the main portal. The barbican is often a miniature fort in its own right, detached from the defensive line of the main fortification to which it is connected by a walled road or tunnel, called the 'neck'.

The mediaeval barbican was an answer to the fundamental problem that the weak point of any fortification is its gate, reflecting the tension between the desire for unfettered civil movement and the need for military security. As a piece of military engineering, its period of significance was relatively short – from the late Middle Ages to the advent of effective gunpowder artillery and the consequent development of star-pattern gun fortresses. These also had detached outworks, often extensive, but took a different form from the mediaeval barbican.

Two of the best surviving examples of barbicans are in Poland, in Krakow and Warsaw. The latter was largely destroyed during the Second World War, like nearly everything else in Warsaw, so what may be seen now is a very good reconstruction. The Krakow barbican is essentially in its original state. Built in 1498, it is a powerful, moated brick structure with walls three metres thick pierced by 130 embrasures for defensive fire. It served the defence of the city in four separate sieges, the last time during the Russo-Polish War of 1792, shortly after which it was meant to be demolished as a military relic but was instead thoughtfully preserved as a place of historical and cultural interest.

Barbicans did not just have an overt military purpose. They were also an integral part of the full assemblage of civil government and policing of the urban enclosure during peacetime. The Krakow barbican well illustrates this secondary function of such constructions, which is perhaps why it was not demolished. Once past the defensive embrasures and through the outer gate, you have not yet entered the city. Instead, you find yourself in a roughly circular courtyard twenty-five metres in diameter, surrounded internally by a high and protected parapet from which guards and customs inspectors once safely monitored traffic before it was permitted to proceed through internal gates that blocked entrance to the 'neck' of the city.

In effect, the Krakow barbican creates a secure zone of control and inspection that is neither in nor out of the city. It is an intramural zone where traffic can be processed (and taxed) before entry into the city proper – or alternatively expelled. This kind of fortified structure is by no means obsolete. In fact, it is one of the most quintessentially modern, most thoroughly 'globalized', and arguably most symbolic forms of architecture in the world today. We call them airports.

Airports as barbicans

As with contemporary citadels, the twenty-first-century version of a barbican usually looks nothing like its mediaeval ancestor, although the Kabul and Mogadishu airports, both ringed by continuous and concentric walls punctuated by guard towers, come close. Yet, ultimately, what else are they except heavily externally guarded installations designed to regulate flows of people by containing them for a period in a secure space which is neither completely in nor completely out of the place being guarded? Looking past the superficial dissimilarities, what started out as a piece of mediaeval military engineering is clearly alive and well.

Similarly to embassies over the last two decades, airports have been dramatically transformed from essentially open places modulating

6.3 The Kabul Airport evacuation
The Airport Road outside Kabul Airport thick with people attempting to flee, hemmed in by concrete walls topped by chain link and razor wire with overlooking guard towers.
Source: Staff Sgt. Victor Mancilla, 2021, US Marine Corps.

movement between ground and air as efficiently as possible into fortified strategic complexes. As late as 1997 the English novelist J.G. Ballard could write an essay on Heathrow which was practically a paean:

> Airports have become a new kind of discontinuous city whose vast populations are entirely transient, purposeful, and, for the most part, happy. An easy camaraderie rules the departure lounges, along with the virtual abolition of nationality – whether we are Scots or Japanese is far less important than where we are going. I've long suspected that people are truly happy and aware of a real purpose to their lives only when they hand over their tickets at the check-in.[22]

What Ballard describes as a discontinuous city comprised entirely of transients would be better described today as a global network of barbicans whose temporary inhabitants exist in a state of guarded 'placelessness', a term used by human geographers to refer to a feeling of lack of attachment to a place caused by the homogenizing effects of modernity, notably commercialism, mass consumption, standardization, alienation, and obsession with speed and movement.[23] Individual experiences obviously vary, but at present it seems clear that the dominant mood of such places is tension and anxiety rather than happiness.[24]

The watershed event was, unsurprisingly, the attacks of 11 September 2001, and the subsequent global reaction of airport security regimes. Perhaps the best illustration may be seen in the fate of the former TWA Flight Centre at New York City's Kennedy Airport. Designed by Eero

6.4 JFK Airport
The TWA Flight Centre at JFK Airport is a masterpiece of architectural design. Unfortunately it proved to be unsecurable by the standards of contemporary regulations and has been converted from a working terminal into a hotel.
Source: Roland Arhelger, 2010, Wikimedia Commons. CC BY-SA 4.0.

Saarinen, who also designed the American embassy in London, it was opened in 1962. A landmark of the jet age, it is featured in an iconic scene of the Leonardo di Caprio film *Catch Me if You Can* in which the young conman, masquerading as an airline pilot, saunters through a cordon of police trying to capture him by surrounding himself with half a dozen glamorous stewardesses.

Externally, the flowing concrete and glass terminal's main building has the sculptural shape of a bird's wings. It is widely regarded as an architectural marvel and has been listed on the National Register of Historic Places since 2005. In Saarinen's words, it was 'a building in which the architecture itself would express the excitement of air travel ... in which the architecture would reveal the terminal, not as a static enclosed place, but as a place of movement and transition'. The curvilinear quality of the building continues to the interior, which is defined by soaring arches and bright open spaces that, to quote the architect again, were meant to make the human being feel 'uplifted, important and full of anticipation'.[25]

TWA went into serious financial decline in the 1990s and ultimately its assets, including the TWA Flight Centre, were sold off to American Airlines, which continued to run it until December 2001 after which the site was abandoned for eighteen years. It has now been remodelled as a luxury hotel.

Opened in 2019, the hotel is now partially encircled by the new JFK Terminal 5, built in 2008, and is the only hotel located on the airport's grounds. It is a coincidence that being turned into a hotel was also the fate of Saarinen's London embassy, but the reasoning behind it was the same: an overtly modern architectural treasure built as a symbol of the liberating quality of flight was deemed by the New York Port Authority to be functionally obsolete and unadaptable to contemporary security requirements.

It should be noted that there were other problems with the terminal, notably that its boarding gates were too small for very large modern aircraft. The main issue, however, was its intrinsic insecurity. It was built in an era that prioritized minimum distances between 'landside', where passengers would arrive by motor vehicle, and 'airside', where they would depart by plane. In other words, the TWA Flight Centre was optimized for mobility and openness, clashing with the highly elevated post-September 11 perception of the risk of attack on the aviation system.

Attacking airports

As a BBC report on the 'tricks' of airport design put it, after the September 11 attacks the airport became a different place both psychologically and physically:

> Today, the airport terminal is more like a fortress containing only verified travellers who have willingly passed extensive security tests – hands swabbed for traces of plastic explosives, passing through enormous x-ray machines that may reveal their internal anatomy to strangers, answering probing questions about their luggage and handing over multiple forms of state-issued identification.[26]

In fact, airports had been under increasing pressure to be 'secure by design' since the 1970s, when international terrorism began seriously to attack the aviation system. One comprehensive study of such attacks worldwide concluded that from 1960–2016 there were 338 ground attacks on airports, 221 hijackings, fifty-six acts of sabotage, and twenty suicide missions, causing a total of 6,814 deaths. Counting only attacks on airport buildings, as opposed to aircraft, in the same period there were 232 attacks causing 648 deaths.[27] Many of these attacks occurred long before September 2001.

For example, in February 1970, terrorists from the Popular Front for the Liberation of Palestine (PFLP) launched a grenade and gun attack on a bus carrying Israeli passengers at the airport in Munich, Germany, killing one person and injuring eleven others. Even worse was the May 1972 attack on Israel's Lod Airport (now named Ben-Gurion International) in which three members of the Japanese Red Army Faction, operating on behalf of the PFLP, murdered twenty-six people and injured nearly eighty more in a gun and grenade attack. In December 1985 the terrorist group Abu Nidal launched a coordinated attack on the airports in Rome (killing sixteen and wounding ninety-nine) and Vienna (three killed and forty injured). The worst year for airport attacks was 2016, with fifteen killed in the Brussels, Belgium airport in March, followed by forty-five more at Istanbul, Turkey.

The June 2007 attack on the airport in Glasgow, Scotland caused relatively little damage, with five people lightly injured and only the attacker killed. That case was significant in combining the use of a civilian vehicle packed with propane canisters in a ramming attack with an attempt to explode a rudimentary IED. Otherwise, the attacks described have taken the form of 'marauding terror' strikes almost always by multiple perpetrators. The 1972 Lod attack set the basic pattern. In that case, the attackers, having just flown in from Paris, retrieved their luggage in which they had packed assault rifles and hand grenades and then immediately started to mow down other passengers in the baggage retrieval hall.[28]

It is important to break down the types of potential attacks on the aviation system. Those described above are 'ground attacks', as opposed to hijacking, sabotage, and suicide operations that are aimed at aircraft in flight. A further meaningful distinction is between 'aircraft attacks' aimed at aircraft whether taxiing, taking off, or landing, usually by a shoulder-fired missile (guided or unguided), and 'airport attacks' aimed directly at people on airport grounds by guns, bombs, stabbing, or ramming with a vehicle.

The discussion that follows focuses largely upon physical countermeasures and mitigation strategies against the latter two forms of ground attack. We have already talked about the ways in which structures and people are secured in a generic urban context. In many ways, airports, being highly symbolic – and fuel-laden, jam-packed aircraft being intrinsically vulnerable – represent the ultimate high-value urban target. They are, therefore, very heavily guarded. But the whole assemblage of surveillance and physical barriers is no different from that seen at the 'Fortress on the Strand'.

There are, however, some pertinent elements peculiar to aviation security, and specifically 'aircraft attacks', that bear mentioning. First, the process of interrogation of aircraft passengers begins far beyond the perimeter of the airport, effectively at the point a ticket is purchased by a named and formally identified person.

Second, the level of scrutiny of passengers exceeds by an order of magnitude that experienced by 'normal' travellers even in heavily monitored places like London. Much of this is required by domestic regulations as well as international treaties, notably Annex 17 of the Convention on International Civil Aviation that sets out a range of 'Standards and Recommended Practices'.[29]

Defending airports

Clearly, the best way to defend against ground attacks on aircraft or airports is to prevent terrorists from getting guns, bombs or missiles near them in the first place. This is the primary focus of airport security efforts and the purpose of most of the overt security screening and scanning with which anyone who has passed through an airport in the

6.5 Armoured security hut, Islamabad Airport
An armoured security hut at the entrance of the international departures section of Islamabad International Airport, Pakistan. While providing solid protection for guards, its aesthetic qualities are unnerving to passengers.
Source: OpenStreet Map, 2022, Wikimedia Commons. CC0 1.0.

last thirty years is familiar. Under normal conditions such defensive measures can be very extensive but they are usually at least somewhat discreet. In certain circumstances, however, the externally oriented physical fortifications of an airport may be extremely overt.

The highly fortified Kabul and Kandahar civilian airports in Afghanistan discussed earlier are cases in point. The best example, however, is probably the airport of Mogadishu, Somalia, run since 2010 largely by the Dubai-based firm SKA Air & Logistics, whose motto 'Doing Difficult Jobs in Difficult Places' is very apposite.[30] This highly fortified installation sits within a larger fortified 'Green Zone', an area which most international visitors never leave. Indeed, foreigners are usually not permitted even to leave the airport to go to a hotel in the Green Zone without private bodyguards costing potentially several thousand dollars per day.

It is hard to know the precise costs of all this defensive infrastructure, let alone the burden on the Somali economy of the perceived need for so much protection. It is practically impossible to get insurance for travel in Mogadishu beyond the airport without contracting a recognized bodyguard, while travelling a distance that might cost £100 in a London taxi is ten or twenty times greater – a serious disincentive. Another indicator of cost: at the time of writing, the best price for a flight from London to Mogadishu (approx. 4,300 miles) was £1,107, whereas a flight to nearby Nairobi, Kenya (approx. 4,200 miles) was £610. The difference represents the cost per passenger of the major flight operator, currently Turkish Airlines, to self-insure against the loss of an aircraft.

Perimeter security affects airports more than almost all other installations, except for places like nuclear power plants, due both to their great size and relative openness. Airport runways are usually between 2.5 and four kilometres long, many airports have several of them, and by necessity they are completely flat and unobstructed. Aircraft on the ground are large, slow-moving, and prior to take off are full of explosive fuel. Physically, airport perimeters are protected by fences and walls usually topped by barbed wire or other anti-climb devices. These, however, are relatively easy to overcome, and climbing or cutting through fences is common at major airports.

At 3.30 a.m. on 13 June 2015, for instance, thirteen environmental activists from the group Plane Stupid, one dressed as a polar bear, cut through the perimeter of Heathrow Airport. Making their way to the northern runway, they then chained themselves together and to a metal tripod which they had brought with them. The incident caused significant disruption to flights, inconvenienced travellers, and increased costs to airlines. Although not itself a violent attack, it showed how easily one could succeed. Subsequently, Heathrow installed the 'Zoneguard Plus' fencing system manufactured by the UK firm Hardstaff Barriers, which is significantly more robust, and resistant to cutting, climbing, and vehicle ramming, than the original chain-link fence.[31]

The overall approach to airport perimeter defence, however, depends more on multi-layered sensors than on physical barriers. The first layer of such systems usually starts with a long-range radar system covering the airfield and its facilities. High-resolution radars can detect people and vehicles in all weather and light conditions at distances of hundreds of metres. They can also cover areas beyond the airport's perimeter, giving advance warning of threats. Once a radar has detected an 'object of interest' it will direct a pan-tilt-zoom (PTZ) camera to gaze directly upon it. This second layer of visual sensors includes a high-resolution daylight camera with thermal imaging capability for night-time use.

Operators can assess the objects the radar detects and determine the level of threat, if any, very rapidly. The word 'operator' might be somewhat deceiving, insofar as most of the work of visually observing and assessing potential threats is now likely done by a convolutional neural network (CNN) rather than by humans. A CNN is a class of artificial intelligence used to analyse visual imagery in real time and in large volume for security purposes. The advantage of CNN-based video analytic systems is that they do not tire, can analyse tens of thousands of images, and over time they can learn what kinds of unusual behaviour need to be flagged to security personnel. The poetic line 'all watched over by machines of loving grace'[32] offers a description of a possible future of humanity that is increasingly obviously real.

Drones, or unmanned aerial systems (UASs), are a more recent addition to the range of threats to airports. Just after 9 p.m. on 19 December 2018, two small commercial drones were sighted at London's Gatwick Airport – one hovering above a vehicle inside the airport complex and another alongside the perimeter fence. Flight take-offs were immediately halted and a dozen aircraft waiting to land, several low on fuel, were ordered to circle at a distance. Throughout the night and into the next day, every time officials attempted to reopen the airport another drone would be sighted (whether they were the same two originally sighted or there were more drones is unknown). At 6 p.m. on 20 December a military anti-drone system was installed on the roof of the South Terminal. The airport was finally reopened, on the tenth attempt, in the early hours the following day.[33]

Again, although not a violent attack, the incident signalled the dread potential in relatively cheap commercial drone technology. The airport was closed for thirty-three hours, and 1,000 flights were cancelled. Since then, as amply illustrated in the war in Ukraine, the ability of cheap drones to deliver militarily significant levels of explosive with a high degree of accuracy has developed rapidly. Even without a 'bang', bird strikes can seriously damage jet engines. How much more damage might be caused by drones? Consequently, a burgeoning area of the airport perimeter security sector is in counter-UAS technologies.

Countering drones is surprisingly challenging. Radars often have trouble detecting and separating them from other small flying objects. Acoustic solutions, i.e., listening for the buzz of the engine, are ineffective in noisy environments like an airport. Jamming a drone's control signals risks affecting the radio communications and control systems of the airport. In any case, as soon as the jamming stops the drone operator can regain control. Shooting drones down is risky in crowded situations where debris could hurt innocents.

A Dutch company, Guard from Above, offers trained hunting falcons to counter drones, as falcons regard drones in 'their' territory as invading bird competitors and attack them.[34] The utility of this tactic would be limited by the risk of injury to the falcons, and their inability to hunt at night or in poor weather.[35] Researchers, however, have profitably studied how falcon strategies of attack might be applied to counter-UAS work.[36]

The state-of-the-art with respect to the defence of facilities like airports against the threat of unauthorized UASs is an integrated system that automatically detects them and identifies their type by known technical characteristics, visually inspects them by long-range camera for signs of any dangerous payload, and then either hijacks the drone's control systems so that it can be landed in a safe area or, if that is not possible, directs a jammer or physical attack against it.[37]

Market size

The global airport security market had an estimated value in 2020 of around $11 billion, with a projected growth to as much as $25 billion by 2028, of which spending on perimeter security accounts for about a third.[38] For comparison, the defence budget of Canada in 2021 was about $25 billion as against a total GDP of $1.6 trillion – just over 1 per cent. The annual value of the airport operations business is reckoned to be $130 billion. In sum, then, the barbican defence of airports amounts to roughly 19 per cent of the annual value of the industry – a figure that, as a percentage of GDP, is more than double that of the defence expenditure of the Soviet Union, a notoriously high spender, at its peacetime peak.

The comparison between airports and states ought not to be overdrawn. The simple point is that security – not only the baggage scanners and x-ray machines with which everyone is familiar but also hard physical defences – makes up a very high fraction of airport operating costs, a number which hints at the fact that functionally they are, as the BBC put it, essentially fortresses. The astonishing and depressing thing is that the costs could get even higher than the already very high growth projection statistics would suggest.

Airports are phenomenally difficult to fully secure because they are massive, vulnerable, and highly symbolic targets. In many ways, all the interlocking tensions we have discussed in other contexts – between security and mobility, economics and aesthetics – are epitomized in the modern airport. Unfortunately, if the goal is to prevent the mass murder of civilians by ground attack on aircraft, then we are probably closer to the beginning of the solution than the end.

Consider two indisputable factors. One is the relative availability of effective shoulder-fired anti-tank and anti-aircraft missiles. The existing literature focuses almost exclusively on the latter – man-portable air-defence systems (MANPADs) – but for attacking a plane on the ground an anti-tank weapon would also be perfectly useful. Tens of thousands of both types of weapons have been delivered to Ukraine since February 2022, mostly unaccountably. At the time of writing, the most optimistic assessment is that they have not reached the European black market in weapons – yet.[39]

The other factor is the geography of the vast majority of the world's airports, which as barbicans of the great cities are by necessity located in peri-urban environments where space is at a premium. Earlier, we spoke of the problem of creating a 'standoff' distance of 100 feet; here, though, we are faced potentially with the need for a distance of thousands of feet. For example, the maximum range of the British NLAW anti-tank missile, designed to destroy a heavily armoured, relatively small, and potentially manoeuvring target, is 900 metres. That happens also to be the distance from the southwest corner of the open-topped car park number two at London's Luton airport to the end of the runway, where fully loaded, fully fuelled, completely stationary aircraft regularly wait for permission to take off at predictably scheduled times.

Since 1973, there have been sixty-five attacks on civilian aircraft using MANPADs, causing a total of over 1,000 deaths. Nearly all these attacks were in war zones.[40] One of the more noteworthy occurred in November 2002 when two Strela-2M missiles were launched against a Boeing 757 passenger jet belonging to Israel's Arkia airline as it was departing Mombasa airport in Kenya. In another incident, in February 2003, it is thought that Al-Qaeda planned to fire a shoulder-launched missile at an El Al plane flying out of Heathrow.[41]

In other words, there are quite available means and opportunities to attack, so the question is motive. Although there have been no such attacks lately, there is no reason to believe the threat of mass-murder terrorism is going away or even diminishing. It is likely that serious ground attacks on aircraft will recur. Moreover, there is no reason to be confident that the problem will be confined to distant war zones, as opposed to the 'zone of peace' in the West. 'This is not a theoretical threat', as Matthew Schroeder, a senior researcher at the Geneva-based Small Arms Survey, put it.[42]

For the obvious reason that airports are phenomenally difficult to guard, the efforts of security forces focus on keeping such weapons out of the hands of non-state actors, but that is a foregone conclusion: the weapons exist in large numbers and a lot of people want them. In the meantime, between now and the next major attack, aviation industry leaders are also preoccupied with guarding against ground attacks on airport facilities and passengers before they even get close to an aircraft.

Invisible Fortresses

Now let's look at the fortification strategies, techniques, and technologies deployed against this other form of ground attack, the 'marauding terror' attack exemplified by the gun and grenade assault on Lod Airport fifty years ago. It should be noted that nothing about these attacks is peculiar to airports per se; it is simply that, for reasons already noted, airports are especially good targets.

Everything discussed in the paragraphs that follow could be applied to any place where large numbers of people gather, whether hotels, sporting facilities, museums, and particularly shopping malls, with which airports are now often compared. Most sadly, even schools have also become important places of 'target-hardening' schemes. At this point, as we look at the internal hardening of civilian facilities, I shall broaden the focus beyond airports. The key feature which typifies all this activity is the structured, focused, and quite ingenious way in which designers have contrived to disguise fortifications as something other than fortresses – effectively to make them seem invisible.

Since the 1990s the designs of new airport 'mega-terminals' have tended to have much in common with the enclosed mega-mall, frequently combining extensive shopping areas, as well as hotel and conference facilities, bars, restaurants, and so on. The reasons are straightforward. Due to the heightened security measures, passengers spend more time in the terminal than they once did. They need to be entertained, and shopping also provides airport operators with another valuable revenue stream. Some airports even increasingly feature terminals that are themselves billed as destinations where passengers may wish to go to spend money.[43]

Examples of such new airports, which a CNN Business Traveller report described as 'modern, stylish architectural statements that banish the dark, crowded travel spaces of the past', include the previously mentioned New York JFK Terminal 5 and London's Heathrow, amongst many others.[44] Although they vary greatly in design, they share many common features, notably a sense of openness conveyed by large, high-ceilinged internal spaces, and a feeling of transparency and lightness created by the dominant materials of construction – glass, especially.

Looks, however, are deceiving. The most visually open airports are still places of division and congestion, and a good deal of what looks to be light and transparent structure is armour-plated. Firstly, there is the hard and necessary division between 'secured' and 'unsecured' areas in any airport. Secondly, there is the transition point between the two – where passengers and their baggage are scanned for weapons and explosives or explosive components – which is a main point of congestion. Ironically, what we tend to call 'security', as in 'after check-in please go through security', is also with respect to a ground attack on passengers the point of maximum insecurity.

To explain why, let us return for a moment to the mediaeval barbican of Krakow, which you will recall was configured such that once travellers had been processed in the guarded courtyard they were permitted to pass through the 'neck' of the fortification into the city proper. A big airport works in much the same way but with a major difference: whereas Krakow's barbican filtered people heading to one destination, the airport does the same job for dozens or hundreds of destinations. An airport is a kind of large sorting machine that processes people as they pass through a series of gates.[45]

Compared to the early days of counter-terrorism security measures, airports today operate relatively smoothly and agreeably. Airport managers have done a good job of distracting people with shopping and other entertainments while they are being processed from check-in through to boarding an aircraft. For comparison, an airport of the 1970s was described by its architect as being a 'funnel leading from its parking garages and drop-off points through a linear concourse directly to its boarding pavilions'.[46]

While the lack of gates or much sense of threshold in those days was very different from the situation now, it was sometimes dismal in its own way. Moreover, when gates and security procedures began to be intensified the result was that the interior spaces of old terminals no longer flowed together; instead, they 'choked to a standstill at security throats', with obvious effects on the temper of travellers. 'Moments of anxiety were aggravated by the sense of being funnelled up another chute like a herd of cattle.'[47] Certainly, regular travellers today will be familiar with such feelings. The point is that things were worse not so long ago.

Crowded places

The situation is prone to create 'bottlenecks' as large numbers of people attempt to enter a restricted number of passageways at the same time. The science of 'queue management' has evolved to mathematically model crowd behaviour to devise optimum times for passenger arrival and suggest the ideal layout for queues.[48] Unfortunately, as much as airport managers seek to avoid it by regulating the flow of people into the airport, people inevitably 'bunch up' at predictable places in unsecured areas before check-in and while waiting to pass through border control and security.[49]

A 2003 study of proposed security changes to Los Angeles Airport explained why these high-density areas are particularly vulnerable to attack:

> a terrorist seeking to kill the greatest number of persons can kill more with a small bomb (e.g., luggage bomb) in a relatively dense area such as inside a terminal than with a large bomb (e.g., vehicle bomb) in a relatively open area such as a sidewalk outside a terminal ... Small bombs detonated inside a terminal, in addition to being a more likely threat and more deadly for a given weight of explosives, are easier to build without detection and to deploy in an airport without suspicion and leave less forensic evidence about perpetrators.[50]

Previously, we have discussed the properties of explosive blast. In the case of a bomb small enough to be concealed in a suitcase, or hand grenades as used in the Lod Airport attack, the main injuries are caused by high-velocity fragmentation, whether shrapnel embedded in the bomb itself or material in the environment propelled by the blast.

For example, in May 2017 a suicide bomber detonated a bomb concealed in a backpack, killing twenty-three people amongst a crowd exiting an Ariana Grande concert at the Manchester Arena. A further 160 people were seriously wounded (forty-four of them children), the vast majority of whom suffered injuries requiring orthoplastic surgery to stabilize heads, limbs, and torsos mangled and punctured by shrapnel.[51] All but two of those killed were within ten metres of the bomber, and over half of them within less than six metres. There was nothing in the roughly twenty-metre-wide foyer where the bomb went off to shield any of the victims.

The problem is that defending against a determined attack on an unarmed crowd densely packed in an open space – whether an airport concourse, a shopping mall food court, or the foyer of a concert venue – is enormously challenging. It is possible, however, to design spaces and places to provide cover against the damage of an attack.

Open spaces and crowded places could simply be striated by rows of stacked sandbags, which would add a large measure of ballistic resistance to the shrapnel of a small bomb attack. Had that been the case in the foyer of the Manchester Arena, the death toll would have been very much lower. As we observed earlier of the guarded street scene, however, such measures would interfere with the normal functioning and aesthetic quality of the spaces protected. Would you relish a visit to an airport or a concert venue that looked like an artillery pit from the First World War?

The trick is to create spaces of protection against ballistic threat, i.e., cover, in places where function and fashion otherwise urge designers towards greater openness. To judge from the direction of the security industry, the answer to this contradiction is threefold.

First, some existing interior structures like partition walls, doors, and the like can be hardened against penetration by high-velocity shrapnel, without much changing their appearance, relatively easily but at substantial cost. Second, to a certain degree, 'invisible' barriers using ballistic-resistant glass can be created in open spaces without too much effect on mobility or appearance. Third, normal objects in the guarded space, such as furniture, wastebins, and so on can be made to some extent bullet-proof, or less likely to be turned into deadly fragments by a blast.

As with the hostile vehicle mitigation measures discussed earlier, there is an industry-recognized standard governing the gradations of ballistic resistance of building components such as windows, walls, barriers, or other objects made from rigid 'bullet-proof' materials. One of the most recognized is the European Union's EN 1063 standard, which has seven levels from BR1, proof against three shots from a .22 calibre pistol, through to BR7, proof against three shots from a NATO-standard 7.62mm rifle. The American NIJ 1018 standard covers the same range of ballistic threat but has eight instead of seven levels. The UL 752 standard, also American, has ten levels from handguns through to .50 calibre rifles, plus two extras for shotguns.

The range and variety of products currently sold claiming a level of ballistic resistance according to one of the above standards, many of which are marketed to parents fearful of the rise of school shootings, is bewildering.[52] Automobiles, blackboards, clipboards, desks, eyeglasses, fence panels, garage doors, hoodies ... that is an alphabetized and incomplete list of examples. I could go on, but suffice to say there is a great and grave demand for ballistic resistance that plenty of manufacturers of all kinds of products are eager to satisfy.

Sticking to the realm of architecture, the industry that has emerged to serve the demand for 'ballistic-resistant' building materials is hard to measure precisely because it is so diverse and widespread. Even if we confined our estimate of its scale to some fraction of the annual global airport security industry it would still be a large industry, at least equal to that of perimeter security. There is no reason, however, to be so restrictive because once you learn to notice it, the target-hardening industry seems almost ubiquitous.

Thirty years ago, the business of fortifying civil structures was a niche industry serving the sort of citadels described earlier. For example, when in 1991 the iconic black door to 10 Downing St was replaced with an armour-plated one in the wake of IRA mortar attacks, this was considered quite exceptional.[53] Nowadays, clients of the industry include practically every sector of the economy, collectively representing billions of dollars of investment in 'hardening' annually – an investment that continues to grow.

To illustrate the scope of the market, consider the American firm ArmorCore, based in Waco, Texas, which specializes in making ballistic-resistant fibreglass panels. They provide marketing materials and case studies of the use of their products in, for example, commercial businesses, banks, government offices, critical infrastructure facilities, hospitals, police stations and courthouses, army recruitment centres and drill halls, safe rooms, schools, and residential constructions of all types.[54]

The UK company Architectural Armour provides a good example of the range of products that typify the industry. Their catalogue includes several types of security glass and windows, including bullet- and blast-resistant variants. They also offer a variety of 'safehavens', including ballistic- and blast-resistant guard houses and armoured panic rooms. In addition to 'bullet boards' (ballistic-resistant panels) they produce 'explosion vents' and 'rupture panels' – devices used to protect buildings against the effects of an inside blast by directing it to the outside. Finally, a range of bullet- and blast-resistant doors are available in various shapes and sizes in timber, steel, or glass.[55]

Fortified schools

It is hard to be euphemistic about a subject that is essentially about making people in public places somewhat less likely to be lacerated by shrapnel or bullets in the event of an attack, though the term 'ballistic resistance' has a certain anodyne quality. Governments tend to use the terms 'hardening' or 'securing' rather than fortifying. For example, in May 2022 Senator Ted Cruz called for more federal spending to 'harden schools' following a mass shooting at a Texas primary school.[56]

Likewise, professional bodies such as the American Institute of Architects, which announced in August 2018 that it would work with the Department of Homeland Security on guidelines for design practices to make schools 'more resistant to violent shootings', are acutely chary about being seen to be designing fortresses.[57] The word has an awkwardly military connotation and sits uneasily alongside 'for children' – though it is not as bad as other ways of describing it, like 'converting our schools into prisons and treat[ing] our students like prisoners', as the head of the American National Education Association put it.[58]

Of course the ideal solution to things like school shootings, airport ground attacks, and assaults by marauding terrorists anywhere is not to have a society in which there are people willing and able to conduct such attacks in the first place. In the world as it is, however, such people do exist and fortifying against them is perfectly sensible. The issue, as we have observed, is to find a productive convergence – a balance – between security and other imperatives.

In the case of schools, as a couple of educationalists put it, we must 'remain aware of the potential negative impact of such practices [target hardening] and weigh them closely against the educational mission' lest we do more harm than good.[59] 'Schools are a microcosm of their broader communities', in the words of Ken Trump, a long-standing American expert on school security. He worries that:

> The security hardware and product industry has hijacked school safety ... They have become increasingly organized in their lobbying of Congress and state governments. Their focus includes taking school

security out of the hands of education agencies and putting it under the authority of homeland security departments, which, by their nature, tend to focus on the physical security measures and infrastructure hardening.[60]

It is undoubtedly true that any for-profit provider of 'solutions' has a vested interest in the existence of the 'problem'. The obvious risk is threat exaggeration. Trump's concerns about industry lobbying are well placed.

In the industry's defence, to judge from its marketing literature it is at least rhetorically aware of the acute need to balance security and function at a reasonable cost. The company Gladiator Solutions, for example, a provider of 'ballistic resistant building and structural fortification' systems, reassures potential customers on exactly this point: 'We design and install bullet-proof solutions that balance safety, cost, and daily operations. Our bullet-resistant doors and windows provide the highest level of protection while still feeling welcoming to employees and visitors.'

On the other hand, there is no debating that schools are microcosms of society. Just as efforts to secure the population in urban environments that proceed from the idea of treating everyone as a potential terrorist imperil the existence of a free society, treating all students as potential terrorists, or conveying the belief that they are major potential targets of terrorism, will impact on their ability to learn.

Here are some specific examples of 'invisible fortresses', starting with Fruitport High School in Fruitport, Michigan, which reopened in 2021 after a $48-million renovation by the American architectural firm Tower Pinkster. The object of the renovation was, in part, to fortify the school against an active shooter attack.[61]

Initially, the intent of the redesign was to renovate the old school and add an extension around it, which required that the corridors be curved. As the school superintendent remarked:

> When we were sitting with the architect during the design phase and were looking at this curved structure, somebody said, 'You know, that cuts down on the line of sight of an active shooter.' From that point, we started to brainstorm what else we could do to keep our kids secure.[62]

The resulting fortified school incorporates many simple but ingenious features. Its curved and glazed front office has a panopticon view of the parking lot, main passageway, vestibule, and some hallways.

Administrators can remotely lock rooms, seriously impeding if not actually isolating any attacker by compartmentalizing them away from students. Classrooms are equipped with ballistic-resistant 'shadow zones' where students can hide in cover. Windows looking onto classrooms use laminated glass, with further coverage provided by cement block 'wing walls' that protrude outside all doors.[63]

The architects of mediaeval castles also designed their fortresses to compartmentalize the defence should any one part of it be captured. The calculation of sightlines and taking account of cover from fire and observation have been basic military engineering tasks since earliest times. From that perspective, the architects of Fruitport High School have done a good job, although the necessity of it is to be deplored.

Fruitport is by no means a one-off in the United States, as the call by Senator Cruz for more funding of such hardening attests. Lest, however, it be perceived as a peculiarly American reaction, it is worth noting a recent British example. Rather like Fruitport High School, Yavneh College, a Jewish faith school in Borehamwood, Hertfordshire, was an older building in need of renovation and an extension. The landscape design of the new school includes a high level of security with outer and inner security fences as well as a double-lock gate entrance. The challenge, in the words of its designer, was to 'provide the required level of security at the same time as creating a welcoming and friendly environment' for the students. The solution was an undulating grassy lawn in front, full of mounds that look like green rolling waves. It appears fun and playful, but its purpose is to stop vehicle ramming attacks on students and staff as well as providing standoff distance against blast.

Yavneh College's focus on hostile vehicle mitigation rather than ballistic resistance is no doubt a reflection of the somewhat diminished threat of shooting attacks in Britain, where guns have been much more tightly controlled since the March 1996 Dunblane massacre in which sixteen students at a primary school near Stirling, Scotland were shot dead.[64] It is a reminder that while the school shootings described above are not incidences of international terrorism, from a terrorist's perspective schools remain an ideal target because they combine vulnerability with acute symbolic potential.

There is no better evidence of this than the September 2004 attack upon the school in Beslan in southern Russia, in which a group of Chechen terrorists held hostage over a thousand people – children, teachers, and parents. By the time of the ensuing three-day siege's violent end, over 300 people including 180 children were dead. If, in terms of numbers, it was not the bloodiest terror attack in history, it was probably the most spectacularly cruel. Thus far it has not been repeated, though there is no good reason to think that will be permanently the case.[65]

Ballistic barriers and security gates

Ballistic-resistant glass plays a large role in contemporary fortification. It is defined by the ballistic standard to which it conforms, normally represented by a rating according to the standards noted earlier. Although specific products vary, it is usually manufactured by laminating layers of toughened glass sheets with an interlayer between each. The layered panes slow bullets up to a given rated power and stop them from passing through, their energy being absorbed across the entire glass panel.[66] It may also be manufactured to be blast resistant.

Again, there is an international standard for such toughened glass, ISO 16935:2007 for ballistic resistance and ISO 16933:2007 for blast resistance, as well as the European standard EN 13541 for blast resistance. Under the latter, glass is classified by blast resistance ranging from ER1 to ER4. The details are highly technical and for our purposes unimportant. The main point is that fortification is not only very typical in contemporary architecture, it is also very highly specified.[67]

Ballistic- and blast-resistant glass walls and windows are evidently useful where visual transparency is a primary design consideration. A see-through barrier impedes movement, which may be a problem or a feature depending on the sort of building in question, but it is at least effectively invisible. It is unsurprising to see such barriers in wide use in places deemed by their owners, insurers, or government regulators to be significantly at risk. In the UK, the main source of regulation for airport designers and operators is *Aviation Security in Airport Development* (ASIAD), a Department for Transport policy document.

The 180-metre-long glass front of London Heathrow's Terminal 4 is a good example. It was refitted in 2008 to bring it into conformity with an ASIAD requirement that the terminal be resistant to the blast of a 100kg bomb exploded at thirty metres distance. This was quite a technical challenge, particularly as the façade had to conform with other considerations, notably visual appeal. In the words of the architect, 'we wanted a clean glass box design that fitted in with BAA's other buildings'.[68]

Similar if smaller blast-resistant schemes are common throughout the transport infrastructure. Recently, the Cardiff Central Rail

Station and Cardiff Queen Street Station in Wales were upgraded with blast-resistant façades as part of a multimillion-pound refurbishment. The prime contractor, Wrightstyle Systems, has 'long experience in both rail and airport projects – for example, for a major rail hub in Hong Kong and the Dubai Metro and, in the UK, at several railway and Underground stations', according to its managing director.[69]

The fundamental problem in the transportation context – whether bus, rail, or aviation – occurs when security is a high priority in the same place where the volume and flow of people is the greatest and needs to be kept moving, lest bunching up and delays occur. A typical solution, seen normally at the junction between 'secured' and 'unsecured' areas – notably at the exit or entrance of any major hub – is known as a 'breach control system' or 'security portal'.

A breach control system is essentially an armoured glass tunnel with automatic gates at each end which provide a secure one-way flow of people, i.e., the doors will open to people approaching from one direction but close to anyone approaching oppositely. It's like a valve in plumbing. The system may be set to operate with one traveller at a time allowed in the tunnel or permit multiple people to enter depending on the operator's estimation of the appropriate balance between movement and security.[70]

Security portals vary greatly in design but commonly they look like a normal revolving door. They are often deployed in high-security places like airports, but also in financial institutions, casinos, high-end hotels, and government buildings. A very powerful one is a feature of the main entrance to the UK Ministry of Defence. A main difference from a breach control system is that a security portal is a very effective man trap.[71]

While a person is isolated in a breach control system or security portal they can be identified, perhaps biometrically, and checked automatically for weapons or explosives visually as well as with scanners. Once deemed safe they may be permitted to proceed through the exit portal. While this is technologically all very impressive, in principle the system, known as a 'chamber gate', is an old one deployed by fortress builders since biblical times. The Jaffa Gate of the Old City of Jerusalem, for example, is an L-shaped variant. Another example, the 'Bloody Tower' of the Tower of London, has two gates, one at either end of a vaulted stone tunnel.

The modern industry producing such systems goes by the term 'access control'. The 'Airport Suppliers' directory lists fifty-seven such companies in the aviation sector alone,[72] while the IFSEC directory includes 398 of them for the access-control sector generally.[73] Again we find that fortification is a big industry, highly innovative, and growing. The access-control market was estimated to have a global value of $8.1 billion in 2021, with a projected growth to $13.1 billion in 2026.[74]

A final element of the discreet target-hardening business involves fortifications that hide in plain sight. We have come across this tactic already in the contemporary street scene's defensive furniture – benches, planters, public art, waste bins, and so on – which often have some intrinsic ballistic resistance due to simple mass. The same pattern is found in interior design but given the lighter quality of normal domestic furniture derives its ballistic resistance from the addition of other materials.

We have already discussed ballistic-resistant panels and glass, each of which is used to construct what we might call fortified furniture. There are also ballistic-resistant fabrics and other flexible materials, usually those used in making body armour. These too are governed by a recognized standard. Most often cited is NIJ 0108.01, which specifies levels of protection ranging from low-velocity small bullets (Type I) through to high-velocity armour piercing ones (Type IV).

The Amulet 'ballistic barrier solution' sold by the American airport furniture company Arconas, for example, is rated against NIJ Type IIIA threats (9mm and .44 magnum pistol rounds). What it looks like, though, is a row of standard airport seats known as a 'Flyaway' unit. In the words of the retailer, in the event of an active shooting the seating 'invisibly transforms' into a 'safe haven':

> We recognize the challenges faced by airports to keep their passengers safe in the event of a crisis. Integrating Amulet ballistic barriers with existing furniture is a discreet way of adding security options to protect the public and first responders, as well as giving peace of mind to airport facility operators.[75]

Airport seating is just one ballistic- and blast-resistant product made by Amulet, whose products also include office desks and worktables, markerboards, reception and information stations, upholstered furniture for hotel and corporate lobbies, and lecterns for public speakers. The company's description of its markerboards is an excellent example of the essential idea:

> The mobile markerboard is a tool common to work and school environments. Now, with Amulet Ballistic Barrier technology hidden inside,

it becomes something dramatically better . . . a life-safety device. Why utilize a markerboard to protect life during an Active Shooter event? Simple. It is the essence of what we do – deliver state-of-the-art ballistic protection to public environments . . . invisibly. Protecting life without disturbing it.[76]

The language of marketing is by nature upbeat, which makes the above feel somehow off kilter. The words 'hidden inside', for me, trigger a childhood mental image of a cheap plastic toy secreted at the bottom of a cereal box, not an armour plate concealed in a classroom markerboard. The logic behind the existence of the 'invisible' fortification products discussed here, however, is perfectly sound.

Compared to the markets in access control, ballistic glass and structural materials, and perimeter security, the scale of the bulletproof furniture market is small. There are several companies which provide rigid ballistic-resistant benches, normally referred to as 'safe benches', which make little or no concession to style or comfort. They are designed for use in security offices, police stations, and other very high-risk areas.[77]

The market in ballistic-resistant soft furnishings, or furniture which is designed at any rate to be attractive and comfortable as well as bullet-proof, is very hard to estimate. A short Bloomberg report on it kicked off with the question 'who buys bulletproof sofas?', the answer to which, it concluded, was small numbers of very rich people.[78] The BBC has also reported on a Scottish company, Osdin Shield, selling ballistic-resistant sofas and chairs.[79] This appears, though, to have been a novelty, as while the company still exists there is no sign of its bulletproof furniture being for sale any longer.

There is no point denying that active shooter and small-bomb attacks occur, and that 'normal' people are directly targeted by such violence, although the statistical likelihood of any individual experiencing such a thing is exaggerated. That said, a common driver of many of these efforts is the expected costs of damages of an attack, which as often as not is a calculation driven by the actuarial calculations of insurers. That's why ballistic-resistant furniture is likely to feature a lot more in places like hotel lobbies and corporate offices, where there is exposure to risk and a stiff price to be paid in elevated insurance premiums without countermeasures.

Consistently, both buyers and sellers of invisible fortification technologies talk about finding an appropriate balance between cost and other factors. Ultimately, the answer to the question is highly specific to local context, rather subjective, and hard to generalize. The size of the relevant industries is surprising, as is their rate of growth. But the perception of need is undeniable.

It would certainly be possible to fill our public and crowded places with plenty of overt and cheap armour plating and bullet-proofing. However, if we can make our fortifications less overt and intrusive then that is not in itself a bad thing. The bottom line is that people wish to do things like travel, attend concerts and festivals, visit galleries and museums, and go to school, and none of those quite innocent things are now without risk. Contemporary fortifications are a result of something rather depressing about human nature, which is our propensity for killing. But they also reflect our ingeniousness and desire to continue to live well.

7

Luxury Forts to Data Bunkers

We have examined in depth how governments and public authorities, or private companies whose activities are strongly bound by regulations, work to secure people in civil contexts through discreet fortification. The guardedness of our age, however, can also be seen in the actions of individuals, families, institutions, associations, and corporate entities. The actions of corporate entities, whose spending is highest, show us most clearly what our society values above all else.

Bastles

The word 'bastle' is a corruption of the French word for fortress, 'bastille', as in 'the storming of the Bastille in Paris marked the beginning of the French Revolution'. The Bastille was a serious fortress, built in the twelfth century as part of the primary defences of Paris, then converted into a prison in the seventeenth century. In English use, a bastle is a more modest structure, essentially a fortified house, sometimes a manor, but often rather smaller and humbler. Bastles are the Volkswagens of fortresses – small, cheap, and useful, often literally a family fort.

Bastles are a common form of construction with variants found all over the world in practically every period of history, as far back as the Iron Age or earlier. The three *brochs* (circular dry-stone-wall towers) of the 'Zenith of Iron Age Shetland' site are an excellent example. The specific forms and local names of bastles differ from place to place. Some, like the famous tower houses (fourteen remaining of seventy-two originally) of San Gimignano, Italy, built between the eleventh and thirteenth centuries by the rich families of the town, are unusually large and grand, but generally bastles were relatively modest.

Usually, they were constructions of the wealthier peasantry, the merchant classes, craftsmen, and low-ranking clergy – not of the great and powerful. In the lawless, warlord-dominated Anglo-Scottish border region from the thirteenth century to the seventeenth century, where the term bastle originated, they took the form of very small castles. Immensely strong for their size, they were intended to protect their owner, perhaps a wealthy farmer or a vicar, and his family against the incessant, low-level raids plaguing the region.

Many can still be seen today, often refurbished as quirky private homes. In the little village of Elsdon, Northumberland there is a lovely example – a miniature three-storey castle, with machicolation and a rooftop parapet, built in the fifteenth century as a refuge for the local vicar. Another, more modest still, is the nearby 'Hole Bastle' (outside the village of Bellingham) – a two-storey fortified farmhouse made of locally quarried stone.[1]

The range of fortified civilian structures in borderlands and other lawless, bandit-ridden areas includes 'defensible churches' and fortified barns and granaries – essentially anything of value was hardened against robbery. Designs and names vary from place to place. In Portugal and Spain, they are known as *pazos* and are extremely common. In the Balkans there is a local variant, known as *kules*, stemming from Ottoman times. In the Svaneti region of Georgia, some magnificently picturesque *Svan* towers remain. They were built between the ninth and twelfth centuries (or possibly earlier) by mountain people who remain to this day famously obstreperous.

It is difficult to estimate the number of such constructions – many have not survived, as they were jury-rigged in the first place. We can guess with confidence, however, that 'target-hardened', to use the modern phrase, civilian structures were extremely common. For point of reference, a gazetteer of confirmed bastles just in the north of England, mainly in Northumberland and Cumberland, lists more than 600, with a further fifty-odd suspected.[2]

Governance

The greatest density and variety of these usually modest private fortifications is probably in Central Asia – particularly Iran and Afghanistan. The reason is simple: bad government, centuries of civil war, and slave raiding by steppe peoples – above all ferocious Turcoman horsemen – up to the late nineteenth century, meant that life in the region was incredibly precarious. People fortified everything they could, as well as they could, with whatever they had. Given their poverty, this often resulted in a rough-and-ready fort. The French officer, diplomat, and adventurer J.P. Ferrier travelled through Central Asia in the mid-nineteenth century, publishing a diary that is interesting from a fortification perspective.

In just one day of travel in a small area of Persia, he described an intensely guarded environment that proved typical over his year-long journey over more than 2,000 miles and back:

> From Karund to Sahadabad the walled villages, situated on the crests of eminences, or rather artificial mounds, are very numerous; the practice of enclosing them in Persia has existed from time immemorial, and became general during the wars of the last century. The supreme authority was so badly maintained, and passed from hand to hand so rapidly, that the Persian Khans cared little for it; they were pretty near absolute in their own fiefs, and their principal occupation was to pillage each other. As a sudden onslaught was their usual system of attack, these walls became necessary for defence, and to give them a chance of living in comparative security.[3]

As Ferrier elaborates further, some of these fortifications, like the famous caravanserais where merchant caravans bunkered at night, were well-prepared for defence, at least against bandits. A typical construction was

> loopholed, and capable of being defended against any sudden attack, for there is no possibility of entrance except by the door, and this is generally made of thick hard wood, covered with nails and clamped with iron. Many of these resting places are indeed almost fortresses, and unless supplies failed, or artillery was brought up, a garrison of thirty determined men would be able to hold out against a large force.[4]

In summer 2010, I stood on the parapet of a semi-ruined caravanserai outside the Maiwand district centre in Kandahar province, Afghanistan. The soldiers guarding me reckoned it was still the safest place in the area to stop for a break. The walls, though crumbled, were still powerful.

One thing common to all these fortifications is their relative detachment from any higher notion of strategy. They are where they are because the people who lived there determined that they needed them, and built them usually of local materials. They are a bottom-up reaction to a particular societal condition that is perceived to be insecure, badly governed, and possibly just anarchic, compelling people to self-help solutions.

I am not simply adding historical colour. Everything I have said above about why people built bastle houses and the like in the past, and to a surprising extent both where and how they built them, is still current. The situation that caused Persian and Afghan peasants to turn their lands into an archipelago of fortified compounds of a bewildering variety of types over many centuries can also be seen in our own times.

Moreover, the fortification *zeitgeist* is in no way exclusive to the efforts of national and local governments. On the contrary, the urge to hunker down, to erect physical barriers around oneself and one's property, can be observed everywhere across the civil sphere in the actions of individuals, families, community associations, and corporations. And criminals, as we shall see below.

People are, in general, aware of the situation. If you live in an urban area, it is a near certainty that you lock the door to your home. You likely have an alarm system. It is increasingly common for people to deploy their own private surveillance system using cameras to watch their property and record all that goes on around it. This level of guardedness is unremarkable to contemporary urbanites, even in 'safe' countries.

It goes further than that, however. Otherwise, why write a book about it?

Enclosed neighbourhoods

My argument is that walled neighbourhoods, towns and the fortified residential enclaves known as 'gated communities' are further manifestations of the fortress mentality that pervades contemporary life. A lot of attention has been paid to gated communities in the West, particularly in the United States, where this type of development has grown very common over the last fifty years. It is hard to say precisely how common, as there is no comprehensive data set. A study based on the 2001 American Housing Survey (AHS) reported over 7 million 'walled and fenced' households in the country with over 16 million inhabitants.[5]

In the urban studies literature, a common way to describe a gated community is as a housing development to which public access is restricted using multiple physical barriers such as gates, boom arms, walls, and fences, as well as (usually) security staff and surveillance systems. Interior spaces that would normally be considered public are usually privatized, and often residents must comply with special internal statutory and social frameworks.[6] They are, in effect, micro-territories wherein the conditions of life (not just material but legal and social) can sometimes sharply diverge from the larger sovereign entity of which they are a part.

As I mentioned earlier, some political sociologists and urban geographers read a great deal into the above that is ominous for the health of our societies. They talk of cities being split, largely by class but also by other forces, into 'fortified fragments' – even of a cold civil war between the rich who live in these fragments and the lumpen mass outside of them, perhaps trending slowly into a hot one.[7]

The reasons for the rise of gated communities may also, however, be summarized on a more pragmatic and individual psychological level. For some, it is a lifestyle choice, as the gates and walls provide security and separation for leisure activities and amenities available exclusively to residents. For others, the main motivation seems to be prestige, signalled through living behind monumental, guarded entrances, with private access to desirable landscapes and vistas, such as a waterfront or mountain view.[8] Neither of these motivations excludes the other.

One author has neatly argued that fortified enclaves have been created in the search for the three P's: 'peace, prestige, and perfect vistas'.[9] I agree with this point of view, as well as with the idea that this activity also reflects a very ill society. To my mind, though, the literature is biased by its focus on the, until recently, secure and prosperous West. This makes me differ with it on three points.

First, it seems to me that the literature underestimates the simple desire for security as the main driver of people hunkering down behind walls and gates, whether their main fear is crime, terrorism, nuclear war, or some other catastrophe. In the West, which has been a 'zone of peace' for many decades, the social cachet and sense of exclusivity of living in a gated community is a greater factor than security concerns, whereas in other parts of the world, notably Africa, large parts of central and south Asia, and to an extent also Latin America, it is the reverse.[10] Second, whatever the reason, it is not always (or even mainly) the rich walling themselves off from the poor – though that certainly is a part of it. The situation is more complex. Outside the West, 'gatedness' is the default condition of urban life for all classes, not just the affluent. Third, there is little that has occurred recently that we can't understand better with some historical context.

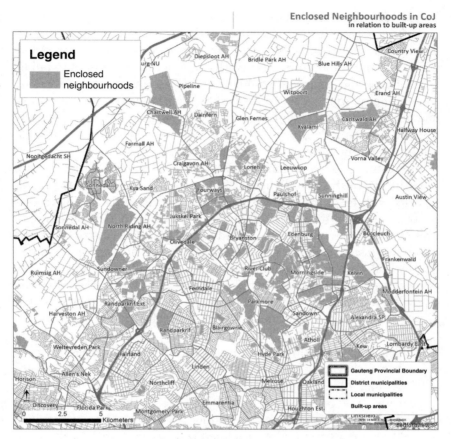

7.1 Enclosed neighbourhoods in Johannesburg
As may be seen here, Johannesburg is a patchwork of guarded enclosed neighbourhoods.
Source: Reproduced with permission from Karina Landman and Willem Badenhorst, *The Impact of Gated Communities on Spatial Transformation in the Greater Johannesburg Area* (University of the Witwatersrand, 2012).

Let us look at some specific examples of fortified residential enclaves, starting with Johannesburg, in post-Apartheid South Africa. For reasons including increased urbanization, economic decline, high levels of crime, and very high levels of fear of violent crime, there has been an explosion of formal and informal fortified settlements across the urban landscape.[11] There are several types of these fortified areas. One of these is known as an 'enclosed neighbourhood', which a look at Johannesburg reveals to be a clearly extensive development.

The distinguishing characteristic of an 'enclosed neighbourhood' is that the roads within it were previously, or remain, public property, and in many cases the city authorities retain responsibility for public services to the community.[12] Notwithstanding this concession to public accessibility, the enclosed neighbourhood is walled off from the surrounding city, with access controlled by security gates sometimes with manned guard posts, and monitored by surveillance systems. It is a fortified space guarded against banditry and crime, with varying degrees of support from the normal sovereign authority.

Interestingly, gated communities like these in South Africa are not just a luxury of the rich. People of all income groups associate greater security with fortification measures including target hardening, access control, and monitoring.[13] The same is true of many African cities, as well as cities generally. A 2017 study of the Soneike district of Cape Town, for instance, found that fully 86 per cent of houses were fortified by physical measures, including walls, spikes, and razor wire as well as motion-activated lights, infrared beams, and CCTV cameras. The report's authors observed, however, that in 2014 the number was only 37 per cent, which is clear indication of a spectacular rate of growth.[14]

This is not to deny that segregated districts, class privilege, and elite spatial exclusivity continue to typify many postcolonial cities, in some cases even as they have grown many times over, long after the departure of white rule.[15] The details, however, are complex.

Consider the retrospectively and imperfectly barricaded suburbs erected by 'residents welfare associations' in Delhi. They are at once central to the construction of a middle-class identity, while at the same time expressing the view of these new middle classes that they are inadequately protected by police and under threat, notably from attack by slum dwellers. 'Gates both produce and assuage anxieties', argued the author of an important study of the phenomenon of gating so prevalent in India.[16]

Or take contemporary Lagos, Nigeria, where the so-called 'government reserved area', built in colonial times for Europeans, remains in effect a fortified enclave of government buildings and residences serving a rich domestic elite. At the same time, enclosed neighbourhoods, fortified family compounds, and the like have proliferated throughout the city in both upper- and lower-class suburbs and streets where some form of 'club democracy gating' is taking place for pragmatic security reasons as well as prestige.[17]

Neither, it should be stressed, is this a uniquely bourgeois middle-class reaction. Consider, for example, the poverty-stricken Ingeniero

Budge district of Buenos Aires, Argentina, where in 2008 it was reported that crimes against persons (e.g., homicide, assault, and battery) were running at 535 per 100,000 residents. 'People here are scared', one person told researchers, 'if you do something, they [the perpetrators] might get you and hit you or your family'. As a result:

> Residents have not only secluded themselves in their homes but have also made physical modifications to their homes that increased their (perceived) level of safety. Like middle-class families in other parts of the Americas, many residents in Ingeniero Budge have built higher walls around their properties, installed stronger doors ('so they can't kick it down and break in'), and added padlocks to their windows.[18]

The situation of these people is dire, but is it categorically different from that faced by Afghan peasants a century ago, or now for that matter? That both groups have reacted in essentially the same way suggests that the answer is no.

Gatedness, social segregation, serious fear of crime, and endemic mistrust of police have become increasingly normalized in Latin America and other places around the world.[19] One could go on practically ad infinitum with examples of poor people responding to insecurity with fortifications like this, selecting cases from every continent.

Prepping

Before we look at the flip side – the global proliferation of large and luxurious guarded settlements for the rich – it is worth dwelling briefly on another form of contemporary civil fortification that is the exclusive preserve of neither the rich nor the poor and, while driven by security concerns, is not primarily about fear of either crime or terrorism.

'Prepping', i.e., preparing for apocalyptic social breakdown, generally involves the stockpiling of critical supplies, keeping firearms for defence, and constructing guarded compounds or survival bunkers usually in rural areas.[20]

'Preppers' have been around for many years, dating back to the Cold War nuclear confrontation, which inspired a minor building boom in fallout shelters. In recent years, however, there has been a large growth in the sector, with increasing sales of preserved food and personal protective equipment. Another signal of growth is the popularity of post-apocalyptic fiction, film, and videogames, as well as television programmes like National Geographic's *Doomsday Preppers*.[21]

In 2020 a CNBC report on the prepping market estimated its value at $10.5 billion annually, a figure which the Covid lockdowns and the increasing perception of a looming climate emergency, combined with fear of a recurrence of the 2008 financial near-collapse, has almost certainly increased.[22] The fraction spent on fortifications is hard to determine, but to judge from anecdotal evidence it is certainly substantial. For example, another media report spoke of a retired Texas chiropractor who spent over $2 million constructing and outfitting a fortified hideout 300 miles from his Houston home.[23] There are many other examples.

Luxury estates

A different sort of fortified enclave is sometimes called a 'security village', which ranges in form from heavily guarded townhouse complexes in existing urban areas to much larger luxury estates located outside or on the edge of them.[24] Our interest is largely with the latter. An important aspect of such places is that they are purpose-built by private developers and marketed to potential buyers as serving both their high security requirements and their lifestyle preferences in relation to health, education, and entertainment.

In short, they offer residents protection and the promise of a 'normal' or idealized civil life – simpler, more bucolic, and pleasanter. Such blandishments resonate well in larger metropolitan or national contexts where security, normality, and pastoral scenes are generally absent. Some of these enclaves are very large and luxurious, catering to a well-off domestic elite.

Estimates of the number of gated communities in the world are impressionistic, partly because they are hard to define, but also simply because there are so many of them, with the number growing rapidly. According to one current estimate, 17 million people in the United States live in a gated location of one type or another. Scattered evidence from other regions of the world suggests that global growth is on a similar trajectory though less advanced.[25] At any rate, there is no existing good global data set.

There is a relatively small, but not insignificant, number of very expensive and highly guarded luxury estates. A recent article of the five 'most notable' of them listed the Royal Palm Yacht and Country Club outside Boca Raton, Florida; Alphaville outside São Paulo, Brazil; Rosinko outside Moscow; Aamby Valley City outside New Delhi; and Dainfern and Diepsloot outside Johannesburg.[26]

The *Guardian* newspaper provided a list of fifteen, including most of the above, in a pictorial essay, the common theme of which was scenes of luxurious houses separated from otherwise dilapidated nearby neighbourhoods by high walls and sharp pointed fences.[27]

Let us stick for the time being with South Africa, as it provides a particularly useful example. In a suburb of Johannesburg called Dainfern, near the shanty town of Diepsloot, there is a new fully walled 'security village', recently completed at an estimated cost of 12 billion rand (around £600 million).[28] It is more commonly known as Steyn City, after its founder and creator, Douw Steyn, the South-African-born head of BGL Group, a UK-based insurance and financial services company.

Its amenities include a health facility, gyms, bars and restaurants, a school, a large swimmable lagoon with waterslides, a golf course, hiking and mountain bike trails, and a heliport providing quick and safe transport to the city centre or international airport. Apartments and houses range in cost from 2.6 to 35 million rand (roughly £128,000 to £1.75 million). It is clearly a very nice place to live.[29] Steyn himself lives there in a magnificent stately home known as 'Palazzo Steyn', alongside approximately 10,000 other inhabitants.[30]

The city is also remarkably well defended with a four-metre-high perimeter wall and a monumental gatehouse with ten lanes for incoming residents and visitors – all well guarded with boom gates and

7.2 Steyn City
The gatehouse of Steyn City outside Johannesburg combines high security with maximum mobility. Multiple lanes of traffic alleviate the potential bottlenecking of residents attempting to enter or leave its guarded confines.
Source: DBM Architects/Steyn City Properties.

electronic sensors. Biometric access controls operate throughout the city centre and round-the-clock patrols guard the perimeter. There is also a fully equipped 24/7 security nerve centre running surveillance systems equipped with the latest video analytics and manned by full-time security personnel.

In the words of the city's chief executive, its design was an 'antidote to big cities like Johannesburg'.[31] This is both fitting and ironic. 'City air makes one free' were the words carved over the city gates of the Hanseatic League of trading cities in mediaeval Europe, one of which was Krakow, whose barbican gate we have already discussed. The reason was that to be a citizen of a city in possession of its own charter freed one from the rigid feudal system that prevailed in the countryside. In other words, people moved to the city because it was practically the only place a prosperous merchant or craftsman could go to escape the strictures of feudalism. It was also a place to become even more prosperous.

Sovereignty and security

Which brings us back to the multiple functions and contradictions of walls. One function of the walls of the mediaeval city, as noted in previous chapters, was the defence of the urban enclosure against a dangerous world. However, as also noted, in normal times these walls were for the most part allowed to degrade and be encroached upon by other buildings that compromised their combat role. Why?

The answer is that even decrepit walls in military disrepair still adequately performed their secondary role of demarcating a sovereign bargain within a single political space, i.e., differentiating the city from the rest of the country bound by feudalism.

It is not that urbanites in the Middle Ages were necessarily removed from the authority of the sovereign. A 'royal city', such as Westminster, still had obligations to the crown, but its inhabitants also possessed privileges not generally available outside the city.[32] In contemporary discourse this situation is often referred to as 'private urban governance' and is decried as a sinister expression of the commoditization of modern life.[33] I agree, but would suggest it is not a uniquely modern problem.

Once again, we observe a tension between two functions of walls: here security and sovereignty. While in many of the examples given above, walls were built primarily for defence against violence and threats, in other cases – which I call 'sovereignty towns' as opposed to 'security villages' – their primary purpose is to provide a space where, compared with the territory outside, different social norms and to an extent legal regimes may apply.

The expatriate compounds in Saudi Arabia are one long-standing example of this type. In their case the walls provide a kind of cultural prophylactic effect: on the inside residents can enjoy a Western lifestyle without openly transgressing the strict cultural restrictions that prevail on the outside. These gated compounds for foreign workers were first built in the 1970s, when the kingdom began a major building boom. By 2000, there were fifty of them in and around Riyadh alone, housing between 6,000 to 8,000 people. After the Gulf War of 1991–92, and the rise of animus against Western presence, they became more guarded, but that was not the original design.[34]

Another example is increasingly found in China, where gated residential developments are encouraged by the government to allow new economic elites a degree of local autonomy on the inside, while constraining it for the wider polity on the outside. Vanke Garden City in Shanghai, for instance, is surrounded by two-metre-high concrete walls, protected by gates, boasts a force of 280 private security guards, and is equipped with all the best electronic security measures and surveillance systems the Chinese tech industry can provide.[35]

If it is perhaps less guarded than Steyn City, it is no less luxurious. Everything is meticulously clean and well presented. Its 20,000 square metres of amenities include branded retail outlets, restaurants, a boutique hotel, and an art gallery, plus an exquisite 'breathing central courtyard' (i.e., a garden). As one review gushed: 'residents are able to enjoy the spacious lush green courtyard spaces, which can usually only be found outside the city today'.[36] Given the levels of industrial pollution in urban China, breathable air is a powerful signal of exclusivity.

The appeal of the walls and gates of communities like this to wealthy Chinese and to the Chinese state, which still maintains control of land, planning, and provision of services, is that they create an environment that is easier to govern in three ways. First, they reduce the potential of social conflict caused by rapid urbanization. Second, they aid the classification, monitoring, and control of the population through lifestyle segregation. Third, the introduction of privately managed but politically reliable urban self-governance eases the transition to private forms of service provision, alleviating the burden on the state.[37]

In addition, in an echo of mediaeval walled cities which used their defensive infrastructure to quarantine their populations against plague, these gated communities have been integral to China's strict segregation efforts to prevent the spread of Covid-19.

At the beginning of this book I argued that a main feature of this guarded age was the explosion of the fortification industry across every facet of the global political economy. As we have seen, it is not only armies and governments but also private entities – from individual families to neighbourhood associations, large and small property developers, and corporations (on which more later) – who are 'forting up' prolifically and ingeniously for a range of interconnected reasons. Before leaving the subject of private fortified structures, let us look at a final example which is not strictly civil since it is in fact illegal.

Fortified drug houses

The fortification of criminal enterprises is a small but significant part of the story. I focus here on what are known as 'fortified drug houses', which are usually located in urban areas close to the market they supply with illegal narcotics. They are a growing problem for police in many countries, including the United States, where several states have specific laws against them, as well as Britain and Canada, where some of the earliest and most notorious examples are found.

The New Jersey criminal defence legal firm John Marshall helpfully advises its clients that state law N.J.S.A. 2C:35-4.1 forbids the fortification and booby-trapping of drug distribution sites. The law defines the former activity as having occurred when

> building materials, dogs or other means are used to inhibit access to the premises. It is a third-degree crime to fortify a structure that is used for manufacture, distribution of [illegal drugs]. The elements of a fortify offense include (i) a fortified structure that is used for controlled dangerous substance; (ii) the fortification is to prevent, impede, delay or provide warning to entry; (iii) defendant maintained, owned, leased, occupied or controlled the structure; and (iv) defendant acted knowingly.[38]

As an illegal enterprise, it is not easy to get a detailed sense of the scale of criminal fortification. While fortified drug houses are certainly well known to their users, they do not advertise their presence in a community too openly. Rather like some of the counter-terrorism measures we have discussed, they are designed to blend in.

While there are no market surveys to draw upon, there are some relevant numbers. The key one is the value of the global drug trade, which in 2005 the UN estimated to be $320 billion – a gigantic number nearly three times the size of the value of global airport operations that we noted earlier.[39]

If the cost to the narcotics industry of the 'target hardening' of its retail end was just 1 per cent of turnover, then it would amount to a quarter of the value of the global licit access-control industry. Clearly, there is no easy way to know the true cost, and perhaps it is a case of comparing the proverbial apples to oranges. Moreover, most drug dens are rather ad hoc affairs, often the homes of vulnerable tenants taken over by dealers, or just those of particularly accommodating users.[40] It stands to reason, though, that security is a large part of an illegal industry, of which physical site security represents a significant part.

Anecdotally, we know that some of these investments are quite large. For example, during the 1994–2002 'Quebec Biker War' between two outlaw motorcycle gangs – the Hell's Angels and the Rock Machine – over control of the lucrative Ontario and Quebec drug trade, both sides extensively fortified their respective clubhouses and drug dens. In 2017, when one of them in Lennoxville, Quebec was finally torn down, the judge who ordered the demolition described it as a fortress. Given that the conflict involved over eighty bombings, some 130 cases of arson and twenty disappearances, with more than 160 people killed and over 200 injured, it is no surprise that they built so many bunkers.[41]

One of the most well-documented fortified drug houses, known literally as 'The Fortress', operated in Edmonton, Alberta for ten years up until 1993 when it was destroyed by fire and police managed to prevent its reopening. The facility was both criminally and architecturally ingenious. Originally a single rooming house, the windows were expensively replaced with ballistic glass. The front door and frame, as well as the window frames, were structurally reinforced with steel and wood beams. Steel-reinforced concrete walls were placed around the entire main floor.

Such was the strength of 'The Fortress', when police attempted to enter they had to use an oxyacetylene torch and the fire department's hydraulic 'jaws of life'. It was thought that the walls would have stood up to a battering by a D9 bulldozer. Inevitably, by the time the police entered, all evidence of serious crime had been destroyed. Buckets of bleach were kept handy for the disposal of cocaine, for instance. As a result, the arrests made tended to be for low-level crimes, mainly of drug users exiting the place rather than the dealers inside.

The owner of 'The Fortress' had also acquired and fortified the building next door. A four-inch sewer pipe connected the two, making it a simple matter to transfer drugs, money, and other contraband from house to house. A concrete pad between the houses became the home of two German Shepherd dogs. Internally, the fortified complex, which became known as 'Twin Manors', featured a series of doors of a quality surpassing prison cellblocks, operated electronically from the inside. Getting to the area where drugs were stored meant passing through three such barriers. Drug buyers rarely saw drug traffickers because transactions occurred through a steel-drawer system.

Ultimately, the Twin Manors burnt down due to causes unknown. The Edmonton Police Service concluded its report, somewhat incongruously entitled 'A Problem Solved', with the warning that it was 'not so naive to believe that the Fortified Drug House problem has been fixed so can now be forgotten'.[42] The problem certainly has not gone away. In 2020, the UK police reported the arrest of a drug kingpin who had been living in a fortified mansion in Staffordshire.[43]

It is fitting that this episode in the history of the modern fortified drug house, the earliest and best documented I have discovered, should have occurred in Alberta. 'The Fortress' in Edmonton is simply a more recent example of an older fortification in the same province, just over 300 miles south in the town of Lethbridge.

This is the site of Fort Whoop Up, a fortification that deserves to be much better known in the history of the international trade in drugs. By the mid-nineteenth century, there was a thriving trade in buffalo robes between Canadian Blackfoot Indians and independent American fur traders using alcohol as their principal item of trade, which they sold out of a network of approximately forty so-called 'whisky forts'. Built in 1870, thirty-five years before the founding of the province of Alberta itself, Fort Whoop Up was the largest and most successful of them.[44]

The liquor had a devastating effect on Blackfoot society, while the operations of foreign drug runners represented an implicit challenge to Canadian sovereignty. Shutting down the whisky trade, which was accomplished in 1874, was one of the reasons for the creation of the North-West Mounted Police (later the Royal Canadian Mounted Police, or Mounties) the previous year. A reconstruction of the fort is now a tourist attraction.[45]

Strongholds

In *A History of Warfare*, a standard reference on the subject with a substantial section on fortification, John Keegan defines a stronghold as 'a place of not merely safety from attack but also of active defence' from which armed forces might sally forth proactively to fend off attackers and to impose military control on an area. By contrast, a 'refuge' is a place of short-term safety, 'of value only against an enemy who lacks the means to linger in the vicinity'.[46] I think that this is incorrect.

It is true that fortresses are frequently harnessed to very active and offensive strategies. In my view, though, a stronghold is a distinct kind of 'refuge'. Unlike a bastle, which is essentially about the preservation of lives, a 'stronghold' is about the safekeeping of a given society's wealth – or its means of production of wealth, which amounts to much the same thing. It is, I think, the oldest kind of fortification there is and arguably its development constitutes the first strategic act of human civilizations.

To understand this, we need to go back, briefly, to the period discussed earlier in this book, when the first people learned to live by agriculture rather than hunting and foraging and decided to settle in one place. While they had a more stable supply of food, they also became more vulnerable to attacks by the still nomadic peoples amongst whom they lived – people who on account of their hunting lifestyle were probably on average better fighters, and whose meat-based diet made them stronger individually.

Their solution was an enclosed compound, initially a very modest structure, likely a simple ditch and berm construction with a wooden palisade on top, perhaps not even having a gate, but simply overlapping the palisade to create a defensible structure. Undoubtedly, where the natural terrain permitted it, like at Medmenham as previously discussed, these forts would be located on high points, adding height to the ramparts and allowing the inhabitants a longer range of visibility, giving them advance warning of attack. That is the most likely origin of the tens of thousands of hill forts whose traces still dot the Earth. In southern England there is a particularly high density of them.

These original strongholds had certain notable qualities suggestive of their strategic function. Most importantly, they were not particularly good places from which to fight. They simply gave settled people a way to hold out just long enough against a raiding party that, if the defenders were lucky, would be forced to move on as its limited food supplies ran out.

In short, when a raid was detected, these early agriculturalists would pack their tools, their livestock, and their women and children into their palisaded compound and attempt to hold strong until the attackers grew hungry or bored and moved on. No doubt anything outside the walls that could be stolen, eaten or burnt would be, but after the immediate danger had passed the farmers could pick up their tools, go back to their fields, and try to build back what had been lost. It was a miserly strategy but in the long run it worked, as evidenced by the fact that nomadism is now rare and generally occurs only on land useless for agriculture.

Guarding treasure

The point is that so long as a given society was able to preserve its tools – its means of production – it stood a good chance of survival. Thus, I would say, a stronghold is a refuge for things, rather like its semantic neighbour the 'strongbox' – a secure vessel in which you place your most valued treasures. That is why the phrase 'as safe as Fort Knox', where the American gold reserve is stored, was once so popular – and why it now sounds slightly old-fashioned. A stronghold is the structure a society builds around its most precious things.

It follows, then, that you can tell a lot about a society by what it keeps inside its strongest of strongholds. Now let us pick up the thread in southern England where, as just noted, there is a marked density of old hill forts. Specifically, we start with one of the most visible – if prosaic – landmarks in all of southern England, very familiar to anyone who has driven the M40 between London and Oxford.

At the top of a ridge about six miles west of the town of High Wycombe is the Stokenchurch BT Tower. Just under a hundred metres in height and built of reinforced concrete, the tower is topped by four galleries, each festooned with telecommunications gear, primarily now microwave drum antennas.

Built in 1962, it is a concrete tower instead of a more conventional guyed mast because it was designed to resist the pressure of a megaton blast on London, about thirty miles away. In the event of a nuclear war, it was hoped that armoured communications towers like this one would preserve the government's ability to manage the war and, after it, serve as the basis of an improvised civil network.

It is not commonly known that the core of Britain's government communications system, known as 'Backbone', was designed in the 1950s to survive a nuclear attack. The problem, according to a once top-secret General Post Office report, was that the existing cable-based system would simply not survive a nuclear attack because the critical nodes were in the major urban areas most likely to be attacked, and burying them would be insufficient protection.[47]

The solution was to build a north–south nationwide network of radio link towers located away from urban areas. They had to be sturdily built and, because microwave transmission requires line-of-sight between the sender and receiver of a message, located on high points. The result was a series of about twenty 'radio relay stations' located at key points across the country.

By the definition I have suggested, the Stokenchurch BT Tower is a classic stronghold: a fortified strategic complex designed to protect a vital tool of production, in this case the ability to communicate, so that after an attack the survivors can employ it to reconstitute society. It was not designed to be attractive but to be durable, and cheap, hence the use of unembellished reinforced concrete. It is fitting that it is in an area full of Iron Age hill forts.

An even more spectacular example of this type of stronghold may be familiar to American readers. Looming over Thomas St in Manhattan there is a twenty-nine-storey skyscraper known as the 'Long Lines' building, which would look more at home in the dystopic *Judge Dredd* graphic novel series than where it is on the edge of the New York financial district. An entirely windowless structure, it is a brutalist masterpiece – nothing about it resembles a place of human habitation, which is deliberate because it was built to house machines and not people. Built in 1974 to safeguard the delicate electronic infrastructure of the American Telephone & Telegraph Company, it was designed to survive an atomic blast on the city. It performs a similar task still, over forty years later, having been taken over by the computers of the National Security Agency.[48]

The UK's Backbone network of communications towers is also still in use today but does not have the same role in the government and civil communications network, which is much more reliant on the fibre-optic cables necessary to handle the speed and volume of data created by today's internet. The significance of Backbone, as well as of Manhattan's Long Lines machine fortress, is that they point us logically in the direction of what are probably the most heavily guarded and ingeniously fortified strongholds in the world today.

Before we look at these *new* fortresses, however, it is necessary to discuss how the 11 September 2001 attacks represent a seminal moment that led to the building of the super-forts of today.

Data centres

The global financial services firm Cantor Fitzgerald's corporate headquarters and New York City office were once located on the 101st through 105th floors of One World Trade Center, which were approximately two to six floors above the impact point of American Airlines Flight 11. Since all the stairwells above where the plane hit were destroyed or blocked by smoke, fire, or rubble, every Cantor Fitzgerald employee who reported for work that morning was killed.[49] In total, 658 of 960 employees, two-thirds of its New York workforce, were gone in a few moments. For comparison, the Newfoundland Regiment on the first day of the Battle of the Somme in July 1916 lost 300 killed from a total of just over 800. It was a truly devastating blow.

Days later, however, when the financial markets reopened, Cantor Fitzgerald was still in business.

How this happened is, on the one hand, a very human story. In the words of Howard Lutnick, Cantor Fitzgerald's chief executive officer and chairman: 'The survival of the business is due to the London office and their superhuman efforts. It is without question the reason our firm is here today . . . it was entirely on the shoulders of our London office that we survived.'

As a global financial enterprise Cantor Fitzgerald had developed the technique of mirroring its data between its offices located in the financial centres of the world, including London. In this way, trading could be conducted worldwide on an integrated round-the-clock basis with one exchange handing over to another as the day progressed. With enormous effort and skill after its New York headquarters was blown away, the employees in the London office were able to rebuild the company's business because their data had survived.

From the perspective of an insurance actuary – and, after all, practically everything we have talked about is about estimation of risk – the lesson is clear: a large and complex company, squarely at the centre of the emerging 'knowledge economy', could lose a major portion of its human workforce and still keep going – so long as its *computers* kept running.

It is easy to overlook the fact that the business of data security is not entirely about intangible 'computer firewalls', good 'data hygiene', and other software metaphors. The actual hardware must be protected too.

Step forward the fortification industry into a new, massive, and growing market. The annual value of the global data security market was $187.35 billion in 2020, projected to rise to $517.17 billion by 2030 – a compound annual growth rate of 10.5 per cent.[50] Investment in the target hardening of data centres is only a fraction of those numbers – a fraction which is difficult to estimate precisely, but is likely large, because it is clear anecdotally that data centres are heavily guarded.

As a personal example: fifteen years ago when I was writing on cybersecurity, my wife was working for Microsoft and helpfully provided introductions to some of her colleagues; the only time I perceived any reluctance to speak with me at all was when I asked, naively in retrospect, to see the inside of the data centre the company had just built in Ireland. The first of its kind outside of the United States, it is located at Grange Castle Business Park in Clondalkin, about seven miles south of Dublin.[51] There is a mediaeval Grange Castle in Kildare, over thirty miles away, but it has no apparent connection to the business park. The name is simply a fitting coincidence, as the data centre is as secure as a castle.

Around the world today there are hundreds of 'data bunkers' – literally bunkers filled with computer servers – many located in ex-military nuclear bomb shelters. For example, a few miles from the Stokenchurch BT Tower, in the village of Warren Row, Berkshire, there is a formerly secret bunker once designated as part of Britain's civil defence scheme to be the home of a 'regional seat of government' charged with maintaining rudimentary government services after a nuclear apocalypse had obliterated the capital. It was bought in 1998 by a data storage company, though it is now partly or completely home to the nation's strategic reserve of very high-end wine. As I said earlier, you can tell a lot about a society from what it hides in its strongholds.

Abandoned mines and large natural caverns are also in high demand for the same reasons: out of fear of natural disaster, terrorism, and security intrusion, and to reduce the costs of insuring against them, big technology firms seek to locate new data centres beyond the range of easy attack.[52] Sometimes, that means going underground. In Butler County, Pennsylvania, for example, the Iron Mountain data bunker is buried 220 feet below the limestone rock surface in a former mine. Another such facility, InfoBunker, is located fifty feet underground in a former military communications bunker near Des Moines, Iowa.[53]

In Britain, a company known as The Bunker operates two ultra-high-security facilities, one in Sandwich, Kent and the other in Newbury, Berkshire both based in ex-military nuclear shelters. Of the former site, Colo-X, a British brokerage company specializing in data centres, enthuses:

> The entire complex is located underground and was built to withstand a 22-kiloton nuclear blast! Thus, with 3m-thick concrete walls and up to 100 feet underground, the building sits on rubber buffer strips to absorb shocks and each room is Faraday caged, with blast doors in the corridors.[54]

Compiling a complete list of these data fortresses, strongholds for computers, would be impossible, as many of these facilities are secret, that being part of their appeal.

One of the most impressive examples is the Green Mountain complex in Stavanger, Norway, billed as the world's greenest data centre. It is also among the most physically secure, sited in a very high security Cold War munitions bunker with the added protection of a granite mountain on top. Its computers are housed in two-storey concrete buildings distributed in six underground galleries. They are cooled by water from a nearby fjord and powered by their own hydroelectric plant, also underground. Needless to say, the site also has biometric access controls and 'intelligent' video surveillance systems.[55]

The ancient builders of hill forts and palisaded villages packed their strongholds with hand tools, ploughs, seeds, and livestock – everything that they needed to continue functioning as an agricultural society after an attack. The essential infrastructure of the knowledge economies of the information age rests on a foundation of delicate physical stuff – computers, routers, fibre-optic cables, and such like – that needs either to be hidden in plain sight or securely guarded.

We should not be surprised that, except for a handful of military headquarters and *maybe* places like Fort Knox, there are few places more highly secured than the locations housing our communications infrastructure and precious data.

The computers of the Green Mountain fortified strategic complex, so long as there is water and gravity to drive it through the underground turbines, will keep whirring away calculating something or other. It used to be said that the only survivors of a nuclear apocalypse would be the rats and the cockroaches. Perhaps that was too optimistic. It might just be the computers, presumably churning out 'customers who bought these items in your shopping history also enjoyed' messages for consumers long since reduced to ash and dust.

Conclusion

The cost of a piece of ballistic-resistant glass is ten to a hundred times greater than that of an equivalent size of normal glazing, depending on the level of 'bullet-proofing'. Fortifying a shopping mall, the concourse of a big museum, or a university building without diminishing the functionality and aesthetic appeal of the place is very difficult. Aside from the cost of robust materials, it requires the ingenuity of creative designers, who also are not cheap.

When the Titanic Museum in Belfast opened in 2012, the designers who created a building evoking the mighty ship's great prow also took care to add anti-vehicle barriers to its entrance, lest a terrorist crash a truck bomb into it. It cost £100,000 for forty-seven 2.2-tonne concrete counter-terrorism blocks, or CT Blocks, which also serve as seating.[1] Such devices are typical of the guarded spaces of our world today.[2]

Nobody spends such sums without a reason. All the fortification discussed in this book has been considered worth the investment by whoever was writing the cheque. Poor and working-class people build walls studded with glass around their homes, install bars, and strengthen their doors because they genuinely fear home invasion. Rich people build more luxurious fortified compounds because they can afford luxury on top of security.

Corporations fortify their headquarters and store their computer servers in ex-military bunkers and underground caverns on the basis of judgments about the likelihood of attack and potential loss. Likewise, airport operators have turned international travel into an experience of passing through what is, in effect, an armoured funnel. In these cases, it might be said that insurance actuaries and government regulators demand such things, but even so, someone is making a rational calculation of risk.

Similarly, the way that armed forces operate out of fortified encampments also comes down to an assessment of risk. In this case, the matter is not only the financial cost of life and limb, but also a clear understanding on the part of governments of the tenuousness of voters' support for wars of choice overseas. Each soldier lost drains away a little bit more of the finite supply of political good will. In the larger sense, the fortification of an army base guards the emotional effort required to sustain a conflict.[3] It, too, is a calculation.

Is it rational?

I do not wish to argue against the proximate reasons for all these instances of fortifying and hunkering down, be they tactical, political, commercial, or individual. In this conclusion, though, I am compelled to wonder about a deeper cause. In fact, I am not wondering. I think there is a deeper cause, it is just that unlike those other causes I cannot measure it. I can only describe it and explain why I think it is important.

The Windsor Castle Pub, Windsor, November 2022

The Windsor Castle Pub, located just a short walk from its Royal namesake in the town of Windsor, is an ideal place to contemplate the issues raised in this book, and not only because, having started it on the shores of Kandahar's Poo Pond, it feels good to end it at a place somewhat more regal – and with a quality beer to hand. What makes it ideal is that from here you can see the past and present of fortification in one place, and in a surprisingly inverted way that illustrates the counter-intuitiveness of this guarded age.

The castle itself is obviously marvellous. Originally built for William the Conqueror in the eleventh century, it has been the main home of the Royal Family for almost a thousand years. Mostly it is a Victorian and Georgian design built around a mediaeval structure. It is essentially a perfectly preserved piece of mediaeval fortification with various subsequent additions, such as palatial living quarters, a large chapel, and a range of decorative embellishments.

As a fortification, however, all that magnificent stonework is mostly irrelevant today. The King would be just as well guarded in Buckingham Palace, or the Savoy Hotel for that matter. Windsor Castle's main function is as a tourist draw. For many people, the high point of a visit here is the Changing of the Guard, a piece of military pageantry in which colourfully uniformed, mounted and dismounted soldiers perform a parade in the middle of the street for crowds lined thickly along its sides.

What is being guarded here is not so much the castle or the King but that whole tableau – the soldiers themselves as well as the people who have come to watch them. They are guarded by steel-bound barge-shaped concrete barriers that have lined the route of the 'guards' since the 2017 Westminster ramming attack. The problem with these concrete guards is that they are ugly additions to a place that earns its way by being attractive.

The council official in charge of security explained the essence of the matter with a nice clarity:

> We're still looking to come up with the balance of protecting crowded places and making them as aesthetically pleasing as can be. This is about protecting not only the military personnel involved in the Changing [of] the Guard but everyone involved including residents and visitors who come to see and watch. At certain times of the day there are potentially queues of people waiting to gain entry to the Castle queuing down St Albans Street. From a terrorist threat perspective, that is potentially going to be a very crowded place where people could drive up the wrong way. If you look at Park Street now there are a series of concrete bollards linked together that don't look terribly pretty. The final solution won't look as ugly as that. It'll be a lot more sympathetic than that.[4]

Not being a designer, I don't know what the solution to prettying a concrete wall is going to look like – possibly the addition of more Gothic ornamentation. I am sure, however, that eventually the term 'CT Block', or something like it – 'hostile vehicle mitigation system' is too cumbersome – will enter the lexicon of fortification alongside words for older things like portcullis, chamber gate, and murder-hole.

The stated object of this book was to explore the interrelationship of fortification and globalization in the context of what I have characterized as our guarded age. Let us reflect for a moment on what we think of each of these things now that we have come to the end. I shall go in reverse order.

The dominant mood of our age, I think it is fair to say, is anxiety – an acute and widespread apprehension of risk at all levels of society. In the most general sense, among Western states particularly, there is a great fear of being overshadowed, a sense that the burgeoning of connectivity has brought along with it several profound challenges to the status quo that defy easy resolution.[5] When it comes down to it, the West is relatively old and relatively rich – two characteristics that in individuals often lead to guarded behaviour. Indeed, behavioural economists tend to explain this general phenomenon as one dominated by patterns of loss aversion and status quo bias.[6]

I have already spoken a great deal about globalization and its characteristics, most notably its massively networked nature that seems to have interconnected practically everything in an accelerating flow of people, things, and ideas. The point I would draw out now is the quality of that acceleration. It is not just that things are moving fast, it is also that the pace of change is accelerating. The essence of 'future shock' is that individuals and societies find themselves overwhelmed by the perception of too much change happening in too short a time.[7] The natural response, when being battered by such a storm, is to hold on tightly to something solid.

In the study of complex networks, the concept of a 'refractory period' is extremely important. In the human brain, for instance, neurons have a refractory period in which they are unable to fire a nerve impulse. In effect, when a given neuron receives an electrical signal it does not simply respond immediately with a signal of its own, but waits for a time, or for the receipt of more signals, before it fires. Without this refractory period, the complex system would collapse into a chaotic mess, with the result that instead of producing coherent emergent behaviour – purposeful action in the case of a human being – it is paralysed by an electrical storm.[8]

This brings me back to fortification, which reduced to its essence is a movement-slowing machine. Fortresses do not stop things per se; rather, they channel movement, slowing it to a rate that the whole assemblage of components – the fortified strategic complex – can handle. They also do many more things of course, but this quality of slowing down is universal in forts. Perhaps, then, the cause of this Guarded Age, beyond and beneath all the proximate factors driving the investment in this or that piece of fortified architecture, is just a very human unconscious urge to slow things down – to the point that some sort of order might be made of a society which seems otherwise to be on the verge of the equivalent of a paralysing global epileptic fit.

Further Reading

The literature on fortification is very large but has a certain tendency to go to one of two extremes. On the one hand, histories of the subject tend to be sweeping – from prehistory to today – and more descriptive than analytical. On the other hand, studies of specific fortresses or periods typically indulge in a level of detail that would tax a general reader. The works noted below are some which I have found exemplary and especially useful.

The French architect and military engineer E. Viollet-le-Duc's *Annals of a Fortress: Twenty-Two Centuries of Siege Warfare* (1875) is justifiably a classic. The way it traces the rise and fall of European fortifications over two millennia is unique and unusual, brilliantly lucid, and nicely illustrated. The British military engineer Sir George Sydenham Clarke's *Fortification: Its Past Achievements, Recent Developments, and Future Prospects* (1907) is narrower in its focus on the nineteenth century, but looks ahead to the future. Its marked quality lies in the author's attempt to analyse the subject from the perspective of first principles which to my mind are still quite valid.

Of the many historical surveys of fortification, two that stand out are Sidney Toy's *A History of Fortification from 3000 BC to the Present* (1955) and Ian Hogg's *The History of Fortification* (1981). An architect and scholar, Toy's work was obviously informed by a deep personal familiarity with the sites he studied, apparent in his meticulously hand-drawn maps and illustrations. Hogg, a Master Gunner in the Royal Artillery, had a fluency with the subject that is remarkable in its depth and breadth as well as its mastery of technical detail.

The two works on urban studies which I have found to be the most consistently useful are Spiro Kostof's *The City Shaped* (1991) and *The City Assembled* (1992). Both are accessible to the non-specialist, genuinely a pleasure to read, while also being superbly scholarly. Horst de la Croix's *Military Considerations in City Planning: Fortifications* (1972) is a rather short work, at just over a hundred pages (half of that illustrations), and yet its findings are so consistently astutely observed, without jargon, that I also recommend it highly.

More specifically on the matter of war and urban environments, G.J. Ashworth's *War and the City* (1991) is still essentially unsurpassed, although J. Bowyer Bell's *Besieged: Seven Cities Under Siege* (2006) is also extremely worthwhile. However, both are focused almost exclusively on the twentieth century.

Work on contemporary fortification is very rare, which is why I wrote this book. The issues involved are dealt with from a range of disciplinary perspectives and are frequently focused on related topics such as resilience, gated communities, migration, surveillance, crime, urban planning, or global political economy more generally. From a philosophical perspective, the work I have found most inspiring is Paul Hirst's *Space and Power: Politics, War, and Architecture* (2005), which stands out as both imaginative and pragmatic.

Regarding gated communities, the classic work is Edward J. Blakely and Mary Gail Snyder's *Fortress America: Gated Communities in the United States* (1999). The one book, however, which I would recommend above all others is an edited volume by Samer Bagaeen and Ola Uduku, *Gated Communities: Social Sustainability in Contemporary and Historical Gated Developments* (2010). Though a relatively short work, it stands out for broadening the debate beyond the contemporary West to other parts of the world where 'gatedness' is a rather different phenomenon. *City Walls: The Urban Enceinte in Global Perspective* (2000), edited by James D. Tracy, is rather longer and more historical but similarly invaluable.

On the urban geography of security, and specifically the architecture of counter-terrorism, no author has been more consistently prolific and insightful than Jon Coaffee of Warwick University. A recent and excellent example of his work is *Security, Resilience and Planning: Planning's Role in Countering Terrorism* (2020). On the related issue of surveillance, *The Routledge Handbook of Surveillance Studies* (2012), edited by Kirstie Ball, Kevin D. Haggerty, and David Lyon, is also an invaluable resource.

Scholarly work on migration and borders has burgeoned in recent decades, a reflection of the controversiality of walls as barriers to movement in our globalized world. However, neither of the two works that I have found most helpful are academic. David J. Danelo's *The Border: Exploring the US–Mexican Divide* (2008) and Marcello di Cinto's *Walls: Travels Along the Barricades* (2012) are both essentially travelogues which describe, humanely and astutely, the barriers in question as well as the people trying to cross them and those trying to prevent them crossing.

Finally, one of the most valuable resources is the estimable Fortress series published by Osprey, currently standing at 113 volumes, dealing with fortifications ranging from the Japanese Pacific Island Defences of the Second World War to the Kremlin in Moscow. For detail on any given period or style of fortification this series provides an essential and authoritative introduction.

Notes

Introduction

1 Jay Price, 'Surreal Afghanistan Boardwalk Fading into Memory . . .', *Star Tribune*, 17 September 2013, https://www.startribune.com/surreal-afghanistan-boardwalk-fading-into-memory-as-u-s-troops-withdraw/224171091
2 Subcommittee on National Security and Foreign Affairs, Committee on Oversight and Government Reform, U.S. House of Representatives, *Warlord, Inc* (Washington, DC: June 2010).
3 David Betz, 'Communication Breakdown: Strategic Communications and Defeat in Afghanistan', *Orbis*, Vol. 55. No. 4 (2011), pp. 613–30.
4 On the matter of trust and credibility in communications, see Francesca Granelli, 'What Does it Mean for a Communication to be Trusted?', *Defence Strategic Communications*, Vol. 5 (2019), pp. 171–214.
5 Matt Chorley, 'Britain Prepares for its Nightmare Scenario', *Daily Mail*, 30 June 2015, https://www.dailymail.co.uk/news/article-3143410/Police-stage-mock-Tunisia-style-marauding-gun-attack-streets-London-biggest-counter-terror-exercise-prepare-atrocity-British-soil.html
6 Lord Toby Harris, *Independent Review of London's Preparedness to Respond to a Major Terrorist Incident* (October 2016), p. 6, https://www.london.gov.uk/sites/default/files/londons_preparedness_to_respond_to_a_major_terrorist_incident_-_independent_review_oct_2016.pdf
7 David Betz, *Carnage and Connectivity* (London: Hurst, 2015).
8 The Global Terrorism Database hosted by the University of Maryland lists 200,000 attacks in the period 1970–2019, https://www.start.

umd.edu/research-projects/global-terrorism-database-gtd; Lord Toby Harris's update of London's counter-terror readiness has a select list which continues up to the end of 2021 – see *London Prepared: A City-Wide Endeavour* (March 2022), pp. 12–16, https://www.london.gov.uk/sites/default/files/harris_review_-_march_2022_web.pdf

9 Jacques Darras and Daniel Snowman, *Beyond the Tunnel of History* (London: Palgrave, 1990), p. 16.
10 See for example the call to resistance in the conclusion of Stephen Graham's *Cities Under Siege* (London: Verso, 2006).
11 Roy Berkeley, *A Spy's London* (London: Leo Cooper, 1994), p. 385.

Chapter 1

1 Michael Dear, *Why Walls Won't Work* (Oxford: Oxford University Press, 2013), particularly chap. 7, 'Fortress USA'.
2 David Danelo, *The Border* (Mechanicsburg, PA: Stackpole Books, 2008), p. 77.
3 Jeremy Harding, *Border Vigils* (London: Verso, 2012), p. 149; also see Matthew Carr, *Fortress Europe* (London: Hurst, 2012), pp. 2–3.
4 Lahcen Haddad, 'Message from The Morocco/EU Joint Parliamentary Committee on the Assault of the Melilla Fence', *Atalayar*, 29 June 2022, https://atalayar.com/en/blog/message-moroccoeu-joint-parliamentary-committee-assault-melilla-fence
5 Marcello Di Cinto, *Walls* (Fredericton, New Brunswick: Goose Lane, 2012), chap. 3 on Ceuta and Melilla is interesting because, unusually, he covers both sides of the barrier.
6 Kolås, Åshild; Oztig, Lacin ldil, 'From Towers To Walls', *Environment and Planning C, Politics and Space*, Vol. 40, No. 1 (2022), pp. 124–42.
7 David Averre, 'New "Iron Curtain" Descends Across Europe', *Daily Mail*, 18 November 2022, https://www.dailymail.co.uk/news/article-11441901/Poland-Finland-Latvia-construct-huge-barbed-wire-fences-borders-Russia-Belarus.html
8 Dexter Filkins, *The Forever War* (New York: Vintage, 2009).
9 Winston Churchill, 'Sinews of Peace, 1946', Fulton, MO, 5 March 1946, National Churchill Museum, https://www.nationalchurchillmuseum.org/sinews-of-peace-iron-curtain-speech.html
10 Gordon Rottman, *The Berlin Wall and the Intra-German Border, 1961–1989* (Oxford: Osprey, 2008), p. 14.
11 See Frederick Taylor, *The Berlin Wall* (London: Bloomsbury, 2006).
12 See Greg Mitchell, *The Tunnels* (London: Bantam, 2016).
13 'Remarks of President John F. Kennedy at the Rudolph Wilde Platz', Berlin, 26 June 1963, John F. Kennedy Presidential Library, https://

www.jfklibrary.org/archives/other-resources/john-f-kennedy-speeches/berlin-w-germany-rudolph-wilde-platz-19630626
14 W.R. Smyser, *Kennedy and the Berlin Wall* (New York: Rowman and Littlefield, 2010).
15 Ronald Reagan, 'Remarks on East-West Relations at the Brandenburg Gate in West Berlin', West Berlin, 12 June 1987, Ronald Reagan Presidential Library, https://www.reaganlibrary.gov/archives/speech/remarks-east-west-relations-brandenburg-gate-west-berlin
16 'Address by Mikhail Gorbachev to the Council of Europe', Strasbourg, 6 July 1989, National Security Archive, https://nsarchive.gwu.edu/document/28341-document-21-gorbachevs-address-council-europe-strasbourg-july-6-1989
17 See 'Chronicle 1989', *Chronik der Mauer* (undated), https://www.chronik-der-mauer.de/en/chronicle/_year1989/_month11/?month=11&year=1989&opennid=182520&moc=1#anchornid182520?type=galerie&show=image&i=176429
18 The best description of Grenzwall 75 is in Rottman, *The Berlin Wall*, p. 14.
19 'Victims at the Wall', *Chronik der Mauer* (undated), https://www.chronik-der-mauer.de/en/victims/
20 Camilo Montoya-Gomez, 'At Least 853 Migrants Died Crossing the U.S.-Mexico Border in Past 12 Months – A Record High', CBS News, 28 October 2022, https://www.cbsnews.com/news/migrant-deaths-crossing-us-mexico-border-2022-record-high/#:~:text=While%20the%20International%20Organization%20for,land%20crossing%20in%20the%20world.%22
21 Jacques Darras and Daniel Snowman, *Beyond the Tunnel of History* (London: Palgrave, 1990), p. 104.
22 Francis Fukuyama, *The End of History and the Last Man* (New York: the Free Press, 1992), p. 4.
23 'Remarks by Chairman Alan Greenspan at the 15th Annual Monetary Conference of the Cato Institute', Washington, DC, 14 October 1997, https://www.federalreserve.gov/boarddocs/speeches/1997/19971014.htm
24 John Ralston Saul, *The Collapse of Globalism and the Reinvention of the World* (London: Atlantic Books, 2005), p. 93.
25 Mohamed Sidique Khan video, 'London Bomber: Text in Full', BBC News, 1 September 2005, http://news.bbc.co.uk/1/hi/uk/4206800.stm
26 'Tony Blair's Conference Speech 2005', *Guardian*, 27 September 2005, https://www.theguardian.com/uk/2005/sep/27/labourconference.speeches

27 See, for example, Carla O'Dell and Cindy Hubert, *The New Edge in Knowledge* (Hoboken, NJ: John Wiley and Sons, 2011); also Christopher Meyer, *Future Wealth* (Cambridge, MA: Harvard Business Review Press, 2000).
28 See William Owens, *Lifting the Fog of War* (Baltimore: Johns Hopkins University Press, 2000); also David Alberts and Richard Hayes, *Power to the Edge* (Washington, DC: Department of Defence, Command and Control Research Program, 2003), and David Alberts, John Garstka, and Frederick Stein, *Network Centric Warfare* (Washington, DC: Department of Defence, Command and Control Research Program, 2003).
29 Arthur Cebrowski and John Garstka, 'Network Centric Warfare: Its Origin and Future', *US Naval Institute Proceedings*, Vol. 124, No. 1 (1998).
30 Thomas Friedman, *The World is Flat* (New York: Farrar, Straus, and Giroux, 2005).
31 Zygmunt Bauman, *Liquid Modernity* (Cambridge: Polity, 2000).
32 Ibid., p. 11.
33 Ibid., p. 14.
34 Ibid.
35 'A Lifeline Through Germany – The Green Belt', Germany National Tourist Board (undated), https://www.germany.travel/en/nature-outdoor-activities/a-lifeline-through-germany-the-green-belt.html
36 Toby Driver, Barry Burnham, and Jeffrey Davies, 'Roman Wales: Aerial Discoveries and New Observations from the Drought of 2018', *Britannia*, Vol. 51 (2020), pp. 117–45.
37 Paul Kennedy, 'History from the Middle: The Case of the Second World War', *Journal of Military History*, Vol. 74 (2010), p. 36.
38 See Lukas Milevski, 'Liddell Hart's Impact on the Study of Grand Strategy', in Thierry Balzacq and Ronald R. Krebs (eds.), *The Oxford Handbook of Grand Strategy* (Oxford: Oxford University Press, 2021).
39 M.L.R. Smith, 'Explaining Strategic Theory', *Infinity Journal*, Vol. 1, No. 4 (2011).

Chapter 2

1 David Frye, *Walls* (London: Faber and Faber, 2018), p. 235.
2 For an example of the former see Jayne Svenungsson, 'The Ages of History', in *Divining History* (Oxford: Berghahn, 2016), pp. 151–202.
3 Alvin Toffler, *Future Shock* (London: Pan, 1971) and *The Third Wave* (New York: Bantam Books, 1980).

4 Klaus Schwab, *The Fourth Industrial Revolution* (Geneva: World Economic Forum, 2016).
5 Martin Van Creveld, *Technology and War* (New York: Touchstone, 1991).
6 Ronald Kline, *The Cybernetics Moment* (Baltimore: Johns Hopkins University Press, 2015).
7 See Jack Levy and William Thompson, *The Arc of War* (Chicago: Chicago University Press, 2011), p. 3.
8 A point argued convincingly by John Terraine, *White Heat* (London: Book Club Associates, 1982).
9 See David Edgerton, *The Shock of the Old* (London: Profile, 2008).
10 See Robert Hassan, *The Information Society* (Cambridge: Polity, 2008).
11 See Rupert Smith, *The Utility of Force* (London: Allen Lane, 2005).
12 See Joseph Nye, *Soft Power* (New York: Public Affairs, 2004).
13 See Quentin Hughes, *Military Architecture* (London: Hugh Evelyn, 1974), chap. 5; also, Ian Hogg, *Fortress* (New York: St. Martin's Press, 1975), chap. 6.
14 Ian Hogg, *A History of Fortification* (London: Orbis, 1981), p. 194.
15 Paddy Griffith, *Fortifications of the Western Front, 1914–18* (Oxford: Osprey, 2004).
16 Simon Dunstan, *Fort Eben Emael* (Oxford: Osprey, 2005), pp. 33–57.
17 William Allcorn, *The Maginot Line, 1928–45* (Oxford: Osprey, 2003); also Vivian Rowe, *The Great Wall of France* (London: Putnam, 1959).
18 See Clayton Donnell, *The German Fortress of Metz, 1870–1944* (Oxford: Osprey, 2008).
19 Gordon Rottman, *Japanese Pacific Island Defences, 1941–45* (Oxford: Osprey, 2012).
20 Rowe, *The Great Wall of France*, esp. chap. 8.
21 R. Ernest Dupuy and Trevor N. Dupuy, *The Collins Encyclopedia of Military History*, 4th ed. (London: BCA, 1993), p. 1113.
22 Quoted in Brian Bond, *Liddell Hart* (London: Cassell, 1977), p. 177.
23 Quoted in ibid., p. 177.
24 Hogg, *Fortress*, p. 1.
25 S.V. Date, 'If Trump's "Travel Ban" was so Great, Then How Come . . .', *Huffpost*, 25 March 2020, https://www.huffingtonpost.co.uk/entry/trump-coronavirus-china-boast_n_5e7bb1f6c5b6256a7a239550
26 George Sydenham Clarke, *Fortification*, 1st ed. (London: John Murray, 1890), p. iii.
27 Stephen Biddle, *Military Power* (Princeton, NJ: Princeton University Press, 2008), p. 30.

28 Robert Leonhard, *The Art of Maneuver* (New York: Ballantine, 1991), p. 293.
29 Isaiah Berlin, 'Two Concepts of Liberty', in Henry Hardy (ed.), *The Proper Study of Mankind* (London: Pimlico, 1998), p. 237.
30 Douglas Murray, *The War on the West* (London: HarperCollins, 2022).
31 Carl von Clausewitz, *On War*, ed. and trans. Michael Howard and Peter Paret (Princeton, NJ: Princeton University Press, 1976), p. 167.
32 Christopher Coker, *War in an Age of Risk* (Cambridge: Polity, 2009), p. 57.
33 Manuel Castells, *The Information Age, Vol. 3*, 2nd ed. (London: Wiley-Blackwell, 2010), p. 388.

Chapter 3

1 Steven Zaloga, *The Atlantic Wall 1* (Oxford: Osprey, 2007) and *The Atlantic Wall 2* (Oxford: Osprey, 2011).
2 'Forte di Bard: The Monumental Complex' (undated), https://www.fortedibard.it/en/the-monumental-complex/
3 Marcus Cowper, *Cathar Castles* (Oxford: Osprey, 2006).
4 Clayton Donnell, *Maginot Line Gun Turrets and French Gun Turret Development 1880–1940* (Oxford: Osprey, 2017).
5 Anonymous, 'Beyond "Iron Dome"', *Forward*, 7 December 2012, pp. 13 and 17.
6 Jan Breemer, 'The Soviet SSBN Bastions: Why Explanations Matter', *RUSI Journal*, Vol. 134, No. 4 (1989), p. 33.
7 Milad Aslaner, 'Air-Gapped Networks: The Myth and the Reality', *Network Security*, Vol. 2 (2022).
8 Daniel Hughes (ed.), *Moltke On the Art of War* (Novato, CA: Presidio Press, 2009), p. 48.
9 See Andrew Lambert, *The Crimean War* (Farnham: Ashgate, 2011), esp. chap. 13.
10 Wolfgang Petersen and Klaus Doldinger, *Das Boot* (West Germany, 1981).
11 See James Davey, *The Transformation of British Naval Strategy* (Woodbridge: Boydell & Brewer, 2012). For detailed studies of forts see Charles Stephenson, *The Fortifications of Malta, 1530–1945* (Oxford: Osprey, 2004); David Fa, *The Fortifications of Gibraltar, 1068–1945* (Oxford: Osprey, 2013); Terrance McGovern, *Defences of Bermuda 1612–1995* (Oxford: Osprey, 2018); Bill Clements, *Fatal Fortification* (Haverford: Pen and Sword, 2013); and Clarence Stuart Mackinnon, *The Imperial Fortresses of Canada* (Toronto: University of Toronto PhD

Thesis, 1965); also Bill Clements, *Britain's Island Fortresses* (Barnsley: Pen and Sword, 2019).
12 See the introduction of John Man's *The Great Wall* (London: Bantam, 2008).
13 Peter Spring, *Great Walls and Linear Barriers* (Barnsley: Pen and Sword, 2015), p. 7.
14 David Frye, *Walls* (London: Faber and Faber, 2018), pp. 145–59.
15 Bruce Lincoln, *The Conquest of a Continent* (London: Jonathan Cape, 1994); see also the illustrations of an *ostrog* in Basil Dmytryshyn et al. (eds.), *Russia's Conquest of Siberia, 1558–1700* (Portland: Oregon Historical Society, 1985), pp. 22 and 41.
16 Ron Field, *Forts of the American Frontier, 1820–91* (Oxford: Osprey, 2005).
17 Daniel Headrick, *The Tools of Empire* (Oxford: Oxford University Press, 1981).
18 See Dierk Walter, *Colonial Violence* (Oxford: Oxford University Press, 2017).
19 Quoted in Geoffrey Parker, 'The Artillery Fortress as an Engine of Expansion', in James Tracy (ed.), *City Gate* (Cambridge: Cambridge University Press, 2000), p. 397.
20 For more detail, see Martin Elbi, 'Portuguese Urban Fortifications in Morocco: Borrowing, Adaptation, and Innovation along a Military Frontier', in Tracy (ed.), *City Gate*, pp. 349–85.
21 Kimberly Sullivan, 'Morocco's Stunning Coastal Fortress of Essaouira', 19 March 2019, https://kimberlysullivanauthor.com/2019/03/19/moroccos-stunning-coastal-fortress-of-essaouira/
22 'Casa del Mar', *UrbexStalker*, 16 May 2017, https://www.urbexstalker.com/2017/05/16/casa-del-mar/
23 Joseph Adjaye, *Elmina, 'The Little Europe': European Impact and Cultural Resilience* (Accra: Sub-Saharan Publishers, 2018); also Flora Beardy and Robert Coutts, *Voices From Hudson Bay* (Montreal: McGill University Press, 2017).
24 'Fortification and Siegecraft', in Richard Holmes (ed.), *The Oxford Companion to Military History* (Oxford: Oxford University Press, 2001), p. 312.
25 'Fortification', in Franklin D. Margiotta (ed.), *Brassey's Encyclopaedia of Land Forces and Warfare* (London: Brassey's, 1996), p. 395.
26 See Beatrice Heuser, *The Evolution of Strategy* (Cambridge: Cambridge University Press, 2010), p. 82.
27 David Betz, 'Citadels and Marching Forts: How Non-Technological Drivers are Pointing Future Warfare towards Techniques from the

Past', *Scandinavian Journal of Military Studies*, Vol. 2, No. 1 (2019), pp. 30–41.

28 David Betz, 'On Guard: The Contemporary Salience of Military Fortification', *Engelsberg Ideas*, 19 November 2021, https://engelsbergideas.com/essays/on-guard-the-contemporary-salience-of-military-fortification/

29 See Simon Pepper, 'Siege Law, Siege Ritual, and Symbolism in City Walls', in Tracy (ed.), *City Walls*, p. 586.

30 See Paul Johnson, *Castles from the Air* (London: Bloomsbury, 2006), p. 101.

31 O.H. Creighton, *Castles and Landscapes* (Bristol: Equinox, 2002), chap. 3.

32 Philip Warner, *The Mediaeval Castle* (New York: Barnes and Noble, 1971), p. 5.

33 David E. Johnson et al., *The Battle of Sadr City* (Santa Monica, CA: Rand, 2013), p. xxii.

34 A point illustrated well by R.C. Smail in his account of the strategy in *Crusading Warfare, 1097–1193* (Cambridge: Cambridge University Press, 1956), esp. chap. vii.

35 Jeremy Black, *Forts* (Oxford: Osprey for the National Archives, 2018), p. 22.

36 Christopher Gravett, *The Castles of Edward I in Wales, 1277–1307* (Oxford: Osprey, 2007), pp. 10–11. See also for insight on the economics of castle-building: Jurgen Brauer and Hubert Van Tuyll, *Castles, Battles and Bombs* (Chicago: Chicago University Press, 2008), pp. 53–68.

37 See Allcorn, *The Maginot Line, 1928–45*, p. 9; Steven Zaloga, *Defences of the Third Reich, 1941–45* (Oxford: Osprey, 2012), p. 27.

38 Kyle Mizokami, 'Medieval Star Forts Are Surprisingly Alive and Well in North Africa', *Popular Mechanics*, 31 December 2020.

39 Andrea Isfeld and Nigel Shrive, 'Discrete Element Modeling of Stone Masonry Walls with Varying Core Conditions: Prince of Wales Fort Case Study', *International Journal of Architectural Heritage*, Vol. 9, No. 5 (2015), pp. 564–80.

40 Seema Guha, '100 Tigers Killed: Jaffna Fort Siege Ends', *The Times of India*, 14 September 1990, p. 1.

41 'Sri Lanka Fort: Out of the Rubble', *Gulf News*, 4 November 2015, https://gulfnews.com/world/asia/sri-lanka-fort-out-of-the-rubble-1.1613005

42 Rene Chartrand, *The Forts of New France* (Oxford: Osprey, 2010) and *The Forts of New France in Northeast America 1600–1763* (Oxford: Osprey, 2013).

43 Kassim Kone, 'A Southern View on the Tuareg Rebellions in Mali', *African Studies Review*, Vol. 60, No. 1 (2017), pp. 53–75.
44 '15 Iconic Furniture Designs Every Highsnobiety Reader Should Know', Highsnobiety (undated), https://www.highsnobiety.com/p/iconic-furniture-designs/
45 Andy Bounds, 'Camp Bastion Company Sells Defensive Barriers to UK High Street', *Financial Times*, 18 July 2017.
46 *Perimeter Security Market Size, Share & Trends Analysis Report by System 2022–2030*, Grandview Research GVR-2-68038-042-2 (2021), https://www.grandviewresearch.com/industry-analysis/perimeter-security-market
47 'Hesco Wins Trademark Infringement Case', *PRNewswire*, 7 December 2015, https://www.prnewswire.co.uk/news-releases/hesco-wins-trademark-infringement-case-560758401.html
48 'Hesco and Maccaferri Share US Expeditionary Barrier System Contract', *Defence Equipment News*, 4 August 2021, https://www.joint-forces.com/defence-equipment-news/45518-hesco-and-maccaferri-share-us-expeditionary-barrier-system-contract
49 Paul Szoldra, 'The Tragic Story of Outpost Restrepo Sums Up the Whole Afghan War', *Business Insider*, 7 March 2013, https://www.businessinsider.com/outpost-restrepo-2013-3?r=US&IR=T
50 Duncan Campbell, *Roman Legionary Fortresses, 27 BC–AD 378* (Oxford: Osprey, 2006), and *Roman Auxiliary Forts, 27 BC–AD 378* (Oxford: Osprey, 2009).
51 Quoted in Charles Knightly, *Strongholds of the Realm* (London: Thames and Hudson, 1979), p. 71.
52 Nick Turse, 'The 700 Military Bases of Afghanistan', *Global Policy Forum*, 10 February 2010, https://archive.globalpolicy.org/us-military-expansion-and-intervention/afghanistan/48737-the-700-military-bases-of-afghanistan.html
53 Terry McCarthy, 'In Mud Fort, Marines Handle "Dust Up" with Afghan Locals', CBS News, 17 August 2010, https://www.cbsnews.com/news/in-mud-fort-marines-handle-dust-up-with-afghan-locals/
54 Technical data and a video of the Balpro system may be seen on the company's website: http://www.kenno-shield.com/balpro/force-protection-balpro-products/
55 Julian O'Neill, 'PSNI Review Recommends Crossmaglen Station Closure', BBC News, 31 August 2021, https://www.bbc.co.uk/news/uk-northern-ireland-58388328
56 Kali Rubaii, '"Concrete Soldiers": T-walls and Coercive Landscaping

in Iraq', *International Journal of Middle East Studies*, Vol. 54 (2022), pp. 357–62.
57 The Erasmus Living Learning Community of 2019–2020, 'Belfast and its Peace Walls', *Peace Review*, Vol. 32, No. 2, (2020), pp. 198–203.
58 Mark de Rond, *Doctors at War* (Ithaca, NY: Cornell University Press, 2017), p. xii.
59 See the description of his mother's early life in a canton in the memoirs of Kenneth Bradley, *Once a District Officer* (London: Macmillan, 1966), p. 18.
60 As noted by Todd Greentree in 'What went Wrong in Afghanistan?', *Parameters*, Vol. 51, No. 4 (2021), p. 16.
61 See 'An Army Wife Experience of Living in an Army Cantonment', *Girl and World*, 24 April 2018, https://girlandworld.com/2018/04/24/an-army-wife-experience-of-living-in-an-army-cantonment/
62 Thomas Gibbons-Neff, 'At Empty Bases, Echoes of War', *New York Times*, 28 May 2021, https://www.nytimes.com/2021/05/28/insider/leaving-afghan-bases.html
63 Yasid El Rifai et al., 'Tegart's Modern Legacy: The Reproduction of Power, a Timeless Paradox', *Jerusalem Quarterly*, No. 69 (Spring 2017), pp. 78–86.
64 United Nations Procurement Division, 'Hesco' search page, https://www.un.org/Depts/ptd/search/node/HESCO
65 See 'Safe Havens for UNHCR' (undated) on the Hesco website, https://www.hesco.com/explore/news/safe-havens-for-unhcr/
66 'Security Forces Successfully Overcome Terrorism, Border Fencing: Report', *Dunya News*, 26 August 2021, https://dunyanews.tv/en/Pakistan/616813-Security-forces-successfully-overcome-terrorism-border-fencing-report
67 'Pakistan Completes Majority of Afghan Border Fence', *Unipath*, 4 January 2021, https://unipath-magazine.com/pakistan-completes-majority-of-afghan-border-fence/; also '500 km Long Trench Dug at Pak-Afghan Border', Such TV, 22 June 2016, https://www.suchtv.pk/pakistan/general/item/39883-500km-long-trench-dug-at-pak-afghan-border.html
68 Robert Birsel, 'Pakistani Forces Say Determined to Seal Afghan Border', *Reuters*, 18 February 2007, https://www.reuters.com/article/uk-pakistan-border-idUKISL33435520070218
69 See the introductory discussion of Roman frontiers in Philip Parker, *The Empire Stops Here* (London: Pimlico, 2010), pp. 1–14, and David J.

Breeze, *The Frontiers of Imperial Rome* (Barnsley: Pen and Sword, 2011), esp. chap. 3.
70 'Western Sahara: The Wall That Nobody Talks About', *South World*, 1 November 2019, https://www.southworld.net/western-sahara-the-wall-that-nobody-talks-about/
71 Shelly Walia, 'The India-Pakistan Border Is So Closely Guarded That It Can Be Seen from Space', *Quartz*, 6 October 2015, https://qz.com/india/516864/the-india-pakistan-border-is-so-closely-guarded-that-it-can-be-seen-from-space
72 'Border Walls to Go Up between India, Pakistan, Bangladesh and Afghanistan', *Global Construction Review*, 30 March 2017, https://www.globalconstructionreview.com/border-walls-go-betw7een-ind7ia-pakis7tan/
73 Andrew Lisa, '30 Border Walls around the World Today', *Stacker*, 31 January 2019, https://stacker.com/stories/2451/30-border-walls-around-world-today
74 'DA Shocked by Amount of People Illegally Crossing into SA', *Lowvelder*, 21 January 2019, https://lowvelder.co.za/645289/da-shocked-by-porous-border-2
75 Patrick Vidija, 'Kenya Suspends Construction of Somalia Border Wall to Ease Tensions', *The Star*, 31 March 2018, https://www.the-star.co.ke/news/2018-03-31-kenya-suspends-construction-of-somalia-border-wall-to-ease-tensions/
76 'Ukraine-Russia Border Fence/European Bulwark', *Global Security* (undated), https://www.globalsecurity.org/military/world/ukraine/border-fence.htm
77 Kyle Mizokami, 'Why the Korean DMZ Would Be One of the Deadliest Battlegrounds Ever', *The National Interest*, 22 November 2017, https://nationalinterest.org/blog/the-buzz/why-the-korean-dmz-would-be-one-the-deadliest-battlegrounds-23337
78 'Turkey-Syria Wall', *Global Security* (undated), https://www.globalsecurity.org/military/world/europe/tu-syria-wall.htm
79 See 'MoDA – Turaif-Hafar al-Batin Border Wall Development – Saudi Arabia', *GlobalData*, 10 July 2017, https://www.globaldata.com/store/report/moda-turaif-hafar-al-batin-border-wall-development-saudi-arabia/
80 'Spanish Toehold in Africa "Under Siege" by Morocco', *The Times*, 17 March 2020, https://www.thetimes.co.uk/article/spain-s-african-outposts-under-siege-from-hostile-neighbours-pvr92bl6b
81 In fact, this is fundamentally the take of most extant scholarship. As an example, see Reece Jones, *Violent Borders* (London: Verso, 2016).

82 Ian Hogg, *Fortress* (New York: St. Martin's Press, 1975), p. 110.
83 Norman Stone, *The First World War* (London: Penguin, 2007), p. 38.
84 Gregory Poling, 'The Conventional Wisdom on China's Island Bases Is Dangerously Wrong', *War on the Rocks*, 10 January 2020, https://warontherocks.com/2020/01/the-conventional-wisdom-on-chinas-island-bases-is-dangerously-wrong/
85 Hanna Beech, 'China's Sea Control Is a Done Deal, "Short of War With the U.S."', *New York Times*, 20 September 2018, https://www.nytimes.com/2018/09/20/world/asia/south-china-sea-navy.html
86 'Col. Dr. David Johnson: "It's a Grinding War of Attrition, and We Need to Give Them the Means to Stay in the Fight"', *Georgia Today*, 9 June 2022, https://georgiatoday.ge/col-dr-david-johnson-its-a-grinding-war-of-attrition-and-we-need-to-give-them-the-means-to-stay-in-the-fight/

Chapter 4

1 See Ruth Whitehouse, *The First Cities* (Oxford: Phaidon, 1977) and Lewis Mumford, *The City in History* (London: Harvest, 1961), chaps. 1 and 2.
2 E. Viollet-Le-Duc, *Annals of a Fortress* (London: Greenhill Books, 2000), p. xii.
3 See Lawrence Keeley, *War Before Civilisation* (Oxford: Oxford University Press, 1996), chap. 2; and Azar Gat, *War in Human Civilisation* (Oxford: Oxford University Press, 2006), pp. 165–75.
4 Two good overviews of siege technology and techniques over time are William Seymour, *Great Sieges of History* (London: Brassey's, 1991) and Reginald Hargreaves, *The Enemy at the Gate* (London: Macdonald and Co., 1948).
5 Carola Vogel, *The Fortifications of Ancient Egypt, 3000–1780 BC* (Oxford: Osprey, 2010), pp. 17–18.
6 Horst De La Croix, *Military Considerations in Urban Planning* (New York: George Braziller, 1972), pp. 15–16.
7 See Gat, *War in Human Civilisation*, esp. part II.
8 Stephen Turnbull, *The Walls of Constantinople, AD 324–1453* (Oxford: Osprey, 2004).
9 Nic Fields, *Ancient Greek Fortifications, 500–300 BC* (Oxford: Osprey, 2006).
10 J.E. and H.W. Kaufmann, *Castrum to Castle* (Barnsley: Pen and Sword, 2018), p. 48.
11 See Victor Vion Hagen, *The Roads that Led to Rome* (London: Weidenfeld and Nicolson, 1967).

12 'Ancient Gate May Unlock New Clues about Jericho', *New York Times*, 28 November 1998, https://www.nytimes.com/1998/11/28/world/ancient-gate-may-unlock-new-clues-about-jericho.html
13 See Ivy A. Corfis and Michael Wolfe, *The Medieval City under Siege* (Woodbridge: Boydell Press, 1995).
14 Spiro Kostof, *The City Assembled* (London: Bulfinch Press, 1992), p. 30.
15 Philip Warner, *Sieges of the Middle Ages* (London: G. Bell & Sons, 1968).
16 See Clifford J. Rogers, *The Military Revolution Debate* (Boulder, CO: Westview, 1995), particularly the chapter by Geoffrey Parker, 'In Defence of the Military Revolution'; also, Geoffrey Parker, *The Military Revolution* (Cambridge: Cambridge University Press, 1988).
17 Christopher Duffy, *Siege Warfare* (London: Routledge, 1979), chap. 1.
18 J.R. Hale, *Renaissance Fortification: Art or Engineering?* (London: Thames & Hudson, 1977).
19 Martha Pollak, 'Representations of the City in Siege Views of the Seventeenth Century: The War of Military Images and their Production', in James D. Tracy (ed.), *City Walls* (Cambridge: Cambridge University Press, 2000), pp. 605–46.
20 For details see Christopher Duffy, *The Fortress in the Age of Vauban and Frederick the Great, 1660–1789* (London: Routledge, 1985), esp. chap. 1 on 'The Apogee of Old Fortress Warfare'.
21 De La Croix, *Military Considerations in Urban Planning*, pp. 54–5.
22 Spiro Kostof, *The City Shaped* (London: Thames & Hudson, 1991), p. 162.
23 Ibid.
24 See Allan Braham, *Architecture of the French Enlightenment* (London: Thames and Hudson, 1980), chap. 14.
25 George Sydenham Clarke, *Fortification* (London: Beaufort, 1990 [1907 reprint]), p. 57.
26 See Walter Benjamin, *The Arcades Project* (Cambridge, MA: Harvard University Press, 2002), p. 23.
27 Paul Hirst, *Space and Power* (Cambridge: Polity, 2005), p. 120; also, Frank Jellinek, *The Paris Commune of 1871* (New York: Grosset and Dunlap, 1965).
28 Clayton Donnell, *The German Fortress of Metz, 1870–1944* (Oxford: Osprey, 2008); *The Forts of the Meuse in World War One* (Oxford: Osprey, 2007); and *The Fortifications of Verdun, 1874–1917* (Oxford: Osprey, 2011).
29 Stanley Baldwin, Remarks to the House of Commons, Hansard, 10 November 1932, para. 632.

30 *United States Strategic Bombing Survey, Summary Report (European War)* (Washington, DC: GPO, 1945), p. 36, and Kenneth Hewitt, 'Place Annihilation: Area Bombing and the Fate of Urban Places', *Annals of the Association of American Geographers*, Vol. 73, No. 2 (1983), pp. 257–84.
31 Alexander de Seversky, *Victory Through Air Power* (New York: Simon and Schuster, 1942), p. 327.
32 Peter Laurie, *Beneath the City Streets* (London: Granada, 1970), p. 182.
33 Andy Emerson and Kick Catford, 'Kingsway Telephone Exchange', *Subterranea Britannica*, 25 February 2008, https://www.subbrit.org.uk/sites/kingsway-telephone-exchange/
34 The last serious research on it was done by the journalist Duncan Campbell, *War Plan UK* (London: Paladin Books, 1983), chap. 8.
35 See Paul Dobraszczyk, Carlos Lopez Galviz, and Bradley Garrett (eds.), *Global Undergrounds* (London: Reaktion Books, 2016), pp. 161–3.
36 John Last, 'What Happened to Europe's Public Bunkers?', *Foreign Policy*, 8 May 2022, https://foreignpolicy.com/2022/05/08/europe-public-bunkers-nuclear-war-russia-ukraine-civil-defense/
37 Steven Zaloga, *Defence of the Third Reich, 1941–45* (Oxford: Osprey, 2012).
38 J. Bowyer Bell, *Besieged* (London: Transaction, 2006 [1966]).
39 On such fortifications see Ian Grant and Nicholas Madden, *The Countryside at War* (London: Jupiter, 1975).
40 Ryan Lavelle, *Fortifications in Wessex, c. 800–1066* (Oxford: Osprey, 2003).
41 Hirst, *Space and Power*, p. 121.
42 G.J. Ashworth, *War and the City* (Abingdon: Routledge, 1991), esp. chap. 5, 'The City as Battle Terrain'.
43 Paul Bracken, 'Urban Sprawl as Active Defence Variable', in Reiner Huber et al. (eds.), *Military Strategy and Tactics* (New York: Springer, 1974), pp. 219–32.
44 Weapons effects upon structures are covered in some detail in military doctrine such as *UK Operations in the Urban Environment*, Doctrine Note 15/13 (Warminster: Headquarters Field Army, Land Warfare Development Centre, 2019). The International Committee of the Red Cross has also published a great deal of useful material, such as *Reducing Civilian Harm in Urban Warfare* (Geneva: International Committee of the Red Cross, 2021).
45 See 'Explosive Weapons in Populated Areas', International Committee of the Red Cross, https://www.icrc.org/en/explosive-weapons-populated-areas

46 *Urban Tactical Handbook* (Warminster: Headquarters UK Field Army, Land Warfare Development Centre, 2019).
47 John Antal and Bradley Gericke (eds.), *City Fights from World War II to Vietnam* (New York: Ballantine, 2003).
48 Martin Coward, *Urbicide* (Abingdon: Routledge, 2009).
49 Jean Edward Smith, *The Liberation of Paris* (New York: Simon and Schuster, 2019).
50 'Major Describes Moves', *New York Times*, 8 February 1968, p. 14.
51 Lawrence J. Vale and Thomas J. Campanella (eds.), *The Resilient City* (Oxford: Oxford University Press, 2005).
52 See Jasper Goldman, 'Warsaw: Reconstruction as Propaganda', in ibid., pp. 135–58.
53 Nathan Vanderklippe, 'Seoul, a Fortress City Built to Repel Invaders', *The Globe and Mail*, 6 November 2017, https://www.theglobeandmail.com/news/world/seoul-a-fortress-city-built-to-repelinvaders/article36850906/
54 Ian Slesinger, 'A Strange Sky: Security Atmospheres and the Technological Management of Geopolitical Conflict in the Case of Israel's Iron Dome', *The Geographical Journal*, Vol. 188, No. 3 (2022), p. 432.

Chapter 5

1 Peter Marcuse, 'Walls of Fear and Walls of Support', in Nan Ellin (ed.), *Architecture of Fear* (New York: Princeton Architectural Press, 1997), p. 104.
2 See Michael Batty, *The New Science of Cities* (London: The MIT Press, 2013).
3 Paul Virilio, *Speed and Politics*, trans. Mark Polizzotti (Los Angeles: Semiotext(e), 2007).
4 London is credited as a 'global city'. See Mark Abrahamson, *Global Cities* (Oxford: Oxford University Press, 2004).
5 *National Security Strategy and Strategic Defence and Security Review 2015* (London: HM Government, 2015).
6 Eelke M. Heemskerk et al., 'Where Is the Global Corporate Elite? A Large-Scale Network Study of Local and Nonlocal Interlocking Directorates', *Sociologica*, Vol. X, No. 2 (2016), pp. 1–31.
7 'Global Cities: Divergent Prospects and New Imperatives in the Global Recovery', *Kearney Global Cities Report 2021*, https://www.kearney.com/global-cities/2021
8 Lewis Mumford, *The City in History* (London: Harvest, 1961), p. 5.
9 See Lars Lessup, *The Continuous City* (Zurich: Park Books, 2017), p. 5.

10 Nigel Penninck and Paul Devereux, *Lines on the Landscape* (London: Robert Hale, 1989), pp. 152–3.
11 See Harold P. Clunn, *The Face of London*, Revised ed. (London: Spring Books, 1946), pp. 97–101.
12 See City of Westminster, 'Plans Underway for a New Reimagined Strand Aldwych', 8 September 2021, https://www.westminster.gov.uk/news/plans-underway-new-reimagined-strand-aldwych
13 Lewis Mumford, *The Culture of Cities* (London: Secker and Warburg, 1938), p. 492.
14 The phrase 'machine for living' is from Le Corbusier's *Towards a New Architecture*, trans. Frederick Etchells (New York: Dover Books, 1986). The concept of the city as a crucible of culture is drawn from Peter Hall, *Cities in Civilization* (London: Weidenfeld and Nicolson, 1998).
15 Spiro Kostof, *The City Assembled* (London: Bulfinch, 1992), p. 37.
16 See 'RhinoGuard 75/40 Protective Bollard' (undated) on the Marshalls website: https://www.marshalls.co.uk/commercial/product/rhinoguard-75-40-protective-bollard
17 See the Centre for the Protection of National Infrastructure, https://www.cpni.gov.uk/
18 See Lawrence H. Keeley, Marisa Fontana, and Russell Quick, 'Baffles and Bastions: The Universal Features of Fortifications', *Journal of Archaeological Research*, Vol. 15, No. 1 (2007), pp. 55–95.
19 'Nice Attack: At Least 84 Killed by Lorry at Bastille Day Celebrations', BBC News, 15 July 2016, https://www.bbc.co.uk/news/world-europe-36800730
20 'Berlin Lorry Attack: What We Know', BBC News, 24 December 2016, https://www.bbc.co.uk/news/world-europe-38377428
21 'Westminster Attack: What Happened', BBC News, 7 April 2017, https://www.bbc.co.uk/news/uk-39355108
22 See Transport for London, 'Protecting London's Bridges' (undated), https://tfl.gov.uk/corporate/safety-and-security/protecting-london-s-bridges?intcmp=58622
23 'Washington Monument Grounds', Olin Studio (undated), https://www.theolinstudio.com/washington-monument-grounds
24 See Vasilis Karlos and George Solomos, *Calculation of Blast Loads for Application to Structural Components* (Ispra: European Commission Joint Research Centre, Institute for the Protection and Security of the Citizen, 2013), https://core.ac.uk/download/pdf/38628317.pdf and *Explosive Weapon Effects* (Geneva: Geneva International Centre for Humanitarian Demining, 2017), https://www.gichd.org/fileadmin/GICHD-resources/rec-documents/Explosive_weapon_effects_web.pdf

25 See Christopher Beanland, *Concrete Concept* (London: Francis Lincoln, 2016), p. 162.
26 'Admiralty Citadel: The Bomb-Proof Bunker in the Heart of London', *Living London History*, 25 March 2021, https://livinglondonhistory.com/admiralty-citadel-the-bomb-proof-bunker-in-the-heart-of-london/
27 Committee on Feasibility of Applying Blast-Mitigating Technologies and Design Methodologies from Military Facilities to Civilian Buildings, *Protecting Buildings from Bomb Damage* (Washington, DC: National Academy Press, 1995), p. 55.
28 Doris Hollander, 'Nairobi Bomb Blast – Trauma and Recovery', *Tropical Doctor*, Vol. 30 (2000), p. 47.
29 Prudence Bushnell, *Terrorism, Betrayal, and Resilience* (Lincoln, NE: Potomac Books, 2018), p. 15.
30 C.A. Biancolini et al., 'Argentine Jewish Community Institution Bomb Explosion', *Journal of Trauma and Acute Care Surgery*, Vol. 47, No. 4 (1999), pp. 728–32.
31 For a sense of what blast feels like, see Christine M. Dang et al., 'Survivor Narratives of the Oklahoma City Bombing: The Story Over Time', *Journal of Contingencies and Crisis Management*, Vol. 30, No. 1 (2022), pp. 102–11.
32 American Institute of Architects, 'Effects of Bomb Blasts', in *Security Planning and Design* (Hoboken, NJ: John Wiley & Sons, 2004), p. 29.
33 See 'House Prices: How Much Does One Square Metre Cost in Your Area?', *Office of National Statistics*, 11 October 2017, https://www.ons.gov.uk/peoplepopulationandcommunity/housing/articles/housepriceshowmuchdoesonesquaremetrecostinyourarea/2017-10-11
34 See Edward Roberts, 'What is PAS 68? The Definitive Guide to PAS 68', *ATG Access*, 14 December 2020, https://www.atgaccess.com/news/guides/what-is-pas-68
35 Alex Wilner and Andreas Wegner (eds.), *Deterrence by Denial* (Amherst, NY: Cambria Press, 2001), p. 2.
36 See UK National Counter Terrorism Security Office, *Working with Counter Terrorism Security Advisers* (30 July 2020), https://www.gov.uk/government/publications/counter-terrorism-support-for-businesses-and-communities/working-with-counter-terrorism-security-advisers
37 Hannah Neary, 'The Strand Could Change Forever as Council Plans to "Splurge" £32 Million on Car-Free Zone', *My London News*, 13 October 2021, https://www.mylondon.news/news/west-london-news/strand-could-change-forever-council-21843529
38 The canteen of the Ministry of Truth where Winston Smith works is supposed to be based on one which used to be in Bush House, just

down the street from St Clement Danes, now in the use of King's College London after many years' service as the home of the BBC World Service.
39 The most important figure in this literature is Jon Coaffee, who has written voluminously on the topic in, for example, 'Rings of Steel, Rings of Concrete, and Rings of Confidence: Designing Out Terrorism in Central London Pre and Post 9/11', *International Journal of Urban and Regional Research*, Vol. 28, No. 1 (2004), pp. 201–11; *Terrorism, Risk and the Global City: Towards Urban Resilience* (Farnham: Ashgate, 2009), and (with Peter Fussey), 'Constructing Resilience through Security and Surveillance: The Practices and Tensions of Security-Driven Resilience', *Security Dialogue*, Vol. 46, No. 1 (2015), pp. 86–105.
40 Kenneth Short, *The Dynamite War* (Dublin: Gill and Macmillan, 1979).
41 The Greenwich bombing may, some suggest, have been a false flag attack. See Nic Panagopulos, 'False Flag at Greenwich: "Bourdin's Folly", the Nicoll Pamphlet, and *The Secret Agent*', *Conradiana*, Vol. 48, No. 1 (2016), pp. 1–24.
42 Rebecca Walker, 'Deeds, Not Words: The Suffragettes and Early Terrorism in the City of London', *The London Journal*, Vol. 45, No. 1 (2020), pp. 53–64.
43 Paul Rogers, 'Britain's Choice: The Provisional IRA Then, ISIS Now', *openDemocracy*, 23 June 2017, https://www.opendemocracy.net/en/britains-security-choice-pira-then-isis-now/
44 George Legg, 'Security Experiments: London, Belfast, and the Ring of Steel', *Divided Society – Northern Ireland 1990–1998*, https://www.dividedsociety.org/essays/security-experiments-london-belfast-and-ring-steel
45 A map of the extent of Belfast's Ring of Steel may be found in Stephen Brown, 'Central Belfast's Security Segment: An Urban Phenomenon', *Area*, Vol. 17, No. 1 (1985), pp. 1–9.
46 To use the arresting description of Neil Jarman in 'Intersecting Belfast', in Barbara Bender (ed.), *Landscape: Politics and Perspectives* (Providence: Berg, 1993), p. 115.
47 Antony A. Thompson's *Big Brother in Britain Today* (London: Michael Joseph, 1970) is depressingly accurate in its apprehensions about where things were headed. The surprising thing is how many of the basic elements of the surveillance state were in place fifty years ago. What was missing was the connections between systems and the computing power required to automate their functions.
48 Thompson, *Big Brother*, p. 190. The Road Research Laboratory was

privatised in 1996 but lives on as the Transport Research Laboratory, doing much the same research on traffic management, automation, and electronic infrastructure for roads. See https://trl.co.uk/

49 See 'History of ANPR', ANPR International (undated), http://www.anpr-international.com/history-of-anpr/

50 See 'Automated Number Plate Recognition', National Police Chiefs' Council (undated), https://www.police.uk/advice/advice-and-information/rs/road-safety/automatic-number-plate-recognition-anpr/#:~:text=At%20present%20ANPR%20cameras%20nationally%2C%20submit%20on%20average,similar%20data%20from%20other%20forces%20for%20one%20year

51 Thomas Brewster, 'London Police Just Turned on Facial Recognition in One of the World's Busiest Shopping Districts', *Forbes*, 20 February 2020, https://www.forbes.com/sites/thomasbrewster/2020/02/20/london-police-just-turned-on-facial-recognition-in-one-of-the-worlds-busiest-shopping-districts/

52 See 'NATO Demonstrates New Technology for Crowded Venues', *Counter Terror Business*, 26 May 2022.

53 Nina Franz, 'Targeted Killing and Pattern of Life Analysis: Weaponised Media', *Media, Culture, and Society*, Vol. 39, No. 1 (October 2016), pp. 111–21.

54 'The Critic – We have more surveillance today than any country of any political persuasion has had in history', *Big Brother Watch*, 10 September 2020, https://bigbrotherwatch.org.uk/2020/09/the-critic-we-have-more-surveillance-today-than-any-country-of-any-political-persuasion-has-in-history/

55 From an interview with Rishi Lodhia, Managing Director, Eagle Eye Networks, 'Revolutionising Surveillance', *Security Buyer*, May 2022, p. 25.

56 *Information Commissioner's Opinion: The Use of Live Facial Recognition Technology in Public Places*, UK Information Commissioners Office, 18 June 2021, https://ico.org.uk/media/2619985/ico-opinion-the-use-of-lfr-in-public-places-20210618.pdf

57 'Video Analytics Market Growth, Trends, COVID-19 Impact, and Forecasts (2022–2027)', *Mordor Intelligence Report* (2021), https://www.mordorintelligence.com/industry-reports/video-analytics-market

58 Anna Minton, *Ground Control* (London: Penguin, 2009).

59 'Choosing the Right Facial Recognition Solution for Access Control', *Thales Group White Paper* (January 2022), https://www.ifsecglobal.com/resources/whitepaper-choosing-the-right-facial-recognition-solution-for-access-control/; see also Debbie Howlett, 'Embracing Innovation

to Address the Changing Security Landscape', *City Security Magazine*, Autumn 2021, p. 15.
60 David Lyon, *Surveillance as Social Sorting* (London: Routledge, 2003), p. 13.
61 KCL's access-control system is featured as a case study on the Gallagher website: https://security.gallagher.com/en-GB/Case-Studies/Kings-College-London
62 Steve Bell, 'Protecting Layer by Layer', *International Security Journal*, No. 30 (2022), p. 53.
63 See Sun Tzu, *The Art of War*, in *Classics of Strategy and Counsel, Vol. 1* (Boston: Shambhala Publications, 2000), particularly chapter 5 in which he talks of the combination of the direct and the indirect forces in war.
64 Gilles Deleuze, 'Postscript on the Societies of Control', *October*, Vol. 59 (1992), p. 3–7.
65 See 'Tech Dispatch #1/2021 – Facial Emotion Recognition', European Data Protection Supervisor, 26 May 2021, https://edps.europa.eu/data-protection/our-work/publications/techdispatch/techdispatch-12021-facial-emotion-recognition_de
66 Alex Buckle, 'More than Meets the Eye', *International Security Journal*, No. 34 (2022), p. 61.
67 See Kevin D. Haggerty and Richard V. Ericson, 'The Surveillant Assemblage', *British Journal of Sociology*, Vol. 51, No. 4 (2000), pp. 606–22.
68 Max Weber, *The Protestant Ethic and the Spirit of Capitalism* (London: Routledge, 2001 [1930]), p. 123.
69 The concept was applied by Michel Foucault as paradigmatic of what he considered a new model of power. This idea, in turn, is the starting point for the emerging field of surveillance studies. See, respectively, Michel Foucault, *Discipline and Punish: The Birth of the Prison* (New York: Vintage Books, 1977) and Kirstie Ball, Kevin D. Haggerty, and David Lyon (eds.), *Routledge Handbook of Surveillance Studies* (London: Routledge, 2012).
70 See 'Ideal City' in Martin Moffett, Michael Fazio, and Lawrence Wodehouse, *A World History of Architecture* (London: Lawrence King, 2003), p. 308.
71 *Working Together to Protect Crowded Places* (London: Home Office, 2009), https://www.gov.uk/government/publications/crowded-places-guidance, was withdrawn in May 2022. *Crowded Places: The Planning System and Counter-terrorism* (London: Home Office, 2012), https://assets.publishing.service.gov.uk/government/uploads/system/uploads

/attachment_data/file/375208/Crowded_Places-Planning_System-Jan_2012.pdf, is still in use, as is *Protecting Crowded Places: Design and Technical Issues* (London: Home Office, 2012), https://assets.publishing.service.gov.uk/government/uploads/system/uploads/attachment_data/file/97992/design-tech-issues.pdf. As of May 2022 the UK Home Office has consolidated most of its counter-terrorism guidance on a central hub called ProtectUK: https://www.protectuk.police.uk/

72 See, for instance, the UK Police Service 'Secure by Design' website https://www.securedbydesign.com/ The best academic treatment is Jon Coaffee's *Security, Resilience, and Planning* (London: Lund Humphries, 2020).

73 Oscar Newman, *Defensible Space* (New York: Macmillan, 1973), p. 3.

74 Quoted in 'Duty of Protection', *Security Buyer*, May 2022, p. 38.

75 David Harvey, *Rebel Cities* (London: Verso, 2013), p. 15.

76 Marcello Balbo, 'Urban Planning and the Fragmented City of Developing Countries', *Third World Planning Review*, Vol. 15, No. 1 (1993), p. 25.

77 Mike Davis, *City of Quartz* (London: Verso, 2006), p. 224.

Chapter 6

1 Spiro Kostof, *The City Assembled* (London: Thames and Hudson, 1992), p. 15.

2 Simon Pepper, 'Siege Law, Siege Ritual, and the Symbolism of City Walls in Renaissance Europe', in James D. Tracy (ed.), *City Walls* (Cambridge: Cambridge University Press, 2000), p. 592.

3 Kostof, *The City Assembled*, p. 75.

4 Quoted in ibid., p. 76.

5 Philip Rucker et al., '"The Need to Fortify Your House Shows Weakness": Heavily Secured White House at Odds with Its Long History as "the People's House"', *Independent*, 5 June 2020, https://www.independent.co.uk/news/world/americas/us-politics/white-house-protection-security-protests-trump-a9550476.html

6 Quoted in Ron Theodore Robin, *Enclaves of America* (Princeton, NJ: Princeton University Press, 1992), p. 155.

7 'The Battle for Grosvenor Square', *Police Journal*, Vol. 41, No. 5 (1968), pp. 191–5.

8 See 'U.S. Embassies Are Under Siege: The Record of Outrages and the Protocols of Protection', *Life*, 19 March 1965, pp. 38–9.

9 Brian Jenkins, *Embassies Under Siege* (Santa Monica, CA: RAND Corporation, 1981).

10 Ibid., p. 20.

11 Report of the Secretary of State's Advisory Panel on Overseas Security, *Inman Report* (Washington, DC: State Department, 1985), https://irp.fas.org/threat/inman/index.html
12 National Research Council, *The Embassy of the Future* (Washington, DC: The National Academies Press, 1986), p. 28.
13 Jane Loeffler, *Architecture of Diplomacy* (New York: Princeton Architectural Press, 1998), p. 250.
14 See William Langewiesche, 'The Mega-Bunker of Baghdad', *Vanity Fair*, 29 October 2007, https://www.vanityfair.com/news/2007/11/langewiesche200711; and Nate Berg, 'What Will Happen to the U.S. Embassy in Kabul?', *Fast Company*, 19 August 2021, https://www.fastcompany.com/90667240/what-will-happen-to-the-u-s-embassy-in-kabul
15 Rajiv Chandrasekaran, *Imperial Life in the Emerald City* (London: Bloomsbury, 2007), p. 13.
16 Jane Loeffler, 'The Identity Crisis of the American Embassy', *Foreign Service Journal*, June 2000, pp. 21–2.
17 Lucien Vandenbroucke, 'Eyewitness to Terror: Nairobi's Day of Infamy', *Foreign Service Journal*, June 2000, p. 34.
18 See BL Harbert website, 'Our Government and Federal Work', https://www.blharbert.com/market-sector/government-federal/
19 John Kerry and William Cohen, 'Concrete Bunker U.S. Embassies Send Wrong Message', CNN, 12 May 2010, https://edition.cnn.com/2010/OPINION/05/11/kerry.cohen.embassies/index.html
20 Tom Wilkinson, 'United States Embassy in Beirut, Lebanon by Morphosis', *Architectural Review*, 9 December 2019, https://www.architectural-review.com/essays/typology/united-states-embassy-in-beirut-lebanon-by-morphosis
21 Oliver Wainwright, 'Fortress London: The New U.S. Embassy and the Rise of Counter-Terror Urbanism', *Harvard Design Magazine*, No. 42 (2016), https://www.harvarddesignmagazine.org/issues/42/fortress-london-the-new-us-embassy-and-the-rise-of-counter-terror-urbanism; see also Larry Malcic, 'Strong and Silent', *Architecture Today* (undated), https://architecturetoday.co.uk/strong-and-silent/
22 J.G. Ballard, 'Airports: The True Cities of the 21st Century', republished in the *Utne Reader*, 1 July 2000, https://www.utne.com/politics/homeiswherethehangaris/
23 Edward Relph, *Place and Placelessness* (Los Angeles, CA: Sage, 1976), p. v.
24 See Rachel Hall, *The Transparent Traveller Security* (Durham, NC: Duke University Press, 2015), p. 7.

25 Quoted in 'Saarinen's TWA Flight Centre', *Architectural Record*, July 1962, p. 129, https://usmodernist.org/AR/AR-1962-07.pdf
26 Addison Nugent, 'The Tricks of Airport Design', BBC Future, 1 May 2019, https://www.bbc.com/future/article/20190430-psychological-tricks-of-airport-design
27 Jacques Duchesneau and Maxime Langlois, 'Airport Attacks: The Critical Role Airports Can Play in Combating Terrorism', *Journal of Airport Management*, Vol. 11, No. 4 (2017), p. 344.
28 See Patricia G. Steinhoff, 'Portrait of a Terrorist: Interview with Kozo Okamoto', *Asian Survey*, Vol. 16, No. 9 (1976), pp. 830–45.
29 International Civil Aviation Organisation, *Safeguarding International Civil Aviation Against Acts of Unlawful Interference*, Montreal, July 2022, https://www.icao.int/security/sfp/pages/annex17.aspx
30 'Who We Are', SKA (undated), https://ska-arabia.com/about-us
31 Josie May, 'Heathrow Installs New Fencing to Increase Security', *Airports International*, 7 July 2021, https://www.airportsinternational.com/article/heathrow-installs-new-fencing-increase-security
32 The title of a 1967 poem by Richard Brautigan.
33 Samira Shackle, 'The Mystery of the Gatwick Drone', *Guardian*, 1 December 2020, https://www.theguardian.com/uk-news/2020/dec/01/the-mystery-of-the-gatwick-drone
34 See Guard from Above, https://www.guardfromabove.com
35 Gretchen Kell, 'Drones and Falcons Don't Mix', *Berkeleyside*, 7 February 2020, https://www.berkeleyside.org/2022/02/07/drones-and-falcons-dont-mix-recent-incident-at-uc-berkeley-proves
36 Caroline H. Brighton, Adrian L.R. Thomas and Graham K. Taylor, 'Terminal Attack Trajectories of Peregrine Falcons Are Described by the Proportional Navigation Guidance Law of Missiles', *Proceedings of the National Academy of Sciences of the United States of America*, Vol. 114, No. 51 (2017), pp. 13495–500.
37 There are dozens of large and small companies selling counter-UAS systems to military and civil markets. The discussion in the above paragraphs is based largely upon information provided publicly by two of them. Dedrone GMBH is a German-based company which bills itself as the 'market leader in smart airspace security', while D-Fend Solutions is a British company that calls itself the 'leading counter-drone takeover technology provider'. The websites of both companies feature a good deal of useful documentation as well as videos explaining the counter-UAS problems and their solution. Dedrone may be found at https://www.dedrone.com and D-fend is at https://www.d-fendsolutions.com

38 'Global Airport Security Market Is Expected to Reach USD 20.34 billion by 2028', *GlobeNewsWire*, 2 June 2021, and Joe Bates, 'Global Airport Security Market to Be Worth $25 Billion by 2028', *Airport World*, 8 February 2022; the share of spending represented by perimeter security is from 'Airport Security Market Size, Share, and Industry Analysis', Fortune Business Insights Report FBI102853 (undated), https://www.fortunebusinessinsights.com/airport-security-market-10 2853

39 Charles Davis, 'Weapons in Ukraine Aren't Flooding Europe's Black Markets, But That Could Change', *Business Insider*, 27 October 2022, https://www.businessinsider.com/no-sign-of-mass-arms-trafficking-from-ukraine-authorities-say-2022-10?r=US&IR=T

40 Sean Ziegler et al., *Acquisition and Use of MANPADS against Commercial Aviation: Risks, Proliferation, Mitigation, and Cost of an Attack* (Santa Monica, CA: Rand, 2019), https://www.rand.org/pubs/research_reports/RR4304.html

41 Martin Landauer, 'The Threat from MANPADS', *Royal United Services Institute*, 14 November 2007, https://rusi.org/publication/threat-manpads

42 Quoted in 'U.S. Chair of Forum for Security Cooperation Spotlights MANPADS Threat', US Mission to the OSCE, Vienna, 17 February 2021, https://osce.usmission.gov/u-s-chair-of-forum-for-security-cooperation-spotlights-manpads-threat/

43 'Destination Airports', *Gensler: Research and Insight* (undated), https://www.gensler.com/blog/destination-airports

44 Matt Falcus, '16 New Airports and Terminals We Can't Wait to Fly Into', CNN Travel, 6 December 2018, https://edition.cnn.com/travel/article/new-airports-and-terminals/index.html

45 See Peter Adey, 'Modalities and Modulations: The Airport as a Difference Machine', in Mark B. Salter (ed.), *Politics at the Airport* (Minneapolis: University of Minnesota Press, 2008), chap. 7.

46 Alastair Gordon, *Naked Airport* (Chicago: Chicago University Press, 2004), pp. 221–2.

47 Ibid., p. 234.

48 See examples such as Francesco Chiti et al., 'An Integrated Software Platform for Airport Queues Prediction with Application to Resources Management', *Journal of Air Transport Management*, Vol. 67 (2018), pp. 11–18; and Rajat Talak et al., 'Strategic Arrivals to Queues Offering Priority Service', *Queueing Systems*, Vol. 92, Nos. 1–2 (2019), pp. 103–30.

49 See, for example, Suzanne Hiemstra-Van Mastrigt et al., 'Identifying

Bottlenecks and Designing Ideas and Solutions for Improving Aircraft Passengers' Experience during Boarding and Disembarking', *Applied Ergonomics*, Vol. 77 (2019), pp. 16–21.
50 Terry L. Schell et al., *Designing Airports for Security* (Santa Monica, CA: Rand, 2003), https://www.rand.org/pubs/issue_papers/IP251.html
51 Ross Craigie et al., 'Manchester Arena Bombing: Lessons Learnt from a Mass Casualty Incident', *BMJ Military Health*, Vol. 166, No. 2 (2020), pp. 72–5; and Paul Dark et al., 'Healthcare System Impacts of the 2017 Manchester Arena Bombing', *Emergency Medical Journal*, Vol. 38, No. 10 (2021), pp. 746–55.
52 See 'Defence Companies Offering "Bulletproof" School Items for Students', *Premier Body Armor*, 15 March 2018, https://premierbody armor.com/blogs/pba/defense-companies-offering-bulletproof-school-items-for-students-1
53 See '10 Downing Street: The Story Behind Britain's Most Famous Door', *Selo blog*, 21 June 2017, https://selo.global/10-downing-street-story-behind-britains-famous-door/#
54 ArmorCore, 'Bullet Resistant Barrier Applications' (undated), https://www.armorcore.com/applications/
55 Architectural Armour, 'Products' (undated), https://www.architectural armour.com/security-products
56 Ben Dreith, 'Texas Senator Proposes Design Measures to "harden schools" in Wake of Uvalde Shooting', *dezeen*, 27 May 2022, https://www.dezeen.com/2022/05/27/ted-cruz-one-door-uvalde-school-shooting/
57 'Where We Stand: School Design and Student Safety', *American Institute of Architects* (undated), https://www.aia.org/pages/206356-where-we-stand-school-design-and-student-sa?editing=true
58 Tim Walker, '"School Hardening" Not Making Students Safer, Say Experts', *neaToday*, 14 February 2019, https://www.nea.org/advocating-for-change/new-from-nea/school-hardening-not-making-students-safer-say-experts
59 Bryan Warnick and Ryan Kapa, 'Protecting Students from Gun Violence', *Education Next*, Vol. 19, No. 2 (2019), pp. 22–8.
60 Quoted in Walker, '"School Hardening"'.
61 Sydney Franklin, 'Michigan High School Upgrades Campus to Combat Potential Active Shooters', *The Architect's Newspaper*, 26 August 2019, https://www.archpaper.com/2019/08/fruitport-high-school-towerpin kster-renovation/
62 Quoted in Omar Abel-Baqui, 'New Michigan High School Will Have

Potentially Life-Saving Design', *Detroit Free Press*, 6 August 2019, https://eu.freep.com/story/news/education/2019/09/06/fruitport-high-school-michigan-active-shooters/2213687001/

63 Eleanor Gibson, 'Michigan High School Designed to Reduce Impact of Mass Shootings', *dezeen*, 5 September 2019, https://www.dezeen.com/2019/09/05/fruitport-high-school-tower-pinkster-michigan-mass-shooting/

64 Meilan Solly, 'How the 1996 Dunblane Massacre Pushed the UK to Enact Stricter Gun Laws', *Smithsonian Magazine*, 12 March 2021, https://www.smithsonianmag.com/history/how-1996-dunblane-massacre-pushed-uk-enact-stricter-gun-laws-180977221/

65 Sue-Ann Harding's *Beslan* (Manchester: Manchester University Press, 2012) provides several harrowing first-person accounts.

66 See 'Secure Ballistic Glass/Security Glass' (undated), webpage of the UK glass company ESG, https://www.esg.glass/esg-secure/

67 Readers interested in specifics may consult Chiara Bedon et al., *A Comparison of Existing Standards for Testing Blast Resistant Glazing and Windows*, European Commission Joint Research Centre, Report EUR 27133 EN (December 2014).

68 Stephen Kennett, 'Flying Fortress: Heathrow Terminal 4's Bomb-Proof Façade', *Building*, 5 March 2010, https://www.building.co.uk/news/flying-fortress-heathrow-terminal-4s-bomb-proof-facade/3159160.article

69 'Cardiff Central Station: New Blast Resistant Facades', *Wrightstyle* (undated), https://www.wrightstyle.co.uk/cardiff-central-station-new-blast-resistant-facades/

70 For a visual example of a breach control system made by the UK company Record, see: 'record FlipFlow – Exit Lane Breach Control', *YouTube*, https://www.youtube.com/watch?v=AVV8ewwCTI0&list=TLGGUkV8kxGzqWkwODExMjAyMg&t=18s

71 To see an example of Record UK's security portal in use go to: 'R65 Security Portal', *YouTube*, https://www.youtube.com/watch?v=P36keMliUjo&list=TLGGrjnNaI34k1YwODExMjAyMg&t=27s

72 See 'Access Control', *Airport Suppliers* (undated), https://www.airport-suppliers.com/suppliers/access-control/

73 See 'Access Control', *IFSEC Directory* (undated), https://directory.ifsecglobal.com/live/search/search40.jsp?name=Access+Control&SugType_val=310&RecordId_val=4781&site=40&type=all

74 See 'Access Control Market Size by Offering', *Markets and Markets*, Report SE 3145, November 2021, https://www.marketsandmarkets

.com/Market-Reports/access-control-market-164562182.html?gclid =Cj0KCQiAmaibBhCAARIsAKUlaKSjVYqWN5xx0PGF92K3YH -MfIwcAJxh4SON9J5B53fNFr1RuXS1H4MaAoL7EALw_wcB

75 'Arconas Launches inPower Flex 3, Bern Aero Lounger, and Announces Alliance with Amulet', *Arconas* (undated), https://www.arconas.com /arconas-launches-inpower-flex-3-bernu-aero-lounger-and-announ ces-alliance-with-amulet/
76 'Amulet in Structures', *Amulet Ballistic Barriers* (undated), https://www .amuletbb.com/amulet-in-structures.html
77 A good example is the American company Defenshield Inc., whose 'ballistic furniture' page (undated) is well illustrated, https://defen shield.com/products/furniture/
78 Polly Mosendz, 'Who Buys Bulletproof Sofas?', *Bloomberg*, 8 March 2016, https://www.bloomberg.com/news/articles/2016-03-08/who-buys-bulletproof-sofas?leadSource=uverify%20wall
79 '"Bullet-Proof" Sofa Targets Safety Fears', BBC News, 25 February 2016, https://www.bbc.co.uk/news/uk-scotland-glasgow-west-356594 84

Chapter 7

1 See Keith Durham, *Strongholds of the Border Reivers* (Oxford: Osprey, 2008), pp. 26–35.
2 'List of Bastles in England', *Gatehouse* (undated), http://www.gateh ouse-gazetteer.info/Indexs/EngCounty/EB.html
3 J.P. Ferrier, *Caravan Journeys and Wanderings in Persia* . . . (London: John Murray, 1857), p. 33.
4 Ibid., p. 74.
5 Nicholas Branic and Charis Kubrin, 'Gated Communities and Crime in the United States', in Gerben Bruinsma and Shane Johnson (eds.), *Oxford Handbook of Environmental Criminology* (Oxford: Oxford University Press, 2017), p. 406.
6 My definition is based on a widely accepted one in Edward Blakely and Mary Gail Snyder, *Fortress America* (Washington, DC: Brookings Institute Press, 1997), p. 2, and the discussion of the legal characteristics of gated communities on pp. 20–2.
7 David Harvey, *Rebel Cities* (London: Verso, 2013), p. 15, and Mike Davis, *City of Quartz* (London: Verso, 2006), p. 224.
8 Again, my understanding here is based largely upon Blakely and Snyder, *Fortress America*.
9 Samer Bagaeen, 'Gated Urban Life versus Kinship and Social Solidarity

in the Middle East', in Samer Bagaeen and Ola Uduku (eds.), *Gated Communities* (London: Earthscan, 2010), p. 15.
10 This point is argued very well by Ola Uduku, 'Lagos: Urban "Gating" as the Default Condition', in Bagaeen and Uduku (eds.), *Gated Communities*, p. 44.
11 Karina Landman, 'Gated Minds, Gated Places: The Impact and Meaning of Hard Boundaries in South Africa', in Bagaeen and Uduku (eds.), *Gated Communities*, p. 54.
12 See Karina Landman, *Gated Communities in South Africa* (Johannesburg: CSIR Building and Construction Technology, 2004), p. 1, https://www.saferspaces.org.za/uploads/files/Gated_communities_case_studies.pdf
13 Karina Landman and Willem Badenhorst, '11 Gated Communities and Spatial Transformation in Greater Johannesburg', in Philip Harrison et al. (eds.), *Changing Space, Changing City* (Johannesburg: Wits University Press, 2014), p. 237.
14 Christian Jacobus Cronje and Manfred Spocter, 'Open-Plan Suburb to Fortified Suburb: Home Fortification in Soneike, Cape Town, South Africa', *Journal of Housing and the Built Environment*, Vol. 32, No. 4 (2017), p. 723.
15 See Mike Davis, *Planet of Slums* (London: Verso, 2006), chap. 5 on 'Haussmann in the Tropics'.
16 Sanjay Srivastava, *Entangled Urbanism* (Oxford: Oxford University Press, 2015), p. 179.
17 Uduku, 'Lagos', in Bagaeen and Uduku (eds.), *Gated Communities*, pp. 40, 44.
18 Javier Auyero and Kristine Kilanski, 'Managing in the Midst of Social Disaster: Poor People's Response to Urban Violence', in Javier Auyero et al. (eds.), *Violence at the Urban Margins* (Oxford: Oxford University Press, 2015), p. 197.
19 See Teresa Caldeira's landmark study *City of Walls* (Berkeley: University of California Press, 2000).
20 Michael Mills, 'Obamageddon: Fear, the Far Right, and the Rise of "Doomsday" Prepping in Obama's America', *Journal of American Studies*, Vol. 55, No. 2 (2021), pp. 336–65.
21 'Doomsday Preppers', *National Geographic*, https://www.natgeotv.com/za/shows/natgeo/doomsday-preppers
22 See Alysha Webb, 'The $10.5 Billion Emergency Preparation Market', CNBC, 19 December 2020, https://www.cnbc.com/video/2020/12/19/natural-disaster-market.html

23 Scott Hines, '"Doomsday Preppers" on Netflix: Do These People Fear the End of the World, or Are They Hoping for It?', *The Decider*, 27 March 2019, https://decider.com/2019/03/27/doomsday-preppers-netflix/
24 See Landman, *Gated Communities in South Africa*, p. 1.
25 See Chris Webster, George Glasze, and Klaus Frantz, 'The Global Spread of Gated Communities', *Environment and Planning B: Urban Analytics and City Science*, Vol. 29, No. 3 (2002), which is an introduction to a special issue of the journal with a series of case studies.
26 Rupert Taylor, '5 Notable Gated Communities of the World', *ToughNickel*, 20 August 2022, https://toughnickel.com/real-estate/Gated-Communities-of-the-World
27 Chris Michael and Jo Blason, '"For Your Protection": Gated Cities around the World – In Pictures', *Guardian*, 5 May 2014, https://www.theguardian.com/cities/gallery/2014/may/05/for-your-protection-gated-cities-around-the-world-in-pictures
28 The cost included 6.5 billion rand for infrastructure plus a 5.5 billion rand build cost, according to Kim Gurney, 'The Mogul, His Meerkat, and the Meerkat's Second Life', *e-Flux Architecture*, December 2021, https://www.e-flux.com/architecture/workplace/430308/the-mogul-his-meerkat-and-the-meerkat-s-second-life/
29 See LivinginSATV, '5.5 billion – Steyn City – City Centre Full Tour – Latest Steyn City's Development', *YouTube*, https://www.youtube.com/watch?v=RNq3xU2NJrg; see also the 'Lifestyle' page on the Steyn City website, https://www.steyncity.co.za/experiences/
30 'A Look Inside SA Billionaire Douw Steyn's R250 Million "Palace"', *BusinessTech*, 18 June 2018, https://businesstech.co.za/news/wealth/252297/a-look-inside-sa-billionaire-douw-steyns-r250-million-palace/
31 David Smith, 'South African "Lifestyle Resort" Endorsed by Nelson Mandela Opens', *Guardian*, 11 March 2015, https://www.theguardian.com/world/2015/mar/11/south-african-lifestyle-resort-nelson-mandela-steyn-city
32 Technically, Westminster was a royal town rather than a city because it did not possess an incorporated government – the legal details are complicated. See, J.F. Merritt, *Westminster 1640–60* (Manchester: Manchester University Press, 2013).
33 See, for example, Michael Sorkin, *Variations on a Theme Park* (New York: Hill and Wang, 1992).
34 Georg Glasze, 'Segregation and Seclusion: The Case of Compounds

for Western Expatriates in Saudi Arabia', *GeoJournal*, Vol. 66, No. 1/2 (2006), pp. 83–8.
35 Choon-Piew Pow, *Gated Communities in China* (Abingdon: Routledge, 2009), pp. 1–3.
36 'Shanghai Vanke/Tsushima Design Studio', *ArchDaily* (undated), https://www.archdaily.com/462567/shanghai-vanke-tsushima-design-studio
37 Luigi Tomba, 'Gating Urban Spaces in China: Inclusion, Exclusion, and Government', in Bagaeen and Uduku (eds.), *Gated Communities*, p. 28.
38 'Booby Trapping & Fortifying Premises Used to Sell Drugs', *The Law Offices of Jonathan F. Marshall* (undated), https://www.newjerseycriminallawattorney.com/drug-crimes/booby-trapping-fortifying-premises-used-to-sell-drugs/
39 James Bradford, 'Twenty-First Century Global Drug Trades and Consumption', in Paul Gootenberg (ed.), *The Oxford Handbook of Global Drug History* (Oxford: Oxford University Press, 2022), https://doi.org/10.1093/oxfordhb/9780190842642.013.35
40 Max Daly, 'Inside London's Secret Drug Dens', *Vice*, 21 September 2015, https://www.vice.com/en/article/kwxgvx/inside-londons-secret-drug-dens-739
41 Taylor Noakes, 'Quebec Biker War (1994–2002)', in *The Canadian Encyclopedia, Historica Canada* (2022), https://www.thecanadianencyclopedia.ca/en/article/quebec-biker-war
42 'Fortified Drug Houses, A Problem Solved', Edmonton Police Service, Alberta, Canada, 1994, https://popcenter.asu.edu/sites/default/files/library/awards/goldstein/1994/94-06(F).pdf
43 Ellie Kemp, 'Mob Kingpin's Fortified Staffordshire Mansion Full of Weapons and Cash', *StaffordshireLive*, 28 March 2022, https://www.staffordshire-live.co.uk/news/local-news/mob-kingpins-fortified-staffordshire-mansion-6872291
44 R.C. Macleod, 'Fort Whoop Up', in *The Oxford Companion to Canadian History* (Oxford: Oxford University Press, 2004).
45 A tour of the site and its history are shown in 'Fort Whoop-Up Orientation Video', *YouTube*, https://www.youtube.com/watch?v=L8TlshGZUOg
46 John Keegan, *A History of Warfare* (Toronto: Key Porter Books, 1993), p. 139.
47 See John Phillips, 'Notes from the Underground: Microwaves, Backbones, Party Lines and the Post Office Tower', in John Beck

and Ryan Bishop (eds.), *Cold War Legacies* (Edinburgh: Edinburgh University Press, 2016), p. 221.
48 Joanna Kloppenberg, 'The Architecture of Surveillance: Manhattan's Brutalist Masterpiece Revealed as NSA Hub', *Architizer* (undated), https://architizer.com/blog/inspiration/stories/33-thomas-street-nsa/
49 'Cantor Fitzgerald . . . the City Firm That Rose from the 9/11 Ashes', *Evening Standard*, 9 September 2011, https://www.standard.co.uk/hp/front/cantor-fitzgerald-the-city-firm-that-rose-from-the-9-11-ashes-6441839.html
50 Josephine Walbank, 'Top 10 Global Data Centre Markets', *DataCentre*, 10 October 2022, https://datacentremagazine.com/articles/top-10-global-data-centre-markets
51 See 'Microsoft Dublin Grange Castle', *Baxtel* (undated), https://baxtel.com/data-center/microsoft-dublin-grange-castle
52 Andrew Donoghue, 'Underground Data Centers are Having a Moment', *Data Center Knowledge*, 1 December 2017, https://www.datacenterknowledge.com/design/underground-data-centers-are-having-moment
53 Sam Steers, 'Top 10 Underground Data Centres', *DataCentre*, 22 March 2022, https://datacentremagazine.com/data-centres/top-10-underground-data-centres
54 'The Bunker', *Colo-X* (undated), https://www.colo-x.com/data-centre/the-bunker-kent/
55 'SVG1-Rennesoy', *Green Mountain* (undated), https://greenmountain.no/data-center/svg1-rennesoy/

Conclusion

1 'Townscape Supplies Anti-Terrorist Protection to Belfast', *Specifier Review* (undated), https://specifierreview.com/2012/05/28/townscape-supplies-anti-terrorist-protection-to-belfast/
2 Jo Carlowe, 'Counterterrorism by Design', *Reader's Digest*, 1 May 2018.
3 David Betz and Hugo Stanford-Tuck, 'Teaching Your Enemy to Win', *Military Strategy Magazine*, Vol. 6, No. 3 (2019).
4 David Lee, 'Anti-Terrorism Plans for Windsor to be Finalised in "Next Few Weeks"', *Slough Express*, 13 September 2017, https://www.sloughexpress.co.uk/gallery/windsor/120944/anti-terrorism-plans-for-windsor-to-be-finalised-in-next-few-weeks.html
5 See Dominique Moisi, *The Geopolitics of Emotion: How Cultures of Fear, Humiliation, and Hope Are Reshaping the World* (New York: Random House, 2009).

6 Dan Ariely, *Predictably Irrational: The Hidden Forces that Shape Our Decisions* (New York: HarperCollins, 2008).
7 Alvin Toffler, *Future Shock* (New York: Random House, 1970).
8 Steven Johnson, *Emergence: The Connected Lives of Ants, Brains, Cities, and Software* (New York: Scribner, 2001).

Index

3xLOGIC, 124

Aamby Valley City, Delhi, 172
Abu Nidal, 144
access control, 132, 160, 162, 170, 174, 184
Admiralty Citadel, 110–11
aerial bombing, 28, 53, 55, 87, 88, 89, 90, 93, 95, 99, 111, 114, 115
aeroplane, *see* aircraft
Afghanistan, 1–3, 12, 65, 134, 146, 165, 166, 167, 171
   fortifications and, 57, 58–9, *59*, 60, 62
   Hesco barrier and, 57
   war and, 4, 5
Age of Walls, 31
Airbus Defence and Security, 67
aircraft, 62, 70,100, 132, 143, 145, 147, 148, 152, 182
   attacks on, 144, 145, 150, 151
   see also aerial bombing
airport, 12, 14, 141, 142, 143, 177, 185

attacks on, 144–5, 153
Bagram, 60
as barbican, 141–4
defending and, 145–53, 159–61
Glasgow, 144
Islamabad, *146*
Kabul, 141, *141*
Kandahar Airfield, 1, 2, 60, 62, 63, 146, 166, 186
London Gatwick, 148
London Heathrow, 11, 142, 147, 150, 152, 159
London Luton, 150
Los Angeles, 153
New York Kennedy, 142–3, *142*, 152
Lod (Ben Gurion) 144, 145, 151, 153
Mogadishu, 11, 141, 146–7
air-raid shelter, *see* bomb shelter
Al-Qaeda, 56, 150
Alberti, Leon Battista, 130
Albuquerque, Alfonso de, 49
Alexander the Great, 3, 59

INDEX

Alfred the Great, 92
American National Education Association, 156
Amulet 'ballistic barrier solution', 161
American Housing Survey, 167
American Institute of Architects, 156
American Telephone & Telegraph Company, 181
Anarchists, 115
Anduril, 121
Annals of a Fortress, 75
anti-aircraft installation, 90, 91
anti-aircraft missile, *see* man-portable air-defence system (MANPAD)
anti-tank barrier, 98
anti-tank ditch, 91, 92
Arab Revolt, 62
Architectural Armour, 155
architecture, 4, 25, 33, 74, 82, 88, 94, 95, 104, 108, 111, 114, 128, 129, 130, 131, 132, 135, *137*, 138, 141, 143, 155
   bunkerized, 107
   defensive, 138 fortified, 4, 82, 107, 108, 159, 188
   military, 25, 56, 85, 109
   securitized, 31
Arconas, 161
Argentina, 112, 171
ArmorCore, 155
Aristotle, 107
Athenians, 78
artificial intelligence (AI), 121, 125, 148, 152
Atlantic Wall, 28, 46
atomic bomb, *see* weaponry
Austria, 74, 86, 90, 91, 144
Automatic Number Plate Recognition (ANPR), 118, 119, 120, 121
Aviation Security in Airport Development (ASIAD), 159

Babylon, 77
Backbone network, 180–1
baffled gate, 109
Balaclan, 7
Baldwin, Stanley, 87
ballistic-resistant glass, 12, 134, 136, 154, 155, 159, 160, 161, 162, 177, 185
ballistic resistant product, 155–6, 157, 158, 161
Ballard, J.G., 142
Balpro system, 60
Bangladesh, 67
barbican, 127, 140, 141, 149, 150, 152, 174
bastion, 45, 46, 81–5, 88, 98
bastle, 164, 165, 167
Bauman, Zygmunt, 25, 26
Beaumaris, 53
Belfast, 60, 116, 124, 185
Belgium, 36, 68, 78, 86, 96, 144
Bellingham Hole Bastle, 165
Bentham, Jeremy, 125
Berlin, 16, 17, 18, 19, 20, 40, 42, 109
   Airlift and 17
   Blockade and 17
Berlin Wall 16, 17, 18, 19, 20, 25, 26, 31
Berlin, Isaiah, 40, 42
berm, 28, 66, *70*, 168, 179
Bermuda, 48
Beslan, 158–9
Biddle, Stephen, 38
BL Harbert International, 135

Blackfoot Nation, Canada, 178
Blair, Tony, 23
blast resistance, 139, 159
blast wall, 61, 71, 134
Blitz, *see* aerial bombing
Bolivia, 132
Bollard, 108, 109, 110, 113, 138, 137
bomb, 36, 62, 89, 93, 110, 112, 114, 116, 124, 135, 139, 145, 153, 154, 159, 185
  incendiary, 88, 114
  see also vehicle-borne explosive device, weaponry
bomb attack, 62, 90, 95, 109, 110, 111, 112, 113, 115, 116, 132, 133, 134, 139, 145, 153, 154, 162
  Buenos Aires and, 112
  by Irish-American Republicans, 155
  by Islamic extremists, 116
  London and, 23, 24, 116
  Manchester and, 153–4
  Mumbai and, 6
  Nairobi and, 111
  Northern Ireland and, 116
  Oklahoma City and, 112, 134
  Paris and, 6
  Quebec and, 177
  US Embassy Beirut and, 132
  US Embassy Dar es Salaam and, 134
  US Embassy Nairobi and, 134
  see also aerial bombing *and* vehicle-borne explosive device
bomb shelter, 68, 88, 89, 90, 99
  Dietel-type, 90
  flaktower, 90, 91
  see also nuclear shelter

border, 13, 14, 20, 22, 26, 54, 59, 64–8, 153
  Afghanistan-Pakistan, 64
  Anglo-Scottish, 165
  Ceuta and Melilla-Morocco, 13–14
  Intra-German (IGB), 16–17, 19–21, 26–7
  India-Bangladesh, 67
  India-Pakistan, 66
  Israel-Palestine, 14, 67
  Korean DMZ, 67, 98
  Mali-Niger, 54
  Morocco-Western Sahara, 66
  Saudi Arabia-Iraq, 67, 70
  Saudi Arabia-Yemen, 12, 67
  Turkey-Syria, 67
  Wessex-Daneland, 28
  Ukraine-Russia, 67
  United States-Mexico, 11, 13, 14, 20, 65, 66, 68
Bourtange, 55, 82
breach control system, 160
Brialmont, Henri-Alexis, General, 36
brick, 16, 46, 59, 65, 76, 83, 93, 101, 111, 140
Britain, 2, 3, 5, 6, 11, 12, 23, 29, 37, 60, 61, 62, 64, 91, 92, 103, 111, 114, 118, 125, 126, 139, 150, 158, 176, 180, 183
  Romans and, 27, 66, 78
  terrorist attacks on, 115–16, 130, 153–4, 158
  World War II and, 15, 87, 89, 93, 114
  see also England
British Empire, 3, 48, 61, 62, 64, 104, 107
British Imperial Police, 62

British Security Industry
    Association, 126
British Transport Police, 125
Brown, R. Allen, vii
Buenos Aires, 112, 171
Bulgaria, 132
bunker, 64, 91, 99, 177
    data, 183–5
    survival, 171
    see also bomb shelter, nuclear
        shelter

camera, *see* surveillance
Cameron, David, 103
Camp Bastion, 60, 61, 62, 63
Canada, 54, 55, 134, 149, 176
    Quebec Biker War, 177–8
canton, 58, 61, 62, 63
Cantor Fitzgerald, 181–2
Cape Town, 170
caravanserai, 166
car bomb, *see* vehicle-borne
    explosive device
castle, viii, 3, 4, 25, 46, 49, 51, 52,
    58, 59, 138, 139, 140, 158, 165
    Beaumaris, 53
    Caernarfon, 53
    Cathar, 46
    Conwy, 53
    Elmina, 50
    Grange, 183
    Harlech, 53
    Krak des Chevaliers, 137
    Neuschwanstein, 46
    Windsor, 130, 186–7
Cardiff, 160
Catal Huyuk, 75
CCTV, *see* surveillance
Ceuta and Melilla, 13–14, 6
chamber gate, *see* breach control
    system

Charles VIII, 80
Charlie Hebdo, 6
Chechnya, 6, 96, 158
China, 11, 21, 71, 72, 79, 122, 175
von Choltitz, Dietrich, 95
Churchill, Sir Winston, 15, 16, 65,
    89, 90, 111
Citadel, 110, 129–30, 131, 134,
    141, 155
    Quebec, 55
    Erbil, 76, 78
City of London, 12, 116–19, *117*
Clarke, George Sydenham, 38
Clausewitz, Carl Phillip von, 41–2
coastal fort, 27, 49–50, 53
Coker, Christopher, 42
Cold War, 16, 17, 18, 46, 65, 89,
    90, 171, 184
    end of, 8, 9, 19–21, 72
    post, 25, 29, 71, 93
Colo-X, 183
Commune of Paris, 86
communications tower, 180–1
concrete, 2, 13, 14, 16, 17, 19, 20,
    36, 48, *52*, 53, *59*, 60, 62, *69*,
    90, 91, 93, 98, 101, 108, 110,
    125, 133, 135, *136*, 137–9,
    141, 143, 175, 177, 178, 180,
    181, 183, 184, 185, 187
Constantinople, 70, 77, 80, 98
Convention on International Civil
    Aviation, 145
convolutional neural network
    (CNN), 148, 152
cost, 9, 43, 186
    of airport security, 147, 149, 150
    of ballistic protection, 154, 157,
        185
    of damages, 116, 162
    of data security, 182
    of US embassies, 134, 136

cost (*cont.*)
  of fortifications and walls, 53, 57, 64, 78, 81, 82
  of insurance, 43, 44, 64, 162, 183
  of narcotics industry, 177
  of travel to Mogadishu, 147
  of modifying buildings, 111
  of Strand redevelopment, 112, 114
  of Titanic Museum security, 185
Council of Europe, 18
counter terrorism, 115, 126
  UK government guides on, 126
Counter Terrorism Security Advisor (CTSA), 114
Covid-19, 38, 100, 172, 175
Crimea, Russian invasion of, 71
  war, 48
Crime Prevention Through Environmental Design (CPTED), 127
Cruz, Ted, Senator, 156, 458
CT (counter-terrorism) blocks, 185
curtain wall, 84, 109
Czechoslovakia, 132

Davis, Mike, 128
Darras, Jacques, 8, 21
data bunker, 183–4
data security, 47, 182
defensible space, *see* Crime Prevention Through Environmental Design (CPTED)
defensive street furniture, 109, 115, 138
Deleuze, Gilles, 123
Delhi, 170
demi-lune, 81
Denmark, 55
Department for Transport, 159

Department of Homeland Security, 156
Detection of Explosives and Firearms for Counter Terrorism (DEXTER), 120
deterrence by denial, 114
ditch, 16, 25, 27, 28, 45, 56, 62, 63, 64, 66, 67, 77, 81, 83, 91, 92, 138, 139, 179
Donbas, 92, 94
Dowding, Hugh, Air Chief Marshall, 115
Downing Street, 130, 155
drone, *see* unmanned aerial system (UAS)
drug house, 176–8
  New Jersey law on, 176
Duffy, Christopher, 75
Dunblane massacre, 158
Dupuy, Trevor N., Colonel, 37
Dynamite War, 115

Eagle Eye Networks, 121
Eastern Europe, 18, 20
economic factors, *see* cost
Edmonton, Alberta, 177–8
Edward I, 53
Egypt, 77, 89, 133
El Al, 150
Eliot, T.S., 41
Elmina Castle, 50
Elsdon, Northumberland, 165
Embassy Design and Security Act, 135
enceinte, 28, *59*, 85, 86, 87, 100
enclave, 11, 78, 128, 167, 168, 169, 170, 172
  Ceuta and Melilla, 13, 68
  Sadr City, 52, *52*
enclosed neighbourhood, 167–75
  Steyn City, 173–4, *173*

England, 27, 53, 91, 92, 165, 179, 180
Erbil, 78
Essaouira, 49
European Rampart, 67
European Union (EU), 13, 14
Exeter, 78
Excellence in Diplomatic Facilities Initiative, 136

facial emotion recognition, 124, 125
Ferrier, J.P., 166
fence, 13, 14, 16, 23, 61, 63, 24, 65, 66, *69*, *70*, 138, 147, 148, 155, 158, 167, 168
Finnish Army, 60
First World War, *see* World War I
Forbidden City, 130
Forever War, *see* Global War on Terror
Forrester, Joseph, 88
Forte di Bard, 46
Fort, Afghan National Police compound, 59, *59*
   Apache, 49
   in Baltic, 48
   Barcha, 59
   Belgium, 36
   Bermuda, 48
   Bourtange, 55
   Casa del Mar, 50–1
   Chartres, 56
   Combat Outpost Castle, 58
   Combat Outpost Coleman, 59
   Dahab refugee camp, 64
   Danesfield Camp, 28
   Eben Emael, 36
   Elmina Castle, 50
   Enhrenbreitstein, 19
   Essaouira, 49
   George, 55
   Forward Operating Base Langman 59
   Forward Operating Base Apache, 59
   Gibraltar, 48
   Halifax, 48
   Hong Kong, 48
   Jaffna, 55
   Kastellet, 55
   Labbezanga, 54, 55, 56
   Lwara, 65
   Maginot, 36–8
   Malta, 48
   Melaka, 49
   Menaka, 54, *54*, 55, 56
   Metz, 37
   Morocco, 11, 66
   Neuf-Brisach, 55
   Prince of Wales, 54
   Qualat tea house, 61
   Quebec Citadel, 55
   Rest repo, 58
   Singapore, 48
   United Nations Multidimensional Integrated Stabilization Mission in Mali, 63
   Whoop Up, 178
   York Factory, 50
   Zara, 49, *see also* Camp Bastion, Kandahar base, whisky fort
fortification, vii, viii, 4, 5, 8–20, 25–31, 35–9, 60, 128–9, 140, 178, 179, 185–8
   Afghanistan and, 58–9, 61–4
   airports and, 141–3, 153, 159, 160, 161
   architecture and, 159–63
   Britain and, 91–2
   Central Asia and, 165–7

fortification (*cont.*)
  cities and, 51, 74–88, 93–4, 96–100, 101–4, 123–6, 129–31, 140
  coastal, 49–50
  communications facilities and, 180–1
  data centres and, 181–4
  definition of, 45–6, 50
  drug trade and, 176–8
  embassies and, 131–9
  grand strategic, 68–71, 72
  Japanese, 37
  London and, 88–90, 98, 104–23, 125
  modern warfare and, 39, 50–1
  NGO fort, 63
  neighbourhoods and, 167–76
  Pakistan and, 64–5
  police fort, 62
  public spaces and, 153–6
  purposes of, 47, 51–2, 58
  risk aversion and, 43–4
  railway stations and, 160
  Roman, 58
  schools and, 156–9
  Seoul and, 98–9
  underground, 88–91
  see also air-raid shelter, Balpro system, bastion, border, bunker, canton, citadel, barbican, castle, hill fort, Hesco Bastion, fort, Intra-German Border, wall, marching camp (fort), palisade, star fortress, stronghold, T-Wall
fortification strategy, vii 5, 8, 9, 10, 51, 53, 73, 100, 151
fortified architecture, *see* architecture
fortified city, 11, 51, 75–86, 166, 174–5
fortified strategic complex, 9, 39, 50, 51, 53, 58, 63, 71, 72, 100, 101, 129
  in American West, 49 definition of, 51
  Maginot Line, 36–8, 46, 53
  Moroccan 'Sand Wall', 66
  ostrog, 49
fortress, *see* fort
Forward Operating Base (FOB), Apache, 59
  Langman, 59
France, 46, 53, 54, 55, 68, 75, 80, 82, 85, 86, 113, 124, 164, 166
  Terrorist attack and, 7, 109
  in World War II, 15, 36
Franco-Prussian War, 33, 34, 75
Friedman, Thomas, 25
French Revolution, 8, 21, 85, 164
Fruitport High School, 187–8
Frye, David, 31
Fukuyama, Francis, 21

gabion, 56, 57, 63
Gallagher, 123
Garibaldi, Giuseppe, 82
gate, 19, *59*, 62, *69*, 76, 78, 81–2, 84, 85, 86, 108, 109, 116, 122, 125, 127, 134, 140, 152, 158, 160, 168, 170, 174, 175
gatehouse, 90, 173, *173*
gated community, *see* enclosed neighbourhood
gatedness, *see* enclosed neighbourhood
Gaza Strip, 67, 68
George V, 89
Germany, 9, 19, 20, 48, 66, 68, 86, 93, 116, 123, 132

East, 16, 18, 21
  terrorist attack on, 144
  World War I and, 86, 89
  World War II and, 12, 15, 16,
    28, 36–7, 46, 53, 87, 88, 90,
    91, 95, 111, 114,115
Gibraltar, 48
glacés, 55, 56, 70, 83
Gladiator Solutions, 157
Gladstone, William Ewart, 104
glass, *see* ballistic resistant glass
global war on terror, 2, 14, 56
globalization, 22, 23, 24, 25, 29,
    66, 187, 188
Gorbachev, Mikhail, 18
grand strategic fortification, 68,
    69, 72
Greece, 5, 15, 78, 131
Green Mountain complex,
    Norway, 184
Green Zone, 134, 147
Greenspan, Alan, 22
Grenzwall 75, *see* Berlin Wall
ground attack, 145, 150, 151, 152
Grozny, 96
Guard from Above, 149
Guatemala, 132

Halifax, 48
hard landscaping, 109
Hardstaff Barrier, 147
Harris, Sir Arthur, Air marshal, 87,
    115
Hart, Basil Liddell, 29, 37
Harvey, David, 128
Hell's Angels, 177
Helmand province, 59, 60
Hesco Bastion, 11, 56, 57, 59, 60,
    63, 64
Heselden, Jimi, 56
Heuser, Beatrice, 50

high-rise building, 94
hill fort, 28, 79, 179, 180, 181, 184
Hitler, Adolf, 93, 95
Holocaust, 41
Home Office (UK), 126
Hong Kong, 48
hostile vehicle restraint system, 110
Hudson's Bay Trading Company,
    54
Hungary, 132

Impact Rated Hostile Vehicle
    Mitigation (HVM) measures,
    see defensive street furniture.
India, 56, 62, 66, 67, 170
Indonesia, 132
InfoBunker, 183
information age, 2, 4, 32, 34–5, 72,
    184
Inman, Bobby, Admiral, 133, 134,
    135
International Security Assistance
    Force (ISAF), 62
Intra-German Border (IGB),
    16–17, 19–21, 26–7
Iran hostage crisis, 132
Iraq, 12, 52, 67, 70, 76, 134
Ireland, Civil War, 41
  Irish Republican Army (IRA),
    116, 130
  War of Independence, 41, *see also*
    Northern Ireland
Iron Age, 11, 28, 58, 79, 164, 181
Iron Curtain, 15, 16, 21, 65
Iron Mountain data bunker,
    Pennsylvania, 183
Islam, 3, 23, 54, 56, 70, 116, 132
Islamic State, 56, 70
Israel, 11, 14, 62, 68, 69, 76, 84,
    100, 132, 144, 150, 160
  Iron Dome, 46, 100

Israel (*cont.*)
  security barrier, 11, 14, 67, 68
  separation fence, 69, *see also* Lod Airport
Italy, 46, 80, 83, 165

Jackson's Fencing, 127
Jaffa Gate, Jerusalem, 160
Jaffna Fort, 55
Japan, 37, 40, 44, 48, 142, 144, 191
Japanese Red Army Faction, 144
Jericho, 75, 78
Jersey barrier, 110
Johannesburg, 169
Johnson, Dave, 72

Kaliningrad, 71
Kandahar base, 1, 2, 60, 62, 63, 146, 166
  Poo Pond, 1, 63, 186
Kastellet, 55
Kearney (global cities index), 103
Keegan, John, 178
Kennedy Airport, New York (JFK), 142–3, 152
Kennedy, John F, 17, 29
Kennedy, Paul, 29
Kenno, 60
Kenya, 64, 77, 111, 121, 134, 135, 144, 147, 150, 157, 160
Kerry, John, 135
Kettering, 127
kibbutzim, 84
Kidwelly, 27
Kieran Timberlake, 138
King's College London, 6, 88, 107, 123
Korea, North, 6, 98, 99
Korea, South 6, 98, 99
Korean Demilitarized Zone (DMZ), 6

Krakow, 140, 152, 174
Kremlin, 130, 131, 191
Kurdistan, 76

Labbezanga, 54
Lagos, 17
  mine, 16, 46, 55, 66, 113
Leicester, 78
Leningrad, 93
Liege, 68, 86
live facial recognition (LFR), 120, 121, 122, 124
London, 3, 6, 7, 8, 12, 23, 26, 78, 88, 89, 90, 91, 97, 98, 103, 104, 106, 107, 109, 110, 111, 125, 126, 130, 143, 145, 160, 180, 182
  Aldwych, 12, 104, 106, 107
  City of, 12, 116, 118–19
  counter terrorism and, 7, 110, 116–23, *117*
  Gatwick Airport, 148
  Heathrow Airport, 11, 142, 147, 150, 152, 159
  King's College, 6, 88, 107, 123
  Luton Airport, 150
  Ring of Steel, 116–22, *117*
  Strand, the, vi, 6, 12, 88, 104, 106, 107, 113, 119, 123, 145, 160, 164, 165, 183, 186
  terror attack, 23, 109, 115–16
  Tower of, 119, 160
  Underground, 23, 89
  World War II and, 12, 88–90, 111, 114
  US Embassy in, 131–2, 136, *137*, 137–9, 143
'Long Lines' building, New York, 181
Los Angeles, 128, 153
Lucerne, 90

lunette, 81
Lutnick, Howard, 182
Lwara Police Fort, 65

Maccaferri Inc., 57
machine-learning, *see* artificial intelligence
Mali, 11, 54, 55, 56, 57, 58
Malta, 48
man-portable air-defence system (MANPAD), 150
Maginot Line, 36, 37, 38, 46, 53
Manchester Arena attack, 153–4
marching camp (fort), 3, 27, 58, 60, 63
Marshalls (hard landscaping), 108
Medmenham Camp, 27, 28, 29, 179
Mehmet the Conqueror, 77, 80
Menaka, 54
Melaka, 49
Mesopotamia, 77
Metz, 37, 86
Meuse River, 86
Mexico, 13, 20
Michelangelo, 82
Microsoft Grange Castle data centre, 183
migrant, 13, 14, 68
Mogadishu, 146–7
Moltke, Helmuth James von, 47
Mombasa, 150
Mongol Empire, 5
Monte San Giovanni, 80
Mordor Intelligence, 122
Morphosis, 136
Morocco, 11, 13, 14, 49, 66
Moscow, 6, 11, 20, 90, 97, 130, 172, 191
Mozambique, 67
Mumbai, 6

Namur, 68, 86
Napoleon III, 40, 83, 85
New France, *see* Quebec
Nigeria, 17, 135
Nairobi, 111, 134, 135
National Research Council, 133
National Security Agency, 181
NATO, 1, 3, 5, 58, 65, 71, 93, 120, 154
Netherlands, 36, 55, 82
network society, 43
Neuf-Brisach, 55, 82
New York, 86, 181
Newman, Oscar, 127
Nice, 7, 109
Normans, 58, 138
Northern Ireland, 60, 116, 134, 130, 185
North-West Mounted Police, 178
nuclear shelter, 37, 38, 89–90, 171, 180, 183
nuclear weapons, *see* weaponry

Offa's Dyke, 66
Office for Communities and Local Government, 126
Oklahoma City bombings, 112, 134
Olin landscape design studio, 110
One World Trade Center, 181
Operation Rose, 16
Operation Strong Tower, 7
Orlando, 7
Orwell, George, 114
Osdin Shield, 162
Ottawa, 134, 135
Ottomans, 86

Pakistan, 64, 65, 66, 146
Palantir, 122
Palestine, 14, 62, 67, 76, 144
palisade, 27, 92, 179, 184

Palmanova, 83, 85, 133
Panama, 132
panopticon, 125, 126, 157
Paris, 6, 7, 85
Parker, Geoffrey, 80
Patton, George S., General, 37
pedestrian, 70, 107, 108, 109, 110, 116
perimeter security, 14, 57, 127, 147, 148, 149, 155, 162
  see also fence
peripheral linear barrier, 65, 66
Persia, 3, 140, 166, 167
Plane Stupid, 147
Poland, 11, 93, 95, 96, 140, 152, 174
Police Scientific Development Branch, 118
Popular Front for the Liberation of Palestine (PFLP), 144
Portugal, 49, 50, 165
post-industrial age, 42
post-modern age, 32, 128
Praesidiad, 57
Prague, 90
Prepping, 171–2

Quebec (New France), 55, 177
queue management, 153

RAF Central Interpretation Unit, 28
ramming attack, 109, 113, 115, 144, 145, 147, 158, 187
RAND corporation, 132
ravelin, 81
Reagan, Ronald, 18
Regional Command South Kandahar (RCS), 2
retrospective facial recognition (RFR), 120
Revolution in Military Affairs (RMA), 4, 24
Rice, Condoleezza, 42
Ring of Steel, 116, 117
risk society, 43
Rocket, vi, vii, 2, 28, 58, 65
Roman Empire, 27, 48, 52, 58, 65, 66, 78, 90, 104, 122, 123
Roman Limes, 48, 66, 123
Rome, 82, 74, 120
Rostow, Walt W., 17
Royal Air Force (RAF), 6, 28, 87, 115
Royal Commission on the Ancient and Historical Monuments of Wales, 27
Royal Institute of British Architects, 126
Royal Navy, 48, 111
Royal Ulster Constabulary, 60
Russia, 67, 71, 72, 92, 96, 100, 158
  Empire, 34, 48–9, 58
Russia-Ukraine War, 71, 72, 92, 94, 99, 100, 148, 150

Saarinen, Aero, 131, 137, 143
Sadr City, 52, 52
San Gimignano tower houses, 164–5
Saudi Arabia, 12, 67, 68, 70, 175
Saul, John Ralston, 22
Saxons, 28, 58, 92
Scotland, 53, 55, 144, 158
Second World War, *see* World War II
security market, 10, 56, 57, 122, 127, 149, 155, 157, 161, 162, 172, 182
security portal, *see* breach control system
shell, 36, 85, 93, 99

siege, 39, 56, 76, 83, 89, 91, 92
  artillery, 36, 55
  Berlin Blockade, 17
  Beslan and, 158
  Colombo, 55
  COP Castle and, 59
  Donbas and, 94
  engine, 52
  Krakow and, 140
  La Roche Pont and, 75
  Madrid and, 93
  Marshal Sebastien Le Prestre De Vauban and, 113
  Monte San Giovanni and, 80
  Moscow theatre and, 6
  tower, 76
  Vienna and, 86
Seoul, 98, 99
September 11 2001 attacks, 14, 110, 112, 135, 142, 143, 144, 181–2
Séré de Rivières, Raymond Adolphe, General, 36, 37
Seversky, Alexander de, 88
school, 14, 95, 151, 155, 156–8
Schroeder, Matthew, 151
Scotland, 53, 55, 142, 144, 158, 162, 165
Singapore, 48
SKA Air & Logistics, 146
Small Arms Survey, 150
Somalia, 67, 146–7
Sonnenberg Tunnel, 90
South Africa, 67, 169–70, 172–4
South China Sea, artificial islands, 69
Soviet Union (USSR), 3, 20, 59, 71, 100, 132, 149
  Cold War and, 45, 46, 90
  World War II and, 15, 16, 18, 93, 95

Spain, 13, 68
Spartans, 78
Special Air Service (SAS), 7
Sri Lanka, 55
Stabilization Mission in Mali (MINUSMA), 63
standoff distance, 111, 112, 126, 133, 134, 138, 150, 158
star fortress, 54, 80–4
State Department, *see* US Department of State
Sri Lanka, 55
St Clement Danes, 114
St Petersburg, 48
Stalin, J.V., 17
Stalingrad, 93
Standard Embassy Design (SED) programme, 135
standards, American NIJ 1018, 155–6
  American UL 752, 155
  EN 1063, 154
  EN 13541, 159
  ISO 16933:2007, 159
  ISO 16935:2007, 159
  NIJ 0108.01 standard, 161
  PAS 68 rating, 113, 138
Steyn, Douw, 173
Stokenchurch BT Tower, 180–1
stone, 46, 49, 55, 56, 77, 82, 111, 115, 137
Strongholds, 178–80
Sudan, 132
Suffragettes, 115
Sun Tzu, 35, 123
surveillance, 14, 51, 66, 98, 101, 107, 114, 121, 122–7, 145, 167, 168, 170, 174, 175, 184, 190
  camera, 12, 13, 64, 70, 98, 118, 121, 122, 124, 125, 126, 149, 167, 170

surveillance (*cont.*)
  live facial recognition (LFR), 120–2
  number plate recognition (ANPR), 118, 119–20
  pan-tilt-zoom (PTZ), 148
  thermal imaging, 61, 63, 70
Sussman, Baron George-super-Ely, 85, 86
Switzerland, 38, 90
Syria, 67, 137

T-Wall, 52, 60, 62, 110
Taliban, 2, 58
target-hardening, 14, 151, 155, 156, 157, 161, 170, 177, 182
Tuareg, 56
technology, 24, 40, 14, 42, 47, 56, 60, 73, 75, 85, 87, 93, 102, 120, 121, 122, 123, 124, 148, 160, 161, 162
  communications, 58
  information, 4, 22, 24
  military, 24, 32–6, 41–2, 47, 56, 58, 87, 93, 101
  see also artificial intelligence, surveillance
Tegart, Sir Charles, 62
Tegart fort, 62, 63
temporary vertical concrete barrier, *see* Jersey barrier
tenaille, 81
terrorism, 23, 122, 124, 127, 132–5, 151, 153, 156–8, 168, 171, 176, 183, 185
  Abu Nidal, 144
  crowded places and, 187
  data centres and, 183
  Irish Republican Army (IRA), 116, 155, 130
  Japanese Red Army Faction, 144

Popular Front for the Liberation of Palestine (PFLP), 144
prepping and, 171
see also terrorist attack
terrorist attack
  Berlin and, 109
  Beslan and, 158–9
  Brussels Airport and, 144
  Buenos Aires and, 112
  Dunblane and, 168
  Glasgow Airport and, 144
  London and, 23, 24, 109, 155
  Manchester and, 153–4
  Moscow and, 6
  Mumbai and, Munich Airport and, 144–6
  Lod Airport and, 144–5
  Nairobi, 111
  Nice and, 109
  Oklahoma City and, 112, 134
  Orlando and, 7
  Paris and, 6
  Rome Airport and, 144
  September 11, 14, 110, 112, 135, 142, 143, 144, 181–2
  Vienna Airport and, 144
  see also bomb attack *and* ramming attack
The Bunker, 183
Toffler, Alvin, 32
Tower of London, 160
Trump, Donald J., 13, 14, 15, 38, 65, 66, 98, 130
Trump, Ken, 156–7
Turkey, 67, 68, 75, 77
TWA Flight Centre, 142–3

UK Centre for the Protection of National Infrastructure, 109
Ukraine, 67

war with Russia and, 71, 72, 92, 94, 99, 100, 148, 150
United Kingdom (UK), *see* Britain
United Nations (UN), 20, 63, 64
United Nations Multidimensional Integrated Stabilization Mission in Mali (MINUSMA), 63
United States (USA), 2, 5, 18, 22, 34, 35, 37, 38, 41, 42, 49, 57, 57, 58, 87, 95, 115, 121, 154, 157, 143, 154, 155, 156, 157, 158, 161, 167, 176, 178, 180, 181, 182
   border with Mexico, 11, 13, 14, 20, 65, 66, 68
   Congressional Research Service, 2
   Department of State, 133, 135, 136, 137
   World War II and, 93, 131
   see also United States embassy
United States embassy, 131, 132, 133, 134, 135, 136
   assaults on, 132, 134–5
   in Baghdad, 134
   in Beirut, 132, *136*, 136–7, 139
   in Cairo, 133
   in Dar es Salam, 134
   in Kabul, 134
   in London, 131–2, *137*, 137–9, 143
   in Nairobi, 111, 134–5
   in Ottawa, 134, 135
   in Tehran, 132
unmanned aerial system (UAS), 148, 149, *214*
urban planning and design, 74, 86, 108, 126–31
urban warfare, 93, 94, 96, 97
Ur, 77

USA, *see* United States
USSR, *see* Soviet Union

Van Creveld, Martin, 32
Vanke Garden City, Shanghai, 175
Vatican, 82
Vauban, Sebastian Le Prestre de, 54, 113
vehicle-borne explosive device, 62, 110, 113, 116, 135, 153, 185
Verdun, 36, 68, 86
Venezuela, 132
Vienna, 74, 86, 91, 144
Vietnam, 132
Vikings, 28, 92
Viollet-Le-Duc, E., 75

Wales, 12, 26, 53, 54, 58, 160
wall, 13–21, 45–6, 48, 53, 60, *61*, 62, 63, 65–70, 91, 92, 98, 99, 101–2, 106, 109, 110, 112, 114, 115, 122, 123, 125, 131, 136–40, *141*, 147, 154, 158, 159, 166, 174, 175, 179, 185
   'age of', 31
   Belfast, 60
   Berlin, 16–21, 25, 26–7
   Ceuta and Melilla, 13–14
   city walls, 75–86, 96, 97, 98, 108
   German Atlantic, 53
   Great wall of China, 48, 53, 66
   Hadrian's, 48, 53
   ha-ha, 139
   Israeli border, 14, 67, 68, *69*
   T-Wall, 52, *52*, 60, 110
   US border, 13, 14, 20, 65, 66
   Western Sahara 'Sand Wall', 11, 66
   see also blast wall, enclosed neighbourhood, fortified city
Wall of the Farmers General, 85

walled city, *see* fortified city
war, 1, 2, 3, 7, 17, 20, 24, 28, 29,
    31, 32–4, 40–2, 47, 50, 52, 63,
    71, 73, 74, 76, 80, 82, 87, 94,
    95, 97, 99, 100, 104, 123, 150,
    151, 165, 166, 168, 180, 186
  Afghanistan, 4–5
  American Civil, 34
  Crimean, 48
  Boer, 34
  English Civil, 28
  Franco-Prussian, 33, 75
  Gulf, 175
  Irish Civil, 41
  of Irish Independence, 41
  Russia-Ukraine, 71–2, 92, 94,
    99, 100, 148, 150
  Russo-Japanese, 34
  Russo-Polish, 140
  Vietnam, 56
  see also Cold War, Global War
    on Terror, World War I,
    World War II
war of ideas, *see* Global War on
    Terror
Wareham, 92
warfare, vii, 2, 4, 12, 14, 24, 32,
    33–40, 43, 47, 52, 55, 60, 72,
    75, 91
  attritional, 39, 92
  industrial, 71–2, 91
  urban, 60, 93–4, 97
Warsaw, 93, 95, 96, 140
Warsaw Pact, 18, 93
Washington DC, 110, 130, 131

wave theory, 32
Washington DC, 110, 130, 131
weapon, *see* weaponry
weaponry, 32, 33, 34, 35, 36, 40,
    45, 46, 50, 56, 58, 60, 76, 80,
    81, 85, 87, 91, 93, 94, 96, 97,
    100, 109, 110, 150, 151, 152,
    160
  atomic, 40
  nuclear, 37, 168, 180, 183, 184
  see also bomb, shell, vehicle-
    borne explosive device
Weber, Max, 125
West Bank, 67, 67, 76
  separation fence, 69
Western Sahara Wall (Sand Wall),
    11, 66
Westminster, 107, 109, 112, 114,
    119, 121, 123, 174, 187
Westminster Bridge, 109, 110
Westminster ramming attack, 187
whisky fort, 178
White House, 130, 131
Windsor Castle, 130, 186–7
World War I, 34, 35, 36, 41, 57,
    68, 72, 86
World War II, 12, 15, 28, 29, 37,
    46, 48, 53, 87, 88, 90, 91, 92,
    93, 95, 111, 131, 140, 191
Wrightstyle Systems, 160

Yavneh College, 158
Yeats, W.B., 41
Yemen, 12, 67
York Factory, 50